CARTOON
SUCCESS SECRETS

CARTOON SUCCESS SECRETS

A Tribute to Thirty Years of *CARTOONIST PROfiles*

Jud Hurd

**Andrews McMeel
Publishing**

Kansas City

04 05 06 07 08 VAI 10 9 8 7 6 5 4 3 2 1

ISBN: 0-7407-3809-7

Library of Congress Catalog Control Number: 2003106553

Book design and composition by
Kelly & Company, Lee's Summit, Missouri

For
Claudia and Philip,
whose help and inspiration
have meant so much to
CARTOONIST PROfiles

CONTENTS

· · · · · · · · · · · · ·

FOREWORD

. . . .

In Part One of this book you will find words and photos relating to some of the many encounters I had with famous cartoonists over the years. The excitement connected with these visits fueled my continuing enthusiasm and love of cartooning. But in those days, I wasn't trying to dig out the nuts and bolts of how they reached comics stardom. I was just basking in their aura and fame.

In Part Two, you will read stories and interviews that are highlights from the pages of *CARTOONIST PROfiles* during its thirty-five-year history. These stories resulted from the answers that famous cartoonist friends gave to my questions. They discuss in great detail the factors that carried them to the top of our profession and might do the same for you. With this book in your hands, you have a college course in comic strip education never before published.

Jack Cassady, left, cartoonist, teacher, and skydiver, who in 1985 produced the thirteen-part public television series *Funny Business: The Art in Cartooning* in conjunction

with WDCN-TV in Nashville, is shown here
beginning the videotaped interview for the
Jud Hurd, right, segment of the series.

CARTOON
SUCCESS SECRETS

PART ONE

THE MASTERS

JUD HURD
1993

LET THE MAGIC BEGIN!

What an exciting phone call I had recently! The CEO of the company that publishes the most books by and about cartoonists called to say they'd like to do one about me and my favorite profession. How come?

I guess it's because I caught the cartooning bug over seventy-five years ago and haven't yet been cured—at age ninety. Throwing modesty to the winds, I'd say—because of the mind-boggling length of time I've been living and breathing cartooning—I've been fortunate enough to know and interview more cartoonists than anyone else on the planet. Plus, a syndicated cartoon drawn by me has appeared in newspapers every weekday for over forty years. To top things off, my magazine, *CARTOONIST PROfiles,* celebrated its thirty-fifth birthday in 2003.

I want to assure you, dear reader, that all the interviews and stories that first appeared in *CARTOONIST PROfiles,* and which are scattered throughout this book, came directly from the cartoonists' mouths. Their unique advice and career-building comments were *never* the result of my researching what had been printed about these cartoonists elsewhere. That's a promise! Before *CARTOONIST PROfiles,* there was never a place where vital information from so many famous and successful cartoonists could be obtained.

I'm often asked, "What attracted you to this unusual business in the first place?" OK, we're talking about the early 1920s, when there was no television, no network radio, no Internet, no video games, and no rock

This is DE BECK'S clever way of telling you that his CORRESPONDENCE CARTOON COURSE is ready. It is a really adequate course of ten lessons and costs only $5. A folder describing this new course will be sent free for the asking.

The Cartoon School of the Chicago Academy of Fine Arts

CARL N. WERNTZ, Director   81 East Madison Street, CHICAGO

stars to capture the attention of an eager twelve-year-old. But most every Sunday newspaper in America was wrapped on the outside with its comics section in glorious dazzling color, so anyone visiting the neighborhood newsstand could see nothing but the exploits of *Bringing Up Father* with Jiggs and Maggie, the antics of *Mutt and Jeff,* and those of other famous funnies characters of the day.

Adding to my rapidly increasing excitement over comic strips was the frequently reported personal appearance of famous cartoonists in my hometown of Cleveland, Ohio. They were royally welcomed by the mayor and given a key to the city. Gala occasions of this sort were reported in many towns. And famous cartoonists also appeared in vaudeville performances, as you can see in the newspaper advertisement included here.

The promise and excitement of a career in cartooning seemed more and more appealing to me, especially when magazine advertisements for correspondence courses in cartooning caught my eye. These assured youthful readers like me that taking the advertised course would result in attaining the same fame and fortune reached by the famous cartoonists who had previously completed the lessons.

It wasn't long before my mother and I visited the downtown Cleveland office of one of the best known of these courses, the one operated by C. N. Landon, who had been art director of the Newspaper Enterprise Association, a distributor of comics and other features. Not wishing to discourage a potential student, Landon assured us, after a brief look at a few of my sample cartoons, that a career in cartooning was just the ticket for me, and a little later, while taking the course, I had the thrill of seeing my first cartoon in print in *The Lantern,* my junior high school magazine. That was in 1925. I was on my way.

Naturally, I continued to draw cartoons for several high school and college magazines and newspapers, and soon after graduation I was thrilled to discover that the Chicago Academy of Fine Arts had professional cartoonists on its faculty, the first school ever to do so. Vaughn Shoemaker, the Pulitzer Prize–winning editorial cartoonist for the *Chicago Daily News* was one of these. Another was Don Ulsh, whose magazine gag cartoons were widely published. After a year of study,

the animated cartoons being made in Hollywood drew me to California, and a couple of weeks later I was lucky to land a job at the Charles Mintz Studio, which produced *Krazy Kat* cartoons.

Once in Hollywood, I was able to combine my love of cartoons with my longtime interest in famous movie personalities in the syndication of *Just Hurd in Hollywood.* Each of these strips featured an amusing anecdote told by my star of the day.

Beginning in 1938, I drew the weekly editorial cartoon for the Newspaper Enterprise Association in Cleveland. My work for this major distributor of comics included doing caricatures and maps and retouching photos.

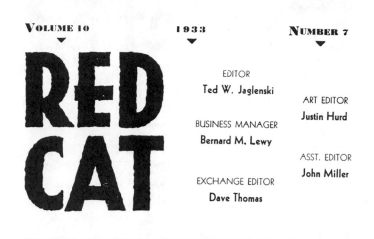

VOLUME 10   1933   NUMBER 7

RED CAT

EDITOR
Ted W. Jaglenski

ART EDITOR
Justin Hurd

BUSINESS MANAGER
Bernard M. Lewy

ASST. EDITOR
John Miller

EXCHANGE EDITOR
Dave Thomas

World War II intervened, and I spent four years in the U.S. Army drawing and writing *Crypto Chris,* a cartoon that regularly emphasized the dangers of handling classified material.

After being discharged from the army at Fort Dix, New Jersey, in April 1946, I returned to Cleveland and opened the Jud Hurd Cartoons Studio. For the next dozen years or more, I produced reams of cartoons that depicted various events involving the business and private lives of the employees of several large corporations, including the Standard Oil Company, the Erie Railroad, and the American Steel & Wire Company. These cartoons appeared in the employee magazines, and I was involved in the layout of many of the pages of these publications.

Skipping quickly to 1959, I was fortunate enough to sell my *Ticker Toons* stock-market cartoon to the *Chicago Sun-Times* syndicate. A couple of years later, a Cleveland doctor, Michael A. Petti, and I began collaboration on the *Health Capsules* cartoon for United Feature Syndicate in New York City, so I was now drawing two syndicated cartoons each day.

In the winter of 1964, in order to be closer to United Feature, my wife, Claudia, and young son Philip moved to Westport, Connecticut. At this point, the late Bob Dunn, the artist for King Features' *They'll Do It Every Time* and then-president of the National Cartoonists Society, asked me to take over the editing of the organization's newsletter.

Following my tour of duty in this assignment, I finally began my magazine, *CARTOONIST PROfiles,* the interviewing, writing, and production of which has consumed about 105 percent of my working time ever since.

Several emotions come back to me as I think nostalgically about school and college cartooning days. The levels of anticipation and absolutely delicious excitement I experienced, when my first published efforts were about to see the light of day in the Patrick Henry Junior High School magazine *The Lantern,* were never topped in following years, no matter what my later cartooning accomplishments. I can still taste the feeling. Exhilarating!

The same was true as I cartooned my way through East High School with cartoons in the school newspaper *The Blue & Gold.* Then, at Adelbert College of Western Reserve University in Cleveland, I eagerly became a staff member of the humor magazine *The Red Cat.*

THE RED CAT STAFF FORMULATES A CLEAN JOKE

E. C. SEGAR AND *POPEYE*

My first contact with E. C. "Elzie" Segar, the famous creator of *Popeye,* was in 1931 when, as *Red Cat* art editor, I wrote to ask him if he'd do a cartoon especially for our publication.

He not only took the time to produce a very funny original *Popeye* page, which has been a cherished possession of mine ever since, he was also careful to see that we weren't violating any syndicate protocol by publishing *Popeye* in our *Red Cat.*

Five years later, when I was living in Hollywood, I would occasionally talk with this giant of our profession. He would always answer all my questions, patiently and graciously.

E. C. Segar

350—17 ST.
SANTA MONICA, CALIF.
JULY 20-1931

DEAR EDITOR—

HERE IS A CARTUNE WITCH I HOPES YA WILL LIKE OKAY— IF THEY IS ENY HOOMER IN THIS PITCHER IT IS AXERDENTIL ON ACCOUNT OF I YAM A SERIOUS SWAB— I ADMITS I GOT A KOMICLE FACE BUT WHAT I LACKS IN LOOKS I MAKES UP IN SEX REPEAL—

YERS TRULIE—
POPEYE.

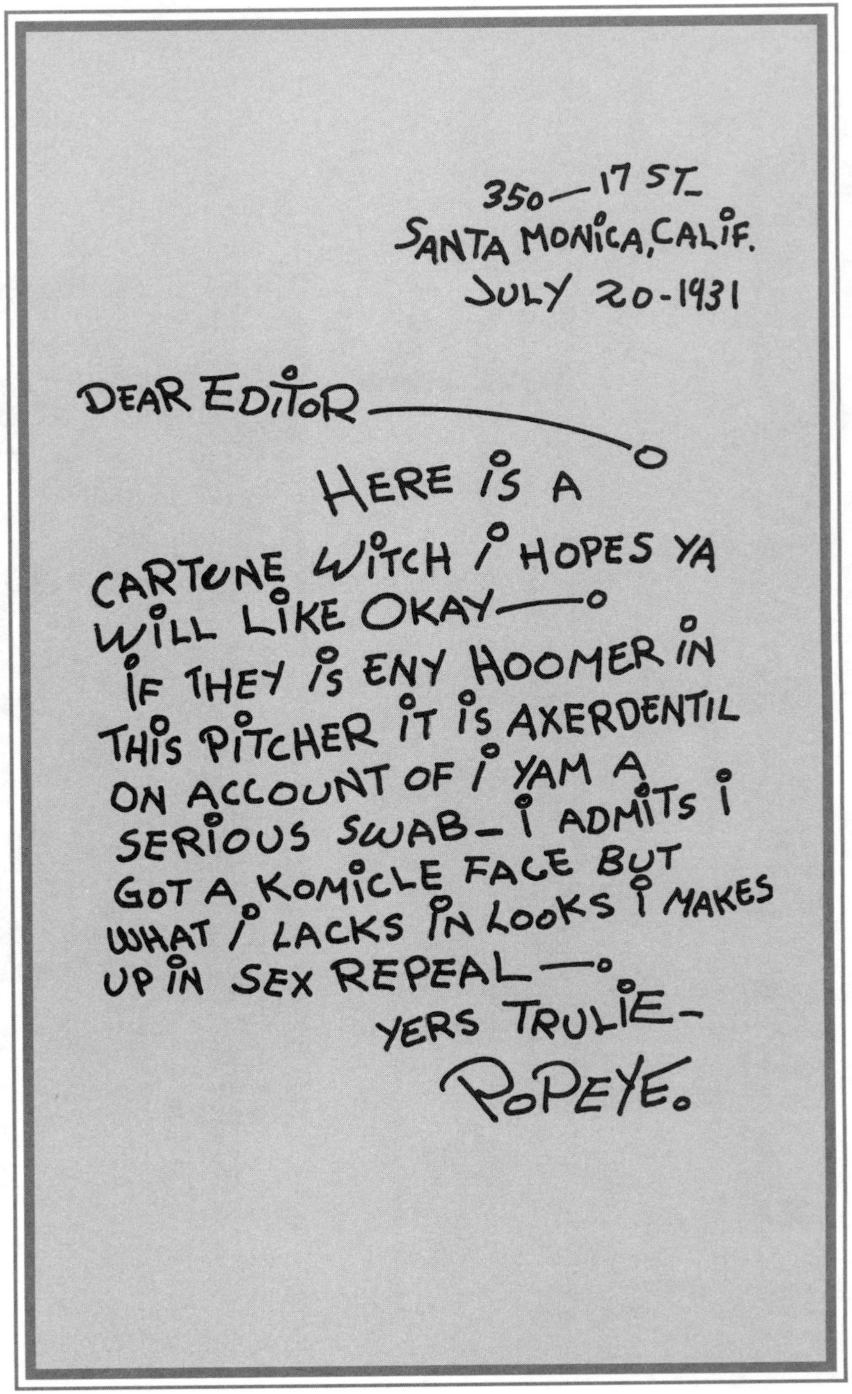

DEAR MR. HURD—

IT WAS NECESSARY TO GET PERMISSION FROM "KING FEATURES SYNDICATE" BEFORE DOING A COMIC FOR YOU — AND A LITTLE VACATION ACCOUNTS FOR SOME OF THE DELAY—

BEST REGARDS TO YOURSELF AND THE "RED CAT" STAFF -

YOURS JERY TRULY

SEGAR

E.C. SEGAR,
350 — 17 ST.
SANTA MONICA,
CALIF.

RUBE GOLDBERG

In 1937 I received a note from Rube Goldberg that was in response to an earlier letter of mine. I lost no time in taking him up on the invitation you see here, and it was with considerable excitement that I went up to his studio on 57th Street in Manhattan for my first meeting with this legendary man. Are any other cartoonists listed in the dictionary? Here's how they put it in *Merriam-Webster's Collegiate Dictionary*, 11th edition: "Rube Goldberg: accomplishing by complex means what seemingly could be done simply."

I was familiar, of course, with Rube's famous inventions, with *Boob McNutt, Foolish Questions,* and others of his zany creations, so the conversation that day was a splendid example of the many battery-charging encounters I've had with great cartoonists.

Fifteen years went by without our meeting again. Then I became a member (in 1952) of the National Cartoonists Society, which Rube cofounded in 1946. Although I was living and working in Cleveland at the time, I managed to attend several of the monthly Lamb's Club meetings in New York City each year, as well as the annual awards dinner, so I came to know him as a good friend.

As he did several times during his long career, Rube had shifted artistic gears in 1938 when he began drawing editorial cartoons for the *New York Sun,* in which

Rube Goldberg enjoying our favorite magazine

capacity he won the 1948 Pulitzer Prize. Once again, in 1965, Goldberg turned his formidable energies toward another art specialty—sculpture—with a one-man show of his work at Brentano's in New York that year and another at the Hammer Galleries in 1968. So great was his enthusiasm for this latest aspect of his career that his wife, Irma, told me that Rube, then in his eighties, could hardly wait to leave their apartment for his studio, bright and early each morning.

I remember being particularly astounded at one of Rube's pieces entitled *The Cocktail Party*, in which a dozen or so colorful characters of every conceivable type are milling around just as we've all done at hundreds of such affairs. One of Rube's *Human Comedy* series, a sculpture of an aging Broadway actor entitled *The Ham*, has graced the foyer of our home in Westport, Connecticut, for a number of years. I think the most valuable lesson I learned from my association with Rube was that it is possible to retain over the years the same boyish enthusiasm for our craft that one has at the beginning. Not many cartoonists manage to do this, but Rube certainly did.

When the Connecticut corporation CARTOONIST PROfiles, Inc., was chartered in 1969, Rube became a small stockholder, and he and Irma continued to express their interest in my magazine from then on. I really appreciated that. And from time to time, after Rube's death, I had some pleasant meetings with his son, George, who is a theatrical producer with a number of Broadway successes to his credit.

In November of 1970 I saw Rube for the last time on an evening at the Smithsonian Institution in Washington when he and his career were honored. I had a copy of the book *Rube Goldberg vs. the Machine Age* in my hand and had planned to ask him to inscribe it, but he looked so very ill that I decided not to bother him. However, several days later I mailed him the book to be signed at his leisure. You can imagine my feelings, after he returned it with the inscription you see on page 14, when I realized that he had written it just four days before his death.

As you may know, the National Cartoonists Society annually honors its Cartoonist of the Year by presenting the winner with a Reuben, named for Reuben Lucius Goldberg.

PROFESSOR BUTTS TRIES TO FIX A LEAK IN THE BOILER AND WHEN HE IS RESCUED FROM DROWNING HE COUGHS UP AN IDEA FOR AN OUTBOARD MOTOR THAT REQUIRES NO FUEL. AS YOU REACH FOR ANCHOR, BUTTON(A) SNAPS LOOSE AND HITS SPIGOT(B) CAUSING BEER TO RUN INTO PAIL(C). WEIGHT PULLS CORD(D) FIRING SHOT GUN(E). REPORT FRIGHTENS SEA GULL(F) WHICH FLIES AWAY AND CAUSES ICE(G) TO LOWER IN FRONT OF FALSE TEETH(H). AS TEETH CHATTER FROM COLD THEY BITE CORD(I) IN HALF ALLOWING POINTED TOOL(J) TO DROP AND RIP BAG OF CORN(K). CORN FALLS INTO NET(L). WEIGHT CAUSES IT TO SNAP LATCH OPENING FLOOR OF CAGE(M) AND DROPPING DUCK INTO SHAFTS(N). AS DUCK(O) TRIES TO REACH CORN IT SWIMS AND CAUSES CANOE TO MOVE AHEAD. IF THE FALSE TEETH KEEP ON CHATTERING YOU CAN LET THEM CHEW YOUR GUM TO GIVE YOUR OWN JAWS A REST.

PROFESSOR BUTTS, WHILE OVERHAULING A 1907 FORD, FINDS AN IDEA FOR A SIMPLE WAY TO SHARPEN ICE SKATES. WIRE BUNDLE-BASKET(A) IN SPORTING STORE HITS FLOOR-WALKER(B) AND KNOCKS HIM DIZZY. AS HE SINKS TO FLOOR HIS KNEES HIT END OF SEE-SAW(C) WHICH TOSSES BASKET BALL(D) INTO BROKEN NET(E). BALL FALLS ON TENNIS RACKET(F) CAUSING GROUP OF TIN CANS(G) TO FLY UP OUT OF REACH OF HUNGRY GOAT(H). GOAT, BEING ROBBED OF HIS DINNER, JUMPS IN FURY AND BUTTS HIS HEAD AGAINST BOXING DUMMY(I). DUMMY SWAYS BACK AND FORTH ON SWIVEL BASE(J), CAUSING TWO ECCENTRIC WHEELS(K) TO PUSH FILE(L) ACROSS BLADE OF SKATE(M) AND MAKE IT SHARP ENOUGH TO USE FOR SKATING IN THE WINTER AND SHAVING IN THE SUMMER. YOU MAY THINK IT CRUEL TO HIT THE FLOOR-WALKER ON THE HEAD. BUT WE ASSURE YOU THERE IS NOTHING INSIDE WHICH CAN BE DAMAGED.

Rube Goldberg

To my very good friend, Judd Hurd, who has done so much for cartoons and cartoonists, bless him—

Rube Goldberg

Dec 9, 1970

Rube's inscription in my copy of *Rube Goldberg vs. the Machine Age*.

A BARBER PUTS A SCALDING TOWEL ON PROFESSOR BUTTS'S FACE AND WHILE HE IS SCREAMING WITH PAIN HE THINKS UP AN INVENTION FOR DIGGING UP BAIT FOR FISHING. THE MAID(A) PEELS AN ONION AND CRIES INTO FUNNEL(B). TEARS(C) RUN THROUGH PIPE(D) AND DRIP INTO PAN(E) OF JEWELER'S SCALE(F), CAUSING END OF BAR(G) TO PRESS AGAINST SMALL BELLOWS(H), WHICH BLOWS INSECT POWDER(I) ON SHELF AND KNOCKS OFF ROACHES(J). ROACHES FALL ON EDGE OF ANTIQUE FAN(K), CAUSING IT TO CLOSE AND EXPOSE SURFACE OF MIRROR(L). SELFISH PALOOKA HOUND(M) SEES HIS REFLECTION IN MIRROR AND, THINKING IT IS ANOTHER DOG, HASTENS TO BURY BONE(N). AS HE DIGS, HE UNCOVERS WORM(O) WHICH IS SEEN IMMEDIATELY BY EARLY BIRD(P) WHO DIVES FOR IT OFF PERCH. WEIGHT(Q) DROPS ON HEAD OF BIRD AND KNOCKS HIM COLD JUST AS HE PULLS WORM FAR ENOUGH OUT OF GROUND FOR FISHERMAN TO GRAB IT EASILY.

WHEN THE EARLY BIRD WAKES UP YOU CAN LET HIM EAT THE ONION JUST SO HE WILL NOT BE GETTING TOO RAW A DEAL.

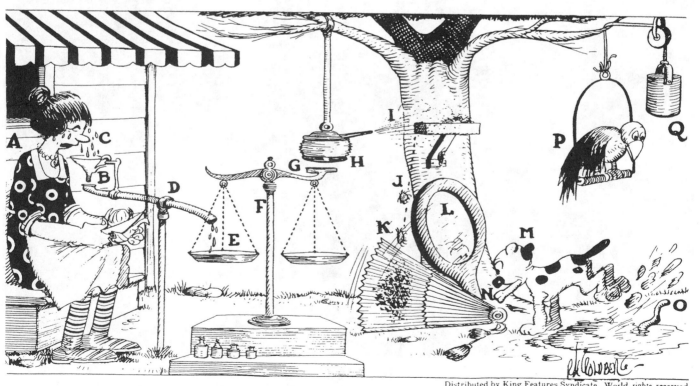

H. T. WEBSTER

I first encountered H. T. Webster, the creator of *The Timid Soul, The Thrill That Comes Once in a Lifetime, Life's Darkest Moment,* and other well-remembered titles, in his studio behind the Webster home on Cresthill Place in the Shippan Point area of Stamford, Connecticut.

He was tall and distinguished-looking and, as I've remarked many times since then, he and the word *gentleman* seem absolutely synonymous. Looking back in memory, I think of him as belonging to a kinder and gentler era, in which many people could easily relate to the Timid Soul's meek reactions to the life around him. The cartoon of his that I've recalled with laughter most often was the one showing this character, who has agreed to meet someone who wants to touch him for a loan, standing on a street corner without a coat, being pelted by a drenching rain. The Timid Soul muses to himself, "Well, I'll wait one more hour and then he can go borrow his hundred dollars from somebody else!" Would most members of today's raucous and less gentle generation split their sides with laughter over *The Timid Soul* as we did in those days? People even blushed in that bygone period. Several times Webster expressed the vain wish that somehow the syndicates would be satisfied with only three panels of his a week. That seems like a reasonable wish until you realize that syndicated cartoonists have always been expected to produce at least six and in most cases seven strips or panels each week, while newspaper columnists can

Harold Tucker Webster and me

Cartoon Success Secrets

The Thrill That Comes Once in a Lifetime. —By Webster

NEW YORK
Herald **Tribune**
European Edition: THE NEW YORK HERALD

September 4, 1937.

Dear Mr. Hurd:

      I will be glad to see you and you might phone me when you reach New York. (Stamford 4-0197) The afternoon is the best time. You will have to come to Stamford I am afraid, for I will not be going to New York until October.

      Sincerely,

take a vacation, with merely a brief editor's note appearing beside a substitute's words, stating that the regular columnist will reappear in a couple of weeks. Only in recent years have Garry Trudeau, Gary Larson, Bill Watterson, and Cathy Guisewite been able to convince their syndicate that they need sabbaticals. Would that Webster were around now to enjoy such a hiatus!

Fishing and bridge were two of H. T. Webster's principal pleasures in life, and hundreds, maybe thousands, of his cartoons dealt with these two pastimes. Boyhood memories formed the subjects of many others. The Websters often wintered on Middle Road in Palm Beach, Florida. Sadly, he died suddenly as he was returning from a fishing trip in 1952.

Claudia and I continued to visit his widow, Ethel, from time to time at her home in New Canaan, Connecticut. And on one occasion I recall taking my mother, Margaret, who had heard us talk about the friendliness of the Websters, to meet her.

FREDERICK BURR OPPER

My first contact with Frederick Opper, one of the all-time giants of cartooning, was via letters from the creator of *Happy Hooligan* and countless other memorable comic characters.

His postscript to the 1933 letter you see here contains a very good piece of advice that, unfortunately, still needs emphasizing. As editor of *CARTOONIST PROfiles,* I often receive letters from students whose teachers apparently never tell them to enclose that necessary stamp for my reply to their cartooning questions.

I finally met Opper personally in 1937 when I visited his home in New Rochelle, New York. And although he had advised me in his 1933 letter to draw from life as often as I could and to fill sketchbooks with my efforts, I was really astounded when he showed me piles of his own sketchbooks. Up to that point I had been familiar only with the bigfoot drawing style he displayed in *Happy Hooligan*. I guess I wondered why some of the style of his sketchbook drawings hadn't been reflected in his Sunday comics pages.

That question was answered for me when I later saw the wonderfully humorous drawings with which he illustrated Bill Nye's *History of the United States*. I'm including a few of them here. Enjoy and laugh!

Sadly, just two weeks after this exciting visit, I read of Opper's death in August of 1937. But my memories of this conversation were pleasantly rekindled in September of 1992 when I met his grandson, Frederick Opper. The Oppers spent years in many cities around the world as he pursued his journalism career. A photo I've included shows him standing in front of a plaque marking the birthplace of his illustrious grandfather in Madison, Ohio, in 1857.

Frederick Burr Opper
DEC 30 1930

Down on the Farm

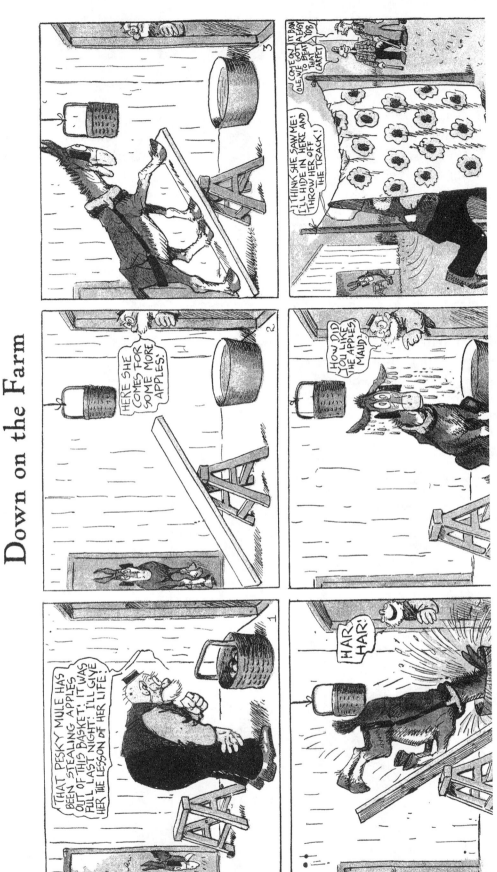

CONVERTING INDIANS.

Opper illustrations

COLUMBUS AT COURT

NOT TOO HAUGHTY TO HAVE FUN SOMETIMES.

Opper illustrations

WALT DISNEY

Since I was earning a salary of $16 a week at the Charles Mintz Studio during the Depression years of 1936 and 1937, the admission charge of 40 cents at the Riviera Country Club polo field seemed the most economical and interesting way to spend a Sunday afternoon. Back east, polo had always seemed the sport of rich society folks, but in Hollywood anyone could combine the excitement of watching the game, played by such celebrities as Walt Disney, with being elbow to elbow with screen luminaries like Spencer Tracy, Boris Karloff, and a number of other stars.

During this period Disney himself played on the Mickey Mouse team. Later on it was said that his employees at the studio finally persuaded him to give it up, arguing that he was too valuable a commodity to thus endanger himself.

A friend and I were usually to be found milling around on the sidelines, keeping one eye on the players and their ponies and the other on the lookout for ever-present celebrities. Early on, during these Sunday-afternoon excursions, we became aware that Disney's father, Elias, was one of those watching the action as he wandered here and there at the edge of the field. Gradually, from Sunday to Sunday, we struck up conversations with him.

I can't tell you how many times during the years since then that I've repeated with great glee the follow-

I took this 1936 photo of Walt and Elias Disney.

ing exchange between the elder Disney and myself. First let me say that he seemed like a dry, unemotional, and very modest man. Walt Disney, of course, was already a world figure, and, in my enthusiasm, I expressed my appreciation of him to his father in very extravagant terms. When I finally finished my tribute, the elder Disney replied quietly, without changing expression or tone of voice, "Yes, Walter's done well." It was no more or less than you would expect from a father who had just been told that his teenager did a good job of sweeping out the local grocery store.

On this and other Sundays, Disney would often come to the sidelines to have a word or two with his father. And since my friend and I were generally hovering around the older gentleman, we probably became fairly recognizable young fellows to Walt. I took advantage of this on one occasion when I met a young Englishman named Osborne Harley who told me he had written a script he would like to submit to the Disney studio. I knew he had little chance of seeing Disney himself, and I guess I wanted to show that I knew the great man personally, so I said I would hand the script to Disney on the following Sunday. When that day came and Disney rode up to his father on his polo pony, I extended the script with a hasty explanation of how I got it. Immediately, Disney waved it off, saying he couldn't look at anything unless the writer had previously signed a release. Looking back, I can't believe

that I expected Walt to stuff the package in his pocket and ride back into the polo match! But I learned that a writer would sometimes claim falsely of having suggested a scene in a Disney cartoon and was now prepared to sue!

As time went on, we noticed that Walt Disney was always among the last to leave the Riviera Country Club when the polo match was finished. Apparently he was seeing that his pony was fed and properly bedded down for the night in the stables. One Sunday I had what seemed like a brilliant idea. My friend and I would station ourselves on the side of the road on which Disney would drive back to Hollywood, with thumbs out, indicating that we were headed in the same direction. Sure enough, on one memorable Sunday that I'll never forget, along he came—at the wheel of a Cadillac, as I recall—and ground to a stop as we waved. I hopped into the front seat beside him, too thrilled to remember how the conversation started. But he talked continually throughout the forty-five minute drive back to the film capital. I was literally awestruck, but I do remember his saying that many fairy tales that couldn't be properly handled by live actors were great for animated films. (The studio was in the midst of making *Snow White* at the time.) Disney also expressed the fervent hope that the bankers, the money men, wouldn't get control of his studio and call the shots. A really exciting forty-five minutes!

GEORGE HERRIMAN AND *KRAZY KAT*

George Herriman/Photo by Jud Hurd

Krazy Kat

Years before I first met George Herriman in 1936, I had read the frequently published story of how he had tried to return some of the money he was being paid by William Randolph Hearst for producing *Krazy Kat*. It was reported that Herriman didn't feel he deserved that much money. Hard to imagine? Of course. But I became a believer of this oft-told tale after meeting the cartoonist personally at his home on Maravilla Drive high in the Hollywood Hills.

I was at the Charles Mintz Studio during that year, and he had invited me to come up and visit him, after I had told him by phone what an eager beaver I was for cartooning! As I recall, the many pots of various sizes and shapes containing different members of the cactus family, which were scattered around in the area in front of his door, immediately put me in a *Krazy Kat* mood. *Krazy Kat* fans have always been fascinated by Herriman's ever-changing southwest backgrounds.

He'd simply been working at a card table, not in an elaborate studio, and as he talked with me he seemed a genuinely modest man. I'm sure, if he were alive today, he'd be more astounded than anyone else to learn that acquiring a Herriman is at the top of every collector's wish list.

I will always remember, and have often quoted in the years since 1936, the classic Herriman reply to a lavish compliment I tried to bestow on him. Said he, "Oh, *I'm* not much of a cartoonist, but Al Capp—*there's* a *cartoonist!*"

I took the rather faded photo of Herriman that you see on page 26 during one of several succeeding visits I made to his home. And on one occasion I watched with delight as Herriman drew the accompanying cartoon for me.

To Jus Hurd—
mitt Luff — Herriman

©King Features Syndicate

Cartoon Success Secrets

THE CHARLES MINTZ STUDIO

As I have said, in May of 1936, after a year at the Chicago Academy of Fine Arts, an interest in animation and the exciting possibility of living in glamorous Hollywood, the movie capital of the world, lured me to California. I went out on the Santa Fe Railroad. Those were the days of Harvey House restaurants at principal stops along the way and of Harvey Girl waitresses, later glorified in a hit movie. At mealtimes the train was scheduled to make perhaps a thirty-minute stop, during which time we passengers would pile into the restaurant and attempt to get our breakfast, lunch, or dinner down in the allotted time. That routine often presented a problem when the train was a few minutes late arriving at one of the meal stations. We were always on edge, wondering if we would hear "All aboard!" at exactly the moment listed in the timetable for leaving or whether we would be allowed the full half hour for eating. On several occasions the train was already rolling as we jumped aboard.

Going from the cold, wind, and snow of a Chicago winter to the warm, balmy, pastel-colored, smog-free (at that time) golden atmosphere of Hollywood made me feel that I was in a wonderful new world. For a short time I stayed at the Hollywood YMCA until, with

great good luck, I landed the job with Mintz. Shortly thereafter, I made arrangements for a room in the home of a Mrs. Hanell, a photo retoucher, who lived with her son, Russell, at 6534 Bella Vista Way, a few minutes' walk north of Hollywood Boulevard, just off Cahuenga. As I recall I had about a thirty-minute walk each morning, down Cahuenga, west on Hollywood Boulevard past such landmarks as the famous Egyptian Theater and Hollywood High School, south on Orange Avenue at Grauman's Chinese Theater, across Sunset Boulevard, and thence to 7000 Santa Monica Boulevard, where the studio was located.

What was Mintz Studio's background and place in the animation scene? In 1923, Walt Disney had signed a contract with Margaret Winkler, a New York film distributor, specifying that Disney would produce a series called *Alice in Wonderland* and would furnish a new Alice story each month for her distribution. Posters for these films advertised a WALT DISNEY COMIC, M. J. WINKLER DISTRIBUTOR, N.Y., WINKLER PICTURES. This arrangement continued for several years.

By 1927, the project had about run its course and Disney's studio had begun work on *Oswald the Lucky Rabbit* films. Meanwhile, Charles Mintz, who had married

KRAZY KAT

THE CHARLES MINTZ STUDIO
7000 SANTA MONICA BLVD.
HOLLYWOOD - - - CALIFORNIA

This photo of me in front of the Mintz Studio was taken in 1936.

Margaret Winkler in 1924, signed an agreement with Disney to turn out a year's worth of Lucky Rabbit cartoons. The cartoons made money, but Disney learned to his dismay that Mintz owned the name Oswald. To top off the situation, Margaret's brother, George, persuaded a few of the Disney animators to go with Mintz/Winkler to produce the Rabbit. Understandably, this finished business relations between them and Disney. By the time I reached California, the Charles Mintz Studio was turning out *Krazy Kat, Scrappy,* and *Color Rhapsody* cartoons.

I guess my ultimate ambition was still eventually to become a newspaper strip cartoonist. Mintz, unlike Disney, did not provide any special instruction or animation art classes that might have turned my career goal more toward animation. Nor did the animators ever take me aside with suggestions as to how I might improve my work, but of course I should have had enough gumption to bring the subject up myself. My $16 salary was for the job; when overtime from seven to ten P.M. was required, the only compensation was 60 cents for supper. Even though these amounts seem ridiculously low in the light of today's prices, let me add that a thick chocolate milkshake on Santa Monica Boulevard cost only 10 cents, and I got my room and a breakfast each day for $7 a week. That 60 cents was more

than enough for all I could eat at a diner in the center of Hollywood. I never seemed to be strapped for money in those days.

After six months of Hollywood, and still excited by the glamour of moviemaking all around me during my hours away from the studio, I told Phil Davis I was planning to leave Mintz. He acquiesced with the gracious letter of recommendation you see on page 32.

Although I had had no contact with Harry Love, one of the original Mintz group to come from New York to set up shop in Hollywood, we met in 1978 when Harry was a producer at Hanna-Barbera and the man in charge of that studio's training program. We had great fun reminiscing, and he was very gracious in showing me all around their facilities. Following that meeting, as some *CARTOONIST PROfiles* readers may remember, Harry wrote a number of animation stories for my magazine. He's now retired and living in Los Angeles.

Leaving the Mintz Studio gave me the opportunity to concentrate on an idea for a strip that I had been thinking about for some time. This was the feature eventually named *Just Hurd in Hollywood.* (You have to be aware that my given name is Justin in order to appreciate the aptness of this title. I can't remember who came up with it.)

SCRAPPY

©Charles Mintz Studio

THE CHARLES MINTZ STUDIO
7000 SANTA MONICA BLVD.
HOLLYWOOD - - - CALIFORNIA

KRAZY KAT

SCRAPPY

October 29th
1 9   3 6

TO WHOM IT MAY CONCERN:

This is to advise that Justin Hurd, who has been employed
as an artist at this studio during the past year, is re-
signing his position to enable him to accept an art scholarship.

I have always found Mr. Hurd to be a quiet conscientious
worker, and very capable in handling the type of work to
which he had been assigned. I have also observed his serious
attitude toward his work; and his pleasing personality makes
him a desirable associate.

Unhesitatingly, I can very highly recommend him to any one
desiring his services.

(Signed)

Philip Davis

Philip Davis

ff

JUST HURD IN HOLLYWOOD AND NEA

Let me set the scene in the late 1930s in the movie capital when I began to think about *Just Hurd in Hollywood*. It was the so-called golden age of the movie business, during which the major studios and their ever-watchful publicity departments controlled everything and churned out tons of copy that always presented their stars and contract players in the very best light. These heroes and heroines had no faults worth mentioning; they were made to seem larger than life. And of course when any of the movie moguls sensed that a potential scandal was brewing, they instantly moved to put out the fire. All this contributed to the feeling that I was in a dream world, and I relished it!

The present-day studio tours, during which the public can see the ordinary routine comings and goings behind the studio walls, were unheard of then. Absolutely no one could get past the receptionist at a studio unless he or she had been duly accredited by the Hays Office.

Will Hays, who had formerly been postmaster general of the United States, was known as the czar of the

movie business. You had to prove to him and his minions that you were actually currently writing for a recognized newspaper or magazine, or had an airtight contract for your project, before the receptionist at Metro-Goldwyn-Mayer, Paramount, Twentieth Century-Fox, Warner Brothers, or any of the other studios would let you get past, even to see someone in the *publicity department*. Naturally, all this secrecy and tight control made the movie business and the people involved in it seem very glamorous.

During the hours when I hadn't been at work at Mintz, I'd been walking the streets in Hollywood, literally rubbing elbows with various character players whose faces had long been familiar to me. So I was gung ho about the idea of my strip. However, before I could draw up some samples to submit to syndicates, and before I was able to get Hays Office accreditation, I had to dig up those humorous anecdotes that were going to be the backbone of the feature on my own, without official studio help.

As an example, I recall standing outside the Universal

What Movie Stars Say About "Just Hurd in Hollywood"

SHIRLEY TEMPLE:
"I like the funny pictures very much!"

TYRONE POWER:
"It's a peach of an idea."

JOHN BARRYMORE:
"Extremely interesting strip idea."

CARY GRANT:
"Hurd's strip is bound to be a success."

BOB BURNS:
"When you need more stories for that strip, see me—I got 'em."

JUST HURD IN HOLLYWOOD—

"I THREW AWAY MY BIRTHDAY PRESENT"

GARY COOPER CONFESSED RECENTLY

YET HE COULD HARDLY BE BLAMED FOR WHAT HAPPENED TO THE HANDSOME AND BEAUTIFULLY ENGRAVED CIGARETTE LIGHTER HIS CHARMING WIFE SANDRA GAVE HIM

FOR GARY HAILS FROM MONTANA WHERE THE BOYS ALWAYS LIGHT UP WITH PLAIN EVERYDAY MATCHES AND THEN USE THE GREAT OPEN SPACES FOR THEIR ASHTRAYS. AND HE WASN'T USED TO NURSING AN EXPENSIVE NEW GADGET LIKE THIS

BUT VALIANT IS THE WORD FOR GARY AND HE TOOK IT ALONG SOON AFTER WHEN HE TRAINED EAST ALONE. ON THE OBSERVATION PLATFORM ONE EVENING HE PULLED THE THING OUT OF HIS POCKET AND SUCCEEDED IN LIGHTING UP

PARAMOUNT PICTURES INC.
West Coast Studios

APPROVED FOR LUNCHEON

TIME _12:50 P._ M. _Nov 26_ 198_7_

M/s _Hurd_

DESIRES AN INTERVIEW WITH

M _John Barrymore_

NATURE OF BUSINESS

Dressing Room # 120

INTERVIEW PASS ONLY

This pass does **NOT** allow you to go on any stage or sets. It only permits you to go to the office of the person you are to interview **AND NO OTHER PLACE.**
Please return this pass to gateman as you leave studio

Form 437-A—X-58   Approved _Terry DeLapp_
Per Hud.

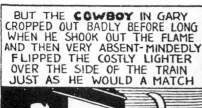

BUT THE **COWBOY** IN GARY CROPPED OUT BADLY BEFORE LONG WHEN HE SHOOK OUT THE FLAME AND THEN VERY ABSENT-MINDEDLY FLIPPED THE COSTLY LIGHTER OVER THE SIDE OF THE TRAIN JUST AS HE WOULD A MATCH

©Central Press Association

AND THOUGH GARY FELT JUST TOO TOO GUILTY THE LIGHTER WAS BEYOND REACH !

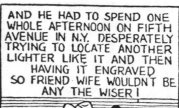

AND HE HAD TO SPEND ONE WHOLE AFTERNOON ON FIFTH AVENUE IN N.Y. DESPERATELY TRYING TO LOCATE ANOTHER LIGHTER LIKE IT AND THEN HAVING IT ENGRAVED SO FRIEND WIFE WOULDN'T BE ANY THE WISER !

JUST HURD

This cleverly drawn feature amusingly depicts funny and interesting incidents in the lives of the leading movie stars—as told to Justin G. Hurd, the artist, by the film stars themselves!

A brand-new series idea certain to interest all types of readers—JUST HURD IN HOLLYWOOD belongs in your newspaper. Three releases each week!

To Justin —
with thanks and
good wishes!
Cary Grant.

JUST HURD IN HOLLYWOOD—

THE TAIL FELL OFF A PLANE

CLAUDETTE COLBERT WAS FLYING IN SEVERAL YEARS AGO!

JUST BECAUSE SHE HAD TO GET TO PARIS FROM CAIRO, EGYPT IN AN AWFUL HURRY, THE PLANE **WOULD** BE GROUNDED BY BAD WEATHER

AND SHE **WOULD** BE STRANDED IN A GOD-FORSAKEN TOWN THAT PROBABLY NOT EVEN THE GEOGRAPHERS' EVER HEARD OF!

AND AFTER A FEARFUL NIGHT IN THE LOCAL HOTEL-SHE **WOULD** HAVE TO BOARD ANOTHER RICKETY PLANE WHICH BUMPED ALONG THE RUNWAY AS THOUGH THE FIELD WERE A GIANT WASHBOARD!

COPYRIGHT 1938 KING FEATURES SYNDICATE, Inc.

New York   # Central Press Association   *Cleveland*

ANITA LOUISE:

"Now all Hollywood can say, "See you in the funny papers.""

CHESTER MORRIS:

"Can I have the original on me? I want to frame it."

NELSON EDDY:

"Just Hurd's strip is truly something different and new."

ZASU PITTS:

"I want to be in Mr. Hurd's strip—but I can't think of a thing, oh, dear!"

meet him at the RKO lot the following morning. His only condition was that I clear this with Perry Lieber, the publicity chief at the studio where Grant was shooting *Bringing Up Baby* with co-star Katharine Hepburn. At this stage I wouldn't even have had access to the publicity department without my OK from Cary Grant. Needless to say, I followed up his invitation and went to the sound stage at RKO.

Fortunately, I soon sold my strip idea to the Central Press Association, which was a subsidiary of King Features Syndicate and distributed *Just Hurd in Hollywood* three times a week to newspapers.

In 1938, *Just Hurd in Hollywood* was canceled and I went to work in the Editorial Art Department of the Newspaper Enterprise Association (NEA) at West 3rd and Lakeside Avenue in Cleveland. One of my assignments was to draw the political cartoon for the NEA Weekly Service, which obviously was sent to weekly newspaper clients. These were the days before Op-Ed pages became regular features in many newspapers, and the feeling was that a syndicated political cartoon should more or less straddle the fence on many issues, so that client newspaper editors having a variety of political opinions wouldn't get mad when a cartoon displeased them and thus consign it to the circular file.

Studios one day and seeing Cary Grant headed toward me. Unabashedly I went up to him and explained that I'd like to elicit some humorous anecdotes from him for *Just Hurd in Hollywood*. I'm sure he sensed that what I was talking about was speculative at that point, but in a very friendly and gracious way, he invited me to

Dance of the Pensioneers

(Copyright 1939, NEA Service, Inc. Printed in U.S.A.)

CRYPTO CHRIS AND WORLD WAR II

Good fortune, during my World War II army service from 1942 to 1946, enabled me to keep my drawing hand limbered up and also to develop a cartoon drawing technique that has stayed with me to this day. How does the army decide on a particular niche for each soldier? After I was drafted in 1942, I was shipped to Camp Crowder in Neosho, Missouri, to be in the Signal Corps. This decision resulted from a listing in an army manual stating that if a soldier's civilian occupation was Animation Artist—Motion Picture, he should be placed in the Signal Corps—that branch being the one responsible for army training films. Since I had been an in-betweener at the Charles Mintz Studio, I did land in the Signal Corps, but as you've already guessed, I never had anything to do with training films during the four years of my service. To make a short story long, sometime later, when I was stationed at Fort Monmouth, New Jersey, I came down with pneumonia while on a weekend pass in New York City and was ambulanced to the army hospital on Governors Island in New York Harbor. During a month's stay at that institution, I ran into a friend from Monmouth who told me there would be an upcoming vacancy in the Signal Intelligence Section of the First Army and Eastern Defense Command on Governors Island.

After my discharge from the hospital, orders were cut transferring me from Fort Monmouth to my new post in the Signal Intelligence Section. The details of that section's activities were so secret that I, being super-conscientious, didn't even tell my folks what I was doing for the remaining three-plus years of my army service. Our duties became public knowledge after the war. Principally my job consisted in receiving from the chief signal officer in Washington the various components—gear wheels, nuts and bolts, and so on—that were constantly being changed, entered, removed, from code machines so that the same message sent out in code a hundred times would appear to the receivers completely different in each instance.

But now to the important stuff. The officer in charge of the section was enthusiastic about my doing a weekly cartoon I named *Crypto Chris,* which was sent to all army installations in the United States and overseas. It was pointed toward those goofballs who might be handling classified documents carelessly and would thus compromise the security of all sorts of units in the field. Unfortunately, examples of this stalwart character Crypto disappeared during a move my family and I made from Cleveland, Ohio, to Westport, Connecticut, in 1964. The moving van company was responsible for this boo-boo. Suffice it to say that Crypto demonstrated each week how *not* to perform the duties of someone entrusted with the handling of classified material. He was obviously a forerunner of the Stew Pidd character I created for the American Steel & Wire Company in the years after the war, when I operated an industrial cartoon studio in Cleveland. Naturally, Stew was bungling his way through an entirely different milieu from Crypto Chris. Stew always got his necktie caught in the machinery, whereas Chris would be shown carefully discarding top-secret papers in the round file rather than shredding them, burning them, or whatever.

And now to the change in technique that has stayed with me. Naturally these just-described cryptographic duties had to be my first priority, with the result that *Crypto Chris,* and another character I later added to my cartoon responsibility, had to be turned out with great speed. Like all good Landon students, I had been slowly making a careful pencil drawing in civilian life, and then laboriously inking it with the famous Gillott 170 or 290 pen. That took time. One fortunate day in the army I picked up a brush and tried to dash off the ink finish with this new tool, which I had used previously only for filling in blacks. (Gradually during the several years when I was putting those army characters through their paces, I discarded the pen altogether and even used the brush for lettering!) Anyhow, since then I've always used a Winsor & Newton Series 7 No. 00 brush for all cartoon drawing, both characters and backgrounds. Only the lettering is done with an Alvin draft liner.

Crypto Chris

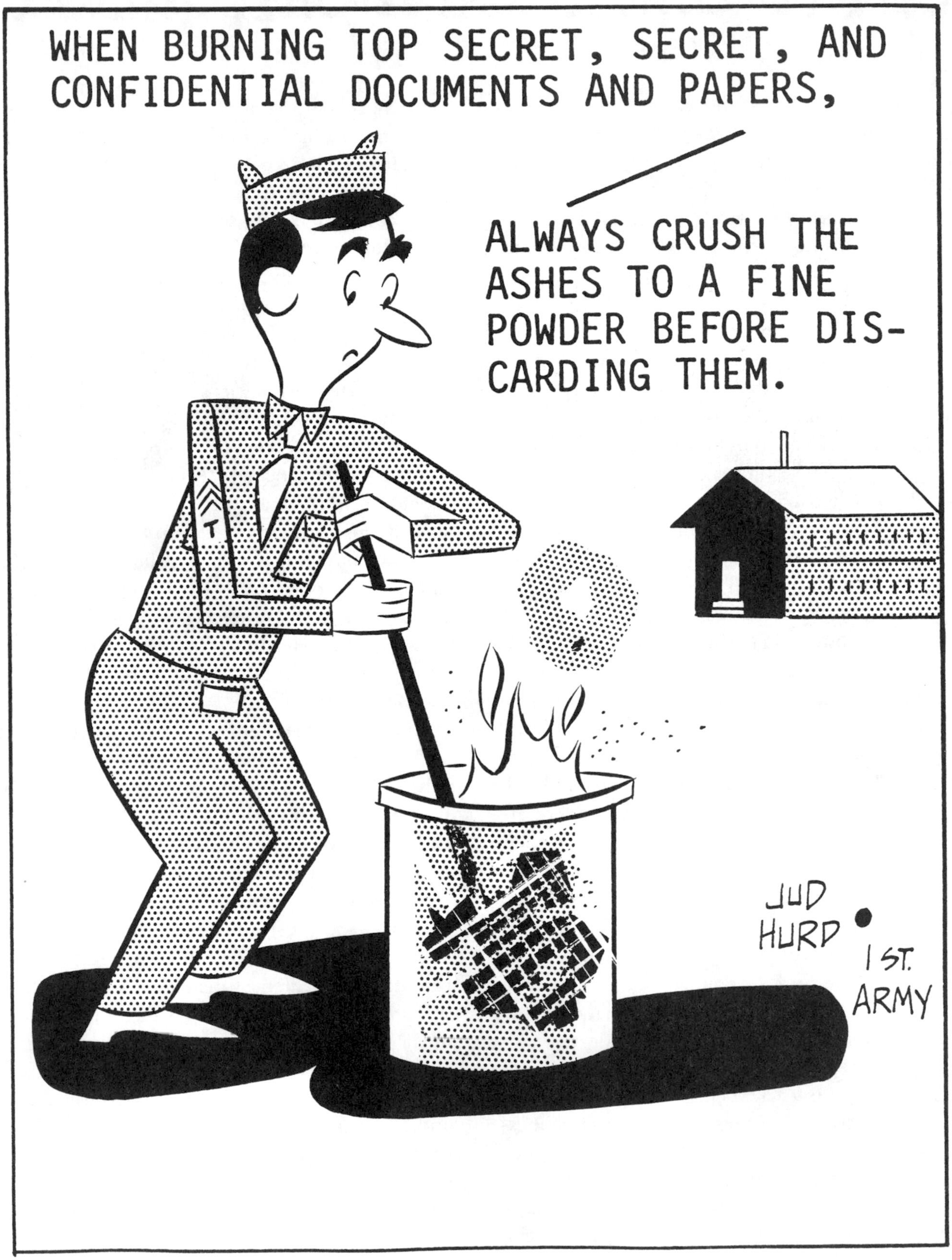

With General Omar N. Bradley in 1965

Originally our headquarters had been designated as the First Army and Eastern Defense Command, since it was frequently reported that German submarines were lurking off our shores. However, sometime after my arrival, some of the people in our group were transferred via the S.S. *Queen Elizabeth* to England to be part of First Army Headquarters. Others of us remained behind as the Eastern Defense Command, commanded by General Hugh Drum, who was reputed to be the highest-ranking general in the army at that time. In Europe General Omar N. Bradley took charge of the First Army.

Which brings me to a very interesting personal encounter that I had with General Bradley in 1965, when the National Cartoonists Society decided to have a War Cartoonists' Night in New York City at the old Astor Hotel on Broadway. Here's how that came about: During my three-month hospitalization at Fort Dix in New Jersey in 1946, a friend in my ward, Bill Biesel, sometimes talked about a friend of his, Chet Hansen, who was an aide to the general and who had helped in writing Bradley's biography. Fast-forward to 1965, when we were all invited to attend the banquet wearing our World War II uniforms. I now learned that the aforementioned Chet Hansen was living in New Canaan near us here in Westport. It didn't take me long to invite him for the big evening, when it was disclosed that General Bradley himself was to be the principal speaker. At some point during the dinner, Chet Hansen said to Bill Biesel and myself, who were sitting next

OFFICE OF

GENERAL OF THE ARMY OMAR N. BRADLEY

WASHINGTON

Dear Mr. Hurd:

Thank you very much for the October 1965 copy of the Newsletter which you edit for the National Cartoonists Society. It will serve as a very pleasing reminder of a most enjoyable evening. You were very thoughtful to send it. I have autographed the picture enclosed with your letter and am returning it herewith.

I thoroughly enjoyed "War Cartoonists Night" on September 22nd. Everything about it was just fine and I don't know when I have enjoyed an evening so much. Vic Herman and his committee are to be congratulated on the splendid program.

Thanking you for your good wishes, and with kindest personal regards, I am

Sincerely,

Omar N. Bradley

Mr. Jud Hurd
281 Bayberry Lane
Westport, Connecticut 06882

to him, "After the banquet is over, the General would like the four of us to have a drink together in his suite upstairs." We lost no time in accepting this invitation to spend a little time with one of the key figures in the war.

Despite General Bradley's becoming the famous army group commander as the Allied Forces plunged forward from Omaha Beach in Normandy, we found immediately, upon meeting him, that he was the same folksy, friendly, unaffected man the news media had always said he was. He quickly took off the much-beribboned jacket you can see in the photo on page 41 and had us sit down while he gathered up a bucket of ice preparatory to mixing us drinks. As we were sampling his old-fashioneds a few moments later, he commented that during days in the field in Europe, he just added orange marmalade to the whiskey to come up with an instantaneous old-fashioned!

General Bradley also told us about a late-afternoon appointment with President Harry Truman in the Oval Office. Truman, appearing tired and weary, reached into the lower drawer of his desk, pulled out a bottle of firewater, and slammed it down with the order, "I've had a hard day—have a drink!"

As a further example of his folksiness, when I told him that I had a young son who, someday, would be proud to have a photo of his dad with the general, he took immediate action. He started moving chairs around, brought a lamp or two into better spots for a photo, put on the jacket with the umpteen ribbons, and we were ready for the shot you see here, all with the utmost graciousness.

One other amusing item about War Cartoonists' Night. My final World War II uniform was in such dilapidated and weatherbeaten shape that I had long since discarded it. Fortunately, being in New York City I was able to go into one of the numerous theatrical costume shops, describe the uniform I had worn, the few routine-type medals I'd been authorized to wear—the whole ball of wax—and come out looking like a carbon copy of the Jud Hurd who had left Tilton General Hospital, Fort Dix, almost twenty years earlier.

Industrial Cartoons, Ticker Toons, and Health Capsules

Late in 1946, after my discharge from the army, I recommenced my civilian cartoon career at an industrial cartoon studio, doing a great variety of cartoon and layout assignments for the house organs and sales magazines published by large industrial companies in the Cleveland area. These included the Standard Oil Company of Ohio (Sohio) with its *Progressive Dealer* and *Bulk Station News,* the Columbia Transportation Company and its *Columbia Shipmate* publication, the American Steel & Wire Company and its *Wireco Life,* the Erie Railroad, and others. Although I didn't realize it at the time, the excitement and battery-charging effects of doing this publication work were the first indication of how much I would later enjoy the years of editing and producing *CARTOONIST PROfiles.*

Take the case of the Standard Oil Company of Ohio: They were the first postwar clients who kept me busy with a great deal of work. Several staff members in their sales publications department constantly traveled around Ohio visiting huge bulk stations and other installations. During each visit they would take a number of photos of employees and make copious notes about any funny or interesting things that had happened since the last visit. When one of these staff members returned to the home office in Cleveland, I would get a rush phone call, during which I would frantically jot down the physical descriptions of all the individuals who were to be involved in each cartoon, the remarks each made, and details as to the background in which each cartoon took place. Whew! It makes me tired, even now, to remember that this procedure was repeated for each of the several cartoons that the staff member expected to have put in his hands later that same afternoon. I don't wonder that

one or two headaches per week were par for the course in those days. After furiously cartooning till late afternoon, I would drive pell-mell five miles to the Sohio offices in downtown Cleveland, desperately try to find that nonexistent parking space, and finally arrive out of breath just in time for my day's output to be handed to the anxiously waiting engraver. This routine was repeated for about a week for each issue of *The Bulk Station News,* and then I would jump to doing layouts of the photos that had been taken and to other cartoons for Sohio publications. I had good relations with all of my industrial clients. The income from Sohio was by far the largest, but the duties were more stressful than my work for some of the other companies.

In the case of the Columbia Transportation Company, which operated a number of ore boats plying the Great Lakes, I would go to their offices, sit down with an editor, and make notes of the details for the half-dozen or so cartoons they would require for a large six-panel strip I named *Columbia Capers.* This was a somewhat more leisurely procedure than was the case with Sohio. I've included here a sample of my work for each of these valued clients. I've always considered myself very fortunate to have found, so soon after my army discharge, a substantial company like Sohio who seemed as eager to get my work as I was to do it for them.

At this point I'd like to tell you about a method for developing accounts with industrial clients that one competitor of mine, during the days I've been talking about, shared with me. After looking over publications of various large companies, he decided to appear personally each morning on the doorsteps of the companies he decided he'd like to cartoon for. Fortunately he was good enough to land an assignment to do a small cartoon at several of them. Thereafter, he would be

Johnny-on-the-spot each day at each company. He soon discovered that if there was an immediate need at "Company A" for a drawing, it was easier to have my friend sit down and do that cartoon than call an art studio. From A he called at Company B, and then C. He built up quite a business in this way. In later years, I discovered that Frank Evers, in the days before he became the editorial cartoonist for the *New York Daily News,* used to make similar calls to several newspapers in New Jersey each day. He'd toss off a cartoon at his first stop, hop into his car, get back on the freeway and off at the second paper, and so on.

©Standard Oil Co. of Ohio

Cover for the Sohio magazine

Cartoon Success Secrets

COLUMBIA CAPERS

by Jud Hurd

O.K. LET'S HAVE EM. THE CHIEF ISN'T COMING!

WOLVERINE

SINCE CAPT. GEGENHEIMER AND CHIEF JOHN-SON GAINED A LITTLE WEIGHT OVER THE WIN-TER, IT'S REALLY SOMETHING TO SEE HOW THEY WATCH EACH OTHER'S CALORIES LIKE HAWKS! THINGS ARE SO BAD THAT THE CAPT. CAN'T EVEN GET HIS HANDS ON ONE LITTLE CRUMB OF CAKE WHEN THE CHIEF'S IN SIGHT!

SIERRA

WONDER WHO THE OFFICER AND MASTER CARPENTER IS WHO BUILT A SET OF STEPS IN THE FORWARD CABIN WITHOUT RECKONING WITH THE WIDTH OF THE DOOR?

HERE HE COMES!

THERE HE GOES!

WHOOSH

C.W. GALLOWAY

IT'S HARD TO TELL IF ANDY WILSON, 3RD ASST. ENG., IS A FORWARD OR AFTER-END MAN. HE SURE HAS BEEN BUSY GETTING THINGS IN ORDER ON DECK!

WELL, THAT'S HAND, GAME, MATCH AND TOURNAMENT. HERE, HECTOR, CHECK OUR ADDING MACHINE TOTALS!

J.H. FRANTZ

THE CANASTA RAGE HAS HIT THE FRANTZ. IN-TRODUCED BY MR. AND MRS. SHOLETTE, IT'S NOW REACHED THE TOURNAMENT STAGE. THE LITTLE WOMAN AND HER PARTNER USUALLY WIN, BUT WE'RE INCLINED TO SUSPECT THAT HER ALWAYS KEEPING SCORE HAS SOMETHING TO DO WITH IT!

R.E. MOODY

HOWARD "SLIM" DOBB, OUR NEW 8 TO 12 A.B. DECKWATCH, WILL BE A PAPA IN AUGUST. FROM THE AMOUNT OF MILK WE'VE SEEN HOWARD DRINK AT ONE SITTING, THE NEW ARRIVAL IS GOING TO HAVE PLENTY OF COM-PETITION FOR HIS COW JUICE THIS WINTER.

HOWARD M. HANNA, JR.

NORWAY 5413 MI.

IT LOOKS LIKE OUR 2ND A.E., MAGNUS GRIPNE, IS PLANNING ON GOING TO NORWAY AGAIN NEXT WINTER. IF HE KEEPS ON PLAYING POKER, HE MAY HAVE TO SWIM OVER!

SUN-TIMES DAILY NEWS
Syndicate

401 NORTH WABASH   CHICAGO 11, ILLINOIS   WHITEHALL 3-3000

Release Monday, Feb. 20, 1961

TICKER TOONS

THE INVESTOR IN A SMALL BUSINESS INVEST-MENT CO. STOCK GETS A SPECIAL TAX ADVANTAGE.

ANY LOSS IN SELLING CAN BE DEDUCTED FROM EARNED INCOME!

IT DOESN'T FIRST HAVE TO BE DEDUCTED FROM CAPITAL GAINS AS IS THE CASE IN SELLING MOST STOCKS.

Release Tuesday, Feb. 21, 1961

TICKER TOONS

ONE 8-MONTH OLD SMALL BUSINESS INVESTMENT CO. HAS ACTIVELY INVESTIGATED OVER 350 DIFFERENT SITUATIONS.

OUT OF THIS GROUP, THEY HAVE INVESTED IN 11 COMPANIES & ARE CLOSING 4 MORE DEALS.

Release Wednesday, Feb. 22, 1961

TICKER TOONS

THE SMALL, NEW BUSI-NESS WHICH IS SUCCESSFUL, OFTEN HAS A PERIOD OF MAX-IMUM GROWTH. THEN GROWTH LEVELS OFF.

A CLAIMED ADVANTAGE OF SBIC'S IS THAT THEY HOLD STOCKS JUST DURING THIS MAX-IMUM GROWTH PERIOD.

Release Thursday, Feb. 23, 1961

TICKER TOONS

PROBABLY THE SMALL BUSINESS CAN'T GET A LONG-TERM BANK LOAN. AND THEY'RE NOT BIG ENOUGH TO SELL STOCK PUBLICLY.

NOW THEY CAN LOGICALLY TURN TO THE SMALL BUSINESS INVESTMENT COMPANY FOR CAPITAL.

Release Friday, Feb. 24, 1961

TICKER TOONS

MUTUAL FUNDS CAN BORROW ONLY 35% OF THEIR NET WORTH.

SBIC'S CAN BORROW 400% OF THEIR NET WORTH IF THEY NEED MONEY TO TAKE ADVAN-TAGE OF GOOD OPPORTUNITIES IN SMALL BUSINESSES.

Release Saturday, Feb. 25, 1961

TICKER TOONS

CHRISTIANA SECURITIES' IS A STOCK OF A DUPONT FAMILY-CON-TROLLED HOLDING CO., WHOSE MAIN ASSET IS 12,200,000 SHARES OF DUPONT COMMON.

NOT A PENNY STOCK!

YOU CAN BUY IT OVER-THE-COUNTER FOR AROUND $14,000 A SHARE.

Scott Davis, floor broker, and James E. Day, president of the Midwest Stock Exchange, examine one of my *Ticker Toons* with me.

With me during a stock exchange conference are (from left) Edward T. McCormick, president of the American Stock Exchange, and Milton J. Stevens, chairman of the board of Republic Transcontinental Industries.

HEALTH CAPSULES ®
by M. Petti, M.D. & Jud Hurd

Dr. Michael A. Petti

Jud Hurd

HEALTH CAPSULES®
by Michael A. Petti, M.D.

IS THERE ANY ADVANTAGE IN HAVING A HERNIA REPAIRED WHEN IT'S STILL RELATIVELY SMALL?

YES.

4/28 JUD HURD

© 1995 UFS, Inc.

HAVING IT DONE EARLY WILL SHORTEN THE TIME FOR SURGERY AND REDUCE YOUR CHANCES OF COMPLICATIONS OR A RECURRENCE.

Health Capsules is not intended to be of a diagnostic nature.

HEALTH CAPSULES®
by Michael A. Petti, M.D.

¿CUÁNTO PESCADO HAY QUE COMER COMO PROTECCIÓN CONTRA LA ENFERMEDAD AL CORAZÓN?

1/20 JUD HURD

© 1995 UFS, Inc.

SÓLO BASTA CON COMER UNA PORCIÓN A LA SEMANA.

HEALTH CAPSULES®
by Michael A. Petti, M.D.

IF YOU TAKE VITAMIN C PILLS, WHICH TYPE IS BEST?

4/25 JUD HURD

© 1995 UFS, Inc.

PLAIN, ORDINARY VITAMIN C PILLS ARE AS EFFECTIVE AS ANY OTHER KIND AND LESS EXPENSIVE.

Health Capsules is not intended to be of a diagnostic nature

HEALTH CAPSULES®
by Michael A. Petti, M.D.

CAN A MOUTHWASH GET RID OF ALL MOUTH ODORS?

NO. FOR EXAMPLE, MOUTH-WASHES CANNOT ELIM-INATE THE ODORS OF ALCOHOL, CIGARETTES, ONIONS OR GARLIC.

Health Capsules is not intended to be of a diagnostic nature.

HEALTH CAPSULES®
by Michael A. Petti, M.D.

HOW DO YOU CHOOSE LOW-FAT, LOW-CALORIE CANNED FOODS?

CHOOSE CANNED FOODS THAT ARE PACKED IN WATER INSTEAD OF OIL OR HEAVY SYRUP.

Health Capsules is not intended to be of a diagnostic nature.

HEALTH CAPSULES®
by Michael A. Petti, M.D.

WILL MELONS RIPEN AFTER YOU BUY THEM?

WATERMELON AND HONEYDEW WILL NOT, BUT CANTALOUPE WILL CONTINUE TO RIPEN ON YOUR COUNTER.

Health Capsules is not intended to be of a diagnostic nature.

Dr. Mike Petti and I are in complete agreement that the more than forty years during which we collaborated in the production of *Health Capsules* were very happy and successful ones for us and for the United Feature Syndicate. Mike supplied the medical questions and answers and I produced the humorous illustrations that accompanied them.

HEALTH CAPSULES®
by Michael A. Petti, M.D.

IS IT TRUE THAT CHIL-DREN SHOULD NOT DRINK MILK?

CHILDREN UNDER ONE SHOULD HAVE BREAST MILK OR FORMULA, NOT COW'S MILK. OLDER CHILDREN SHOULD DRINK LOW-FAT COW'S MILK.

Health Capsules is not intended to be of a diagnostic nature.

HEALTH CAPSULES®
by Michael A. Petti, M.D.

WHAT IS THE BEST WAY TO PRESERVE YOUR HEARING?

AVOID LOUD NOISE WHENEVER YOU CAN AND USE ADEQUATE EAR PLUGS WHEN YOU CAN'T AVOID THE NOISE.

Health Capsules is not intended to be of a diagnostic nature.

HEALTH CAPSULES®
by Michael A. Petti, M.D.

WILL EATING EXTRA PRO-TEIN OR AMINO ACID SUPPLEMENTS INCREASE YOUR MUSCLE SIZE?

NO. A NORMAL DIET GIVES YOU ALL THE PRO-TEIN YOU CAN USE. TOO MUCH PROTEIN CREATES PROBLEMS.

Health Capsules is not intended to be of a diagnostic nature.

NATIONAL CARTOONISTS SOCIETY

For a number of years after its founding in 1946, the National Cartoonists Society had been holding monthly meetings in New York City, culminating in a one-night Reuben Awards Dinner each April. In 1963 an attempt was made to start a tradition of holding a several-day convention, during which out-of-town members would have more time to talk shop, reminisce, and have fun with colleagues. We all had a great time at the initial gathering, but the idea lapsed for some time after that, and it wasn't until recently that three- or four-day affairs became an NCS habit.

As part of the first convention in 1963, the City of New York erected the street sign you see here on Broadway, in front of the old Astor Hotel, which was the site of the meetings. Shown in the accompanying photo are, left to right: Jerry Robinson (of *Batman* Joker fame); Harry (*Abie the Agent*) Hershfield; Bob *(They'll Do It Every Time)* Dunn; Ed (*Cleveland Plain Dealer* Pulitzer Prize–winning editorial cartoonist) Kuekes; me; and Bill *(Smokey Stover)* Holman.

Cartoon Success Secrets

NATIONAL CARTOONISTS SOCIETY

NEWSLETTER
NOVEMBER 1965

Editor:
JUD HURD
281 Bayberry Lane
Westport, Conn.
06882

NCS 5 Meet LBJ !

Shown on the cover of one of these early newsletters I edited are (left to right) Bill Mauldin, Don Sherwood, Mort Walker, President Lyndon Johnson, Milt Caniff, and George Wunder.

Dik Browne loved to refer to himself as a "cottage industry" during his days in Wilton, Connecticut. He's shown here working amid the laundry in his basement studio.

NCS Goes National

Although the National Cartoonists Society has borne that name since its founding in 1946, it has been truly national only in very recent years. From 1946 until approximately 1983, the monthly meetings were always held in New York City, as was the annual Reuben Awards Dinner. Florida and West Coast members, and all those whose bases of operation were scattered throughout the United States, felt that their thoughts and suggestions never really percolated through to the Board of Governors in New York. As far as they were concerned, they were outsiders.

Nowadays, the situation is different. Regional chapters hold meetings in various parts of the country, and the annual Reuben affair has been celebrated in such widely separated spots as Washington, D.C., San Francisco, Toronto, Nassau in the Bahamas, and Scottsdale, Arizona. With that said, I'll risk blowing my own horn a bit and show you a letter from the late, great Dik Browne about these meetings.

HÄGAR
The Horrible

DIK BROWNE

1611 Clower Creek Drive
#H-136
Sarasota
Florida 33581

April 19, 1983

Mr. Jud Hurd
281 Bayberry Lane
Westport
Connecticut 06880

Dear Jud:

    I just talked to Mort Walker who tells me that the
Los Angeles meeting was a huge success, with the biggest
turnout they've had in years. This is just a note to the
man who really made it possible.

    A few years ago it seemed like a comedy of frustration
getting your very clear and rational proposal for a national
chairman to a reality. As you remember, your objective was
eventually for a convention on the West Coast. It was frozen
for a few years, then had to be maneuvered through a minefield
but finally the laws of inertia were overcome and it became
a reality. I had hoped you would attend this year's ball so
you could see the fruit of your labors, and was sorry to
learn you did not attend.

    I am sorry to say that work such as yours is seldom
appreciated. Indeed, most men are unaware of it. More's
the pity. But as a disinterested party, I want to thank
you for this added service which you have given to the
cartoonists' society. Give my best to Claudia and stay
well.

                              Sincerely,

                              DIK

                              Dik Browne

DB/'s

HAROLD GRAY AND LITTLE ORPHAN ANNIE

A few cartoonists have always been told they look like the principal characters in their comic strips; George McManus and Jiggs in *Bringing Up Father* comes to mind, as does Dik Browne and *Hagar the Horrible*. Although Harold Gray, the cartoonist father of *Little Orphan Annie,* didn't particularly remind me of his Daddy Warbucks in looks, his energy, drive, and his strong opinions most certainly resembled Daddy's character traits in spades!

Harold Gray was born in Kankakee, Illinois, in 1894, graduated from Purdue University, served as a lieutenant in World War I, assisted cartoonist Sidney Smith on *The Gumps* in Chicago, and created *Little Orphan Annie* in 1924 for the New York News–Chicago Tribune Syndicate. Over the years he lived in a number of homes in Westport, Connecticut, but I first met him around 1937, when he was living in a mansion on Green Acre Lane. He had responded to my letter, asking for an audience, by inviting me to visit him if and when I happened to be in town.

I was much impressed, during our first meeting, that this master comic strip storyteller shared with me, a complete stranger, some techniques I might use in coming up with comic strip continuities. He hinted that I could read the novels of Charles Dickens, for instance, and perhaps modernize characters and situations that had proved intriguing and effective in Victorian days. It sounds simple to state it here, but this opened up a whole new world for me, in plot and character construction.

Harold Gray donated his *Little Orphan Annie* originals, the datebooks in which he wrote his strip's dialogue in the space provided for each day of the week, and his correspondence and other effects to Boston University. These materials are housed in the Special Collections Department. It was there some years ago that I began reading the very first strips, which appeared in 1924. I was enormously impressed by the speed and

the certainty with which Gray made the individual personalities and characteristics of each of the people in *Annie* so clear. His masterful touch reminded me very much of the same skill demonstrated by Charles Dickens!

Several other visits with Gray followed in succeeding years, and then in 1964, when my family and I moved to Westport, we began to see more of him. Happily, during the years before Harold's death in 1968, he and his wife, Winifred, would join my wife, Claudia, and our son Philip, for a lunch full of good conversation about once a month. (By this time, the Grays were spending their winters in La Jolla, California.)

For my part, I enjoyed immensely listening to Harold talk enthusiastically and at length about his Chicago days and his work on *The Gumps* with Sidney Smith and a great variety of other subjects. And I believe *he* got a kick out of these meetings because of my keen interest in all *his* activities. Incidentally, my enthusiasm for hearing the details of friends' vocations and avocations has always seemed to go far beyond the usual. This probably explains the excitement I get from producing *CARTOONIST PROfiles*. When acquaintances return from a trip, for instance, I always belabor

them with questions such as "What airline did you take? What time of day did you arrive? How did your on-the-spot impression of such-and-such a city compare with what you'd previously read of it? Do most of the people in the city you visited live in apartments or individual houses?" So I suppose my unusual degree of interest in Harold Gray's methods of work and his other activities was music to his ears.

The energy that Harold projected in any conversation was also responsible for his many enthusiastic auto trips from coast to coast, during which he did all the driving. I remember his showing me a map of the United States one year, on which he had indicated with a red marker all the highways and byways he had traversed on that year's treks. He was submitting a copy of this to the IRS as an exhibit in connection with business expenses for that year's income tax report.

HEY! WITH ALL TH' UPROAR "POLECAT" PEW HAS BEEN STIRRIN' UP, I DON'T EVEN KNOW TH' NAME O' OUR CAND'DATE!

I IMAGINE A LOT OF VOTERS DON'T KNOW HIS NAME, EITHER, ANNIE! WHAT DIFFERENCE WILL IT MAKE?

BUT, LEAPIN' LIZARDS! Y'GOTTA KNOW WHO YER VOTIN' FOR!

THE HEAVY VOTE TURNS OUT TO VOTE AGAINST SOME CANDIDATE! FEW BOTHER TO VOTE FOR ANYONE!

OUR MAN IS NO SPELLBINDER! JUST A QUIET, HONEST, COMPETENT MAN WITH A HEART AND BRAINS, WHO'LL RUN THIS TOWN FOR THE DECENT PEOPLE HERE: HIS NAME'S JOHN Q JONES!

GEE! I NEVER EVEN HEARD OF HIM!

I BEEN SNOOPIN' AROUND; HARDLY ANYONE SEEMS TO KNOW MUCH 'BOUT OUR CAND'DATE, JOHN Q JONES... NOT EVEN HIS NAME!

THEY'LL KNOW A LOT ABOUT HIM IN THE NEXT FOUR YEARS!

AND THEY'LL BE GLAD THEY ELECTED HIM MAYOR!
HM·M·~ SURE; ONLY... ONLY SHOULDN'T HE BE OUT MAKIN' SPEECHES?

HE'S MADE A FEW, WHERE THEY COUNT! IT TAKES MORE THAN SOUND TRUCKS AND LOUD, EMPTY PROMISES TO WIN ELECTIONS ... AT LEAST IN MY TOWN, ANNIE!

GEE, BIG AUGUST!
I SURE HOPE SO!

Sample pages from the Gray datebook in which he wrote each day's Annie *dialogue*

Harold loved to stop at corner stores, gas stations, and diners in towns everywhere and, without disclosing his identity, get into conversations with the natives, to find out what people were talking about. Incidentally these efforts to project authenticity into *Little Orphan Annie* remind me of how Gray's drawing style also made his characters stand out. While cartoonist readers of comic strips have always been interested in the quality of line demonstrated by the creator, in the kind of a pen or brush that he or she uses, the shading and the cross-hatching, the average reader *isn't* concerned with these details. I believe that, while reading *Annie,* I always thought of the characters as real people, and never once as two-dimensional *drawings* of Annie, Daddy Warbucks, or any of the other memorable characters. Gray wasn't cluttering things up with a fancy display of penwork, in other words. In this connection I think you'll be fascinated by a letter I uncovered ten years ago at Boston University. Among Gray's papers was a letter written to him by John Updike when the famous author was just *fifteen* years old. Personally. I've never read a Gray critique by a writer of any age to equal the youthful Updike's skillful comments on the work of Annie's creator. I'm including Updike's postcard reaction after I sent him a copy of his boyhood letter.

An epilogue: Bob Leffingwell, a cousin of Harold's, had been doing the lettering and the filling in of the blacks in *Annie* for a number of years but was no longer involved with the strip after Gray's death in 1968. Philip (Tex) Blaisdell, a versatile and experienced cartoonist, assumed the drawing duties. Blaisdell told me at the time that he considered this assignment as the culmination of his career. He loved drawing it. The strip was then written by Elliott Caplin (brother of Al *Li'l Abner* Capp). Caplin, incidentally, is noteworthy on several counts. I believe at one point he was writing the continuity for four or five strips simultaneously; *Big Ben Bolt, Juliet Jones,* and others were on his list. Another of Elliott's specialties was his ability to create a concept and the characters for a proposed strip, select a cartoonist

January 2, 1948

Mr. Harold Gray
c/o New York News Syndicate
220 East 42cd Street
New York 17, New York

Dear Mr. Gray:

I don't suppose that I am being original when I admit that ORPHAN ANNIe is, and has been for a long time, my favorite comic strip. There are many millions like me. The appeal of your comic strip is an American phenomenon that has affected the public for many years, and will, I hope, continue to do so for many more.

I admire the magnificent plotting of Annie's adventures. They are just as adventure strips should be--fast moving, slightly macabre (witness Mr. Am), occasionally humorous, and above all, they show a great deal of the viciousness of human nature. I am very fond of the gossip-in-the-street scenes you frequently use. Contrary to comic-strip tradition, the people are not pleasantly benign, but gossiping, sadistic, and stupid, which is just as it really is.

Your villains are completely black and Annie and crew are practically perfect, which is as it should be. To me there is nothing more annoying in a strip than to be in the dark as to who is the hero and who the villain. I like the methods in which you polish off your evil-doers. One of my happiest moments was spent in gloating over some hideous child (I forget his name) who had been annoying Annie toppled into the wet cement of a dam being constructed. I hate your villains to the point where I could rip them from the paper. No other strip arouses me so. For instance, I thought Mumbles was cute.

Your draughtsmanship is beyond reproach. The drawing is simple and clear, but extremely effective. You could tell just by looking at the faces who is the trouble maker and who isn't, without any dialogue. The facial features, the big, blunt fingered hands, the way you handle light and shadows are all excellently done. Even the talk balloons are good, the lettering small and clean, the margins wide, and the connection between the speaker and his remark wiggles a little, all of which, to my eye, is as artistic as you can get.

All this well-deserved praise is leading up to something, of course, and the catch is a rather big favor I want you to do for me. I need a picture to alleviate the blankness of one of my bedroom walls, and there is nothing that I would like better than a little momento of the comic strip I have followed closely for over a decade. So--could you possibly send me a little autographed sketch of Annie that you have done yourself? I realize that you probably have some printed cards you send to people like me, but could you maybe do just a quick sketch by yourself? Nothing fancy, just what you have done yourself. I you cannot do this (and I really wouldn't blame you) will you send me anything you like, perhaps an original comic strip? Whatever I get will be appreciated, framed, and hung.

Sincerely,
John Updike
Elverson R. D. #2
Pennsylvania

Future author John Updike wrote this perceptive *Annie* critique to Harold Gray at the age of fifteen.

John Updike
675 Hale Street
Beverly Farms, MA 01915

Healy Hall
Georgetown
Washington, DC
HISTORIC PRESERVATION

© USPS 1988

Mr. Jud Hurd
Cartoonist Profiles
P. O. Box 325
Fairfield, CT   06430

ΙΙΙ····ΙΙ··Ι·Ι·Ι··ΙΙΙΙΙ··ΙΙ····ΙΙ··Ι·Ι·Ι·Ι··ΙΙ

July 23

Dear Mr. Hurd:

My goodness, what a busy fellow & I
was! It was a hobby of mine, to coax cartoons out
of people, and I laid it on thick. I was fifteen
when I wrote this letter. Of course you have my
permission to quote it. How sweet that it has sur-
vived the years. And thanks for the   copies of
your magazine; I looked into one and found a profile
of my old comrade at the Ruskin School of Drawing
and Fine Art, Tom Engelhardt. He once babysat for
my infant daughter so my wife and I could have lunch
with the E.B.Whites.

Best wishes,

John Updike

Here is John Updike's response when I sent him a copy of his 1948 letter.

MAYOR GEORGE GULL

DOC. C.C. JONES.

DAN DANDELION HANDYMAN

REV. MEEK

MYRNA MAY

← DICK DEMIJOHN SALOON

← GUY GULF SWAMPER AT DICKS

Gray character sketches

to do the drawing, and then sell the feature to a syndicate. *Broom Hilda* was one of his creations. However, Caplin's personal political position was very different from Gray's, and he took the strip in a different direction from the Gray version. Eventually the Chicago Tribune-N.Y. News Syndicate (now Tribune Media Services) decided to try a new tack and put the strip in the hands of a young and untried cartoonist, but this didn't work for long. Next, reruns of some of the Gray strips of the 1930s were distributed to newspapers for a while. The writing and drawing of *Annie* was then continued for a number of years by Leonard Starr. Upon his retirement, several artists and writers became involved in the production of the strip.

Now, in 2003, it is being written by Jay Maeder and illustrated by Alan Kupperberg.

These six strips are part of a sequence Gray developed after reading the above newspaper clipping. © Tribune Media Services.

Harold Gray strips, courtesy of the Boston University Special Collections Department.
© Tribune Media Services

HARRY HERSHFIELD
AND *ABIE THE AGENT*

HARRY HERSHFIELD

Angelo

Hershfield by Emidio Angelo

Harry Hershfield's earliest comic strips, *Homeless Hector* and *Desperate Desmond,* were before my time, but I was well aware of his most famous strip, *Abie the Agent,* long before I first met him at meetings of the National Cartoonists Society. The thing that I remember most about this multitalented cartoonist is that no matter what subject was being talked about at any given moment, Harry could instantly dredge up a funny story concerning that particular topic. No public meeting or banquet he attended was complete unless he was called upon to keep the audience laughing at the endless fund of appropriate jokes that he was able to pluck from his enormous mental inventory. No less a person than Bob Ripley once noted in *Believe It or Not* that Hershfield had attended 260 affairs in a period of six months and had given one of his humorous talks at every one of them.

During one particularly delightful morning that several of us cartoonists spent with Harry in his West 57th Street apartment in New York City, we asked him how he was able to get up before a large crowd anywhere without the slightest trace of self-consciousness. His answer was that a large gathering of people isn't any more formidable than a single individual, so he talks man to man with just one person in his audience. He told us of the time when he was working on the *Chicago Daily News* and a women's club asked the editor to send over a cartoonist as guest speaker for one of their functions. Harry got the assignment and planned to tell the ladies how a cartoon was processed before it reached the printed page. He began by saying, "Ladies, I'm going to talk to you today on reproduction." This opening drew laughs Harry hadn't expected, and thus began the humorous Hershfield platform career. A number of years before I got to know him at National Cartoonists Society meetings, I'd heard countless Hershfield funny stories during his appearances on the 1940s radio program *Can You Top This?*

Harry Hershfield and *Abie the Agent*

With me from left to right: Bob Dunn of *They'll Do It Every Time* fame,
Harry, and noted lightning caricaturist Jack Rosen

In the photo you see here, Harry was in the midst of giving Bob Dunn, Jack Rosen, and me a tour of his memento-filled apartment, which included paintings by Rubens, a self-portrait by Goya, authentic French Provincial antique tables, and pictures of Harry with various world figures. Harry had lived in this same 57th Street apartment for many years with his wife, Sarah Jane, a Ziegfeld Follies girl who had died six years before our visit.

PART TWO

PROFILES

STAN DRAKE AND
THE HEART OF JULIET JONES

Story from Issue No. 4, December 1969

Stan Drake, the much-admired artist who has drawn *The Heart of Juliet Jones* for King Features Syndicate for seventeen years, not only tells about many of his experiences in the profession, he also was interested enough to write comments about a number of his dailies that are included here. He speaks of his methods and of the different effects he was trying to achieve. We appreciate especially Stan's extra effort to pass on some of the tricks he has learned along the way.

HURD: Would you say something about your beginnings in the art business?

DRAKE: Well, I sold my first illustration to a pulp magazine when I was seventeen years old, before I went to art school.

HURD: Did you have any special art instruction in high school?

DRAKE: I'm a dropout—I left high school in my first year and got a job as an usher in Hackensack, New Jersey. This was during the Depression. My father had been in the theater—on the stage in vaudeville—before I was born. The Depression hit us badly, and he had lost everything he had. We were very poor. We were living in River Edge, New Jersey, and my mother had to go to work at Hackensack Hospital. Finally, my dad got a job from an old friend on a radio program called *Dangerous Paradise*—this was in 1934.

From this point he started working in radio and built himself up to be a very fine character actor—for eighteen or twenty years he was one of the top people in the field. He did all the soap operas, and he was on many big programs like *The Kate Smith Show*. But back in '34 he hadn't really started to make a lot of money, and we owed so many bills that for years the money went to pay back what we owed. We had to move closer to the hospital in Hackensack where my mother worked. I found myself in this crummy little neighborhood and decided I'd have to get a job and pay my way if I wanted to go to art school. I had decided to go into art of some kind. I didn't know the pitfalls—maybe I figured there would be the same number of pitfalls in any job—and I liked art.

Those days found me looking at old pulp magazines that don't exist today—*Cowboy Stories, Love Stories, Breezy Stories*—and they had these little black-and-white illustrations. At seventeen I decided to do some illustrations like the ones I saw, so I did half a dozen, took them into a publishing company in New York, and managed to sell them. Just about this time, or a little

later, I started at the Art Students League with a course under George Bridgman in anatomy. Speaking of the pulps, I had a theory that the men who made these beautiful-looking drawings knew what they were doing, and they looked good, so I used to take tracing paper and trace the lines. In this way I thought I would get a feeling in my mind as to how to draw people. After doing hundreds of tracings of heads, say, I would try it on my own, freehand. By doing this so much, I came to realize how heads were constructed.

It was about this time—1935 and 1936—that the original comic books came out. Bob Lubbers, who now does the *Robin Malone* strip for the Newspaper Enterprise Association, and I were classmates at the League, and, following the example of another one of the art students, we went down to try and get a job on one of these comic books. We landed the jobs. We wrote stories, drew the pictures, and did the lettering, all for $7 a page—and there were about nine panels to a page! Each month we would do one of these comics; the characters were all heroes or detectives. Finally the place went out of business.

HURD: Going back a bit, I believe you once said you also copied portraits to improve your art ability, didn't you?

DRAKE: Yes. the big guys in the movies at that time were people like Robert Taylor and Clark Gable, and I used to copy portraits of them that appeared in movie magazines.

Stan Drake

HURD: Would you advise a young person starting out to educate himself in the art field, using some of the same methods you did?

DRAKE: To advise anyone as to a method for learning art would be very difficult today because they're doing so many different things now—the styles and the

Stan Drake's comments for *CARTOONIST PROfiles* readers follow, based on some of his daily strips.
Halftone effects are difficult in line art—they tend to look mechanical and dead—
so I tried a carbon pencil for the leaves here, and it reproduced well.

Sometimes I am intrigued by one expression that, for me, tells the story that day. When I achieve it, I can be quite flip with the rest of the art—not doing all I could to make the strip complete. This is not good, of course.

techniques are way out. For instance, I can't sell anything today in New York in the style in which I worked only fifteen years ago. Right after World War II, I went to a friend of mine who worked in an art studio and said to him, "What do I do to get into this business?" He told me to make about a dozen black-and-white spots and show them to him. Newspapers and magazines were using thousands of them. Drawings showing people holding up cans of fruit or packages of soap were everywhere. Nowadays you can't find one; they're all photographs or full-color paintings. There is no more work being done today in the style I started with. In 1950, I could get as much as $1,800 a week making line drawings; the business was flourishing. Of course, I didn't earn that much every week, but some weeks I

did. But let's not talk about money; I just mentioned that figure to show the change that has occurred in art.

World War II had drained the art pool from New York, and when I got out of the service in 1946, there was literally one artist for every hundred artists there are today. You could find work without any training. I learned on the job—I was at an art studio—they gave me $80 a week to start and I worked up from there. I worked twenty hours a day. I would sleep flopped across my bed with all my clothes on for four hours, and then I'd go back to New York again. It got so I had to take a hotel room across the street from the studio because I would work till two or three A.M., get up at seven, and go in to the studio before anybody was there to finish up. The jobs were piled up on my desk.

Here is an example of just plain pen lines for clean reproduction. This treatment is the best overall technique to use but it gets boring, so occasionally I rebel and do things that don't reproduce as well but make *me* happier.

In scenes where not much action takes place, efforts to give visual meaning can strain the imagination. I used the man's hands in the first panel; they are placed in a nervous, hopeful, unconscious position. His eyes and sweat beads do it for panel two, as does the hip finger-snap in panel three.

There was so much work that eventually I started my own studio. Our slogan was THE BEST IN LINE. I had ten people working for me, and we did nothing but line art for agencies. Today, no one wants that type of thing.

HURD: What were some of the factors that gave you the drive to succeed in art?

DRAKE: Well, we were poor. I had this psychological drive *not* to be poor, so I could never turn down a job; it was almost a neurosis with me. I would take anything and try to make money. I think *anyone* who is a creative type of person can learn 75 percent of what the top artists know, and the secret of doing good *top* work lies in your attention span. If you can be interested *long enough* in this business, you can learn *all* the tricks. There are so many tricks to learn in art. It's not

talent, it's tricks. You can learn how to rule with a brush instead of a pen, for instance.

The point is, you can't get everybody to be that interested. Most people who paint apply only so much attention to that painting—not enough. If they were really interested and had the attention span that was required of them, they would be much better. In my own case, I *had* this attention span—I enjoyed my work—so I spent many more hours than the average man would spend in learning my craft. In the old days when a job came through, I would know what paper to use, and I would know what the client was talking about because I had observed other people handling that type of work. You don't have this knowledge unless you do all this observing. Very few people can

Love-story strips are notorious for lack of action—so I tried to jazz up the visual impact here with unusual positioning in the first two panels.

Drake took these photos of a model's hair for future reference in drawing
the attractive girl characters he enjoys putting in *Juliet Jones*.

Cartoon Success Secrets

In a loose vignette composition, I tried a felt-tip pen for most of the background in an attempt at an illustrative approach rather than filling the entire panel.

This work was done on Craftint in a very tentative approach practically owned by Roy Crane's use of this chemically treated paper. He is the master of Craftint and—one disclosure I encountered—I am not.

maintain their interest in something long enough to be tops in their field.

HURD: In spite of your interest, after seventeen years of doing a strip, it must get a little boring and lonely at times, doesn't it?

DRAKE: Well, I've reached the stage where what I do doesn't give me a lift anymore. I've drawn over 55,000 figures in seventeen years of *Juliet Jones*—you take six or seven figures a day on a daily strip, and about the same number of figures in a Sunday page as in three dailies, and multiply these numbers by fifty-two weeks in a year, and then by seventeen years, and you arrive at the 55,000 figure. There is no position, no layout, that I haven't done. All the strip men reading this will laugh because it's so true. I can lay out a panel without even thinking about it after all this time. It's not difficult for me to conceive a setting anymore. You look at the paper. The balloons go in first because they have to be there. Then you look at the blank space and think who's talking first and do you want a close-up or a long shot, and then you say to yourself, "Well, a long shot means I'll have to draw all the trees, the houses, and the cars," so you draw a close-up of the guy's nostril. In this way, you wipe out a whole city block!

Seriously, though, in my type of work, the illustrative strip, the artwork grabs the readers—causes them to look at it—after that, the story is important. I believe that good drawing and realistic people and settings pique your interest, but if it's a lousy story you can be the best artist in the world and you can't really get into it. But if it's a good story, then the artwork becomes more important because you don't want the reader to say, "It's such a neat story; why the heck is this or that guy drawn so badly, or why is the girl so ugly?" I think it's kind of a tip in favor of the writer on a story strip, but to be really successful with a feature, you have to have a good writer and a good artist both.

HURD: What is your normal weekly schedule like?

DRAKE: Hell. My schedule is nothing like Mort Walker's. He is the most organized guy in the world in this business, a fabulous exception to a lot of us. His stuff is professional, it's beautifully done, and it's very funny—exceptionally, consistently funny. Mort is one

in a million. I work during the day, at night, at odd hours; I'll play golf, come back, force myself to do some more work. Editors who might read this will say, "Oh, the poor soul—he has to work after he plays golf—my goodness!" But this is a very demanding type of work; a certain number of hours have to be spent on a strip to complete it. For instance, if you're drawing three people in the living room having a conversation, first of all you should have an interesting composition. You then have them sitting in chairs, with bookcases behind them: there's a lamp, a portion of the rug, pictures on the walls, doorjambs—all these things have to be done.

Funny thing. I was talking to Charlie Schulz on the phone, and I mentioned that it takes so much time to

Expressive hands seem to do something extra for non-action scenes;
I use them when I can. In these frames it was necessary.

Rain and gloom may be approached by a loose, undefined "sloppy" technique, as I tried to do here.

Cartoon Success Secrets

For this night-city scene I used a photograph out of a magazine; blacked in the grays with a felt-tip and whitened in the whites. It would have taken many more hours to do it the conventional way.

do this, and he said he felt that the people were the important thing; the backgrounds weren't that important. And I chuckled while talking to Charlie, who is one of the great geniuses of the business today, because his backgrounds consist of a little wavy line. But in my kind of strip, you have to have the people in a setting so that the mind says, without thinking consciously about it, "I know where the people are, and it's realistic." Do you know how long it takes to do a realistic doorjamb? It sounds so stupid but it has to be in perspective, it has to be ruled in pencil, and all the little wood layers in a doorjamb, in order to look real, must be there the way it looks. Then you have to ink all this in—a lot of little tight ruling that has nothing to do with creativity—it's just coolie labor. Ninety percent of my work is coolie labor.

What I would like to do is lay the strip out in pencil with this great flair which I wish I had more of, and perhaps do a few of the pretty girl heads, since they attract me, and then hand it over to somebody and say, "Here—finish this up." To me, the creative work is done in laying out the strip; after that, it's coolie labor. There is nothing creative about my work anymore for the simple reason that the style was set years ago. A handsome man or a pretty girl in pen line, or brush line, a realistic person, can be just so realistic—after that it can't be any more realistic; it begins to look too tight, too much like an old woodcut illustration if you overwork it. It begins to look as though it had too much hair in it. You've got to get yourself down to the

This panel was accomplished with the technique Stan Drake talks about in our interview. A shot of these New York City buildings was photocopied and the halftones dropped out. Stan then pasted the copy into his strip and inked the line work that remained.

point where you can ink in a figure that isn't overdone. If it's too tight, you're not adding anything. A chair in a strip shouldn't be drawn as meticulously as an ad in a Sears, Roebuck catalog. You want to get just the effect of the chair; you're not trying to sell it. Well, that's harder than it sounds—to strike this balance.

HURD: Changing the subject for a moment, you said you wanted to say something about the business of figuring out what line of work your main character should be in, didn't you?

DRAKE: Yes, It happens that I'm very interested in sports cars—I've had one of every sports car, I guess, ever made over the years—and one time I suggested to Sylvan Byck, the editor at King Features, that I do a sports-car strip. Sylvan made a very succinct remark, I think, when he said, "It isn't so much what job your character has that's important, it's what he says and does and thinks—what kind of a character he is." He said that after a race-car driver had won all the important races, then what? It's important to know that the reader is identifying with the character, and not his job.

A while back I completed a sequence in which a bobsled racer was involved. I had shots for two or three weeks of him actually going down the run. He didn't win the race—as a matter of fact, he had an accident on his first run. But the more important thing was what the character was himself. It turned out that he had problems with his family—that he was a born loser—that he had made himself that way, and he didn't have to be that way. The story was of the man; he was more important than the bobsled race. It was neat to have the shots of the run, because that made it attractive to the reader, but the most important aspect of the sequence was the man's personality. It happens that a friend of mine, Bob Said, is one of the U.S. Olympic bobsled drivers—we call him "Bobsled," obviously. Well, Bob and his wife, Valerie, and my wife, Bunnie, and I took off a couple of years ago for the site of the Winter Olympics in France. I went down the run on one of the sleds, and I can tell you it was a hairy experience. But that's a story in itself.

HURD: You like all kinds of athletics, don't you?

Above left: Stan's very attractive wife, Bunnie.
Left: Stan acts as his own model.

Cartoon Success Secrets

DRAKE: Yes, I really feel at my best when I'm moving my body—swimming in the pool, or playing golf, or going down a bobsled run, or bowling—doing something like that. I've never been able to understand how I'm able to sit at the drawing board for all those hours, considering that I enjoy moving around so much. I would have expected that someone like me would be literally climbing the walls—sitting at the drawing board for thousands of hours.

HURD: Would you say something about that new method of drawing backgrounds that you figured out?

DRAKE: Well, in my never-ending search for easier ways to do things, I hit upon this idea to be the only man in the business using electronic machinery in the production of my comic strip. I found, if I copied a halftone photograph on a Xerox machine, that often the halftones were washed out and very light and that just the basic black lines remained. In other words, the machine would, in effect, turn out what amounted to a line drawing of whatever subject was involved. You see, this particular machine was designed to copy letters and not halftone photos.

When I first discovered this, I was doing a sequence where the characters were out at sea in a big ship. I wanted to show a drawing of this ocean liner, but I couldn't conceive of myself sitting down there, penciling and then inking, this huge ship with all the windows and the superstructure. It got me thinking. For my first experiment I got hold of a photo of one of the big liners and ran it through a friend's Xerox. As I said before, the halftones were almost entirely washed out,

leaving this incredibly detailed line drawing of a ship. I proceeded to cut it out, and I pasted it right into a panel of *Juliet Jones*. Then I simply inked in the ship, going right over the lines that appeared on the photocopy and strengthening them. In about forty-five minutes I had this complete, absolutely accurate, fantastic rendition.

On another occasion—Juliet and Eve were living in New York at the time—I went through my files and got a photo of the entire city of New York, taken from a blimp. By this time I had rented a Xerox copier, and I ran this photo through. Immediately, I pasted the photo onto my artwork and inked it in. I'll give you a sample of this technique that you can include with the report of our conversation. I ended up with a drawing that would have taken four days to pencil in the old-fashioned way. Nowadays I use a Pitney-Bowes copier, because they use a coated paper, and I can take a razor blade and scrape out the few traces of gray halftones that remain after the photo is copied.

HURD: Would you tell us what you did about the business of lettering your strip?

DRAKE: I was paying a considerable amount of money to a lettering man to letter my strip each week, and I began to think, Wouldn't it be neat if I could just type it out and save all that money for the lettering? So I got in touch with IBM and wanted to know, if I had a lettering man letter up the alphabet, whether they could make a set of keys for their Executive typewriter with these hand-drawn letters. My hope was that I could then sit down and type out my balloons and save the

Here's another example of a copied and inked city scene.

cost of a lettering man. But IBM told me it would cost as much as $7,000 to make a set of keys like that. I realized finally that they didn't want to do it because such a machine would be the only one in existence, and if it needed repairs they'd have to be done specially. I did actually settle for one of their standard typefaces that looked something like comic strip lettering, but it was just too perfect to be hand lettering. I did strips with it for a while and finally gave it up when the syndicate decided they didn't like it as well as hand-drawn lettering. But I guess I saved something like $1,400 in lettering costs during the period when I used it.

HURD: You wanted to say something about newspapers, didn't you?

DRAKE: Yes. I feel that a newspaper is essentially two things—it's information and it's entertainment. Now, the comics are an integral part of the entertainment portion of the paper. Your comics do not pretend to be anything but pure entertainment—they are pictorial show business. And I believe thoroughly in the therapeutic value of entertainment.

HURD: Have you ever carried a sketchbook around with you? Do you keep a morgue and continually add to it?

DRAKE: No, I've never carried a sketchbook. However, I do subscribe to about eighteen magazines—the national ones—and I clip them all in order to add to my morgue. You have to, in my type of work. I clip background stuff mostly; people, I don't have any

This represents the slightly different approach I use with the Sunday page.
Most areas are left open—with little black—so the colorist may use color to its fullest.

problem with. I may take Polaroid pictures of a particularly difficult pose. No matter how many figures I've drawn, and I mentioned 55,000 earlier, I still cannot draw the human figure to look as good without copying a photograph as if I had taken one. I probably do 80 percent of my stuff with no copying, but there are occasional pictures where a girl is bending down, she's kneeling, or reaching, or doing something like that, that I just can't seem to visualize without taking a Polaroid of the pose. There's an impact of realism given to the work if a photo is used. And since I am concerned mainly with time, I feel that occasionally Polaroids are necessary to speed up the time I take to get a certain pose just right. I could do it without the photo, but it would take longer. I've used my wife, Bunnie, as a model many times, and I have a self-timer so I can photograph myself when necessary.

HURD: What advice would you like to give to an aspiring young cartoonist?

DRAKE: My advice would be to call up a syndicate, ask to speak to the comics editor, and try to get an interview with him. Many of them will give you their time—they may be brutally frank if it is necessary—but they often will be quite kind. Ask the comics editor if you can see what is being done—ask him if you can see some originals. Somebody probably will be sent with you down to the morgue, and you can look over all the originals and see just what you're up against. Go to the heart of this comics business. Don't go to some guy for advice who may be prejudiced or envious. Go to the top—to the syndicates. The syndicate people won't be emotional with you, as friends might. They'll say, "This is so, and that is so, and this is what we're buying." Show them samples of your present work and say to the editor, "This is what I'm doing today. How does it look? What will I have to do to make the grade?" Ask some questions.

I'm going to do exactly the same thing myself sometime in the near future. I'm interested in doing some book illustrations to relieve the monotony of doing what I've been doing for so many years. So I asked a friend where I should go. He suggested that I go up to three or four publishing houses, which he named, with samples of my illustrations. When you get to a syndicate or, as in this latter case, to a publishing house, the ball starts rolling. The man looks at your work, and if it's got any value he'll sit down with you. He'll show you what he's buying. He may take you into a room where there are a lot of originals so you can make comparisons. You may say, "Oh, I'm not this good," or, "Boy, am I off-base—I've got to change my whole approach." In other words, go right to the place you want to work for.

ROY CRANE AND *BUZ SAWYER* ON ARTISTIC ATMOSPHERE

Story from Issue No. 5, March 1970

In the third issue of *CARTOONIST PROfiles* we reproduced some pages from Roy Crane's great scrapbook entitled "How to Draw *Buz Sawyer*" (*Buz Sawyer* being the strip that Crane did for King Features Syndicate for many years). Here are some additional selections from what is in reality a big textbook on how to use the Craftint shading medium effectively. It was prepared originally as a guide for the use of his artist assistant, Hank Schlensker, and was donated by Roy to the Syracuse University Manuscript Collection some years ago. Once again, we'd like to explain that, as a rule, Crane pasted newspaper clippings of *Buz Sawyer* in the scrapbook to illustrate his points, and time has taken its toll on some of the newsprint. Regretfully, we've had to omit many drawings. Even the clearer ones don't always do full justice to the Crane technique. Note: The comments under the drawings are Roy Crane's words.

When atmosphere can add interest to a strip, use it. Use any device that will attract the attention of readers.

Dark, foreboding atmosphere

Regal atmosphere: note depth obtained by placing objects in different planes.

Sitting in with (left to right) Roy Crane (*Buz Sawyer*) and Bob Montana (*Archie*) in 1962

When they're talking about a boat, draw a boat.

Use atmosphere for variety in a talking strip. Note pen lines on roofs to the left, benday dots on the roof to the right.

Make the most of odd shapes.

Honeymoon charm

Backwoods

Night. I may be the only cartoonist who doesn't avoid night scenes.
I love them because of the brilliant contrasts and color.

Lantern light

Use white where it will
be most effective.

Spotlight

Shaded figures with light beyond them

Ah, the moon!

Cartoon Success Secrets

Water

More mud

Mud

Foam is always colorful and interesting.

Splash

Reflections

Self-caricature

Roy Crane by Bob Zschiesche

Roy was disturbed about the diminishing sizes in which comic strips appear in newspapers.
Roy drew this strip especially for us to illustrate his point.

ART AND CHIP SANSOM AND *THE BORN LOSER*

Story from Issue No. 9, March 1971

Art Sansom, who drew a number of illustrative-type strips—*Chris Welkin, Vic Flint, Martha Wayne*—for the Newspaper Enterprise Association over the years, switched to writing and drawing a very humorous strip, *The Born Loser,* in 1965. It became quite popular. *CARTOONIST PROfiles* was interested in talking with Art about the change in his style and in hearing his thoughts about our profession. He lives and works in Lakewood, a suburb of Cleveland, Ohio.

"Hi! I'm Art Sansom, I do *The Born Loser* comic strip for NEA."

"In it I try to portray the universal human experience of falling flat on one's face."

"I've observed that many people suffer one pratfall after another."

"I watch everybody. I take notes. I've become a student of the human condition."

"Still, I can't explain why some people seem destined to be losers."

"But thank heaven for the losers. They give me an endless source of inspiration for my strip."

"I hope you're considering *The Born Loser* for your newspaper. Hundreds of newspapers use it, and I'm proud to report, my strip is number one in most recent surveys."

Art Sansom

HURD: During the 1960s you made the switch from drawing purely illustrative strips to doing a strictly humorous one. Would you say something about how that came about?

ART SANSOM: Well, between 1943 and 1945, while I was working at a drafting job with GE, I was ruining my eyes during the evenings, drawing what I thought was the greatest illustrative cartoon ever done. I had been greatly influenced by Leslie Charteris and *The Saint* and various blood-and-thunder tales, and I finally submitted this strip to Ernest (East) Lynn, who was then the director of comic art for the Newspaper Enterprise Association in Cleveland, Ohio. Following this, I had a call from Lynn, who didn't want my strip, but it seems he wanted *me*—thought I had some flair for writing and that some artistic ability showed through.

Thus began a twenty-year period during which I drew several realistic strips for them. I started as a staff artist in the Comic Art Department, pasting up, coloring Sunday pages, and so on. Around '48 or '49 I inherited a weekly strip called *Peggy,* and then, about 1950, NEA decided that cowboys were on their way out and spacemen were the coming thing. So I began to draw the *Chris Welkin* strip, which was daily and Sunday for a couple of years, and then Sunday only for about eight years after that. During some of this period I was drawing both *Chris Welkin* and a soap-opera type of feature, *Martha Wayne,* at the same time; then, commencing in 1960, I began to do *Vic Flint.*

By 1965 I guess I got sick and tired of trying to compete with guys who were ten times better than I was at the illustrative thing, and I was ready for a change. When I started *The Born Loser* in 1965, it was a great relief to get into a medium I thought I could conquer.

In the years before that, I did what they gave me at NEA—I seemed to be typecast and didn't get a shot at straight cartooning. It was an effort to do the illustrative strips and it wasn't really fun. Incidentally, the drawing habits I acquired during those years sometimes carry over a little to *The Born Loser*. In other words, I have to watch myself that I don't get a bit too arty in drawing women, and I have to remember to give a woman character a comic-art type of figure.

Well, as you can gather, I had become completely fed up with the Great American Novel and the spooky stuff in comic strips and I thought there was room for something light. I think that East Lynn, who was about to retire, wanted to see me with my own feature before leaving. Other people had done most of the writing on several of the illustrative features that I had been drawing. When I came up with an idea for a comic called *The Loser*, NEA thought this title would give rival syndicates too much ammunition, so Meade Monroe, vice president and general manager in Cleveland, came up

with the final name, *The Born Loser*. The late Bob Molyneux, who succeeded Lynn as comic art director, thought a lot like I did, and I drew for six or eight months to get it ready.

At the beginning, there wasn't going to be a main character—just a *lot* of losers were going to be involved. I'm very glad now that we decided to have just one. Molyneux, by the way, named several of the characters himself. He had happened to pass a sign reading Thornapple Lane somewhere, so my main character became Brutus Thornapple because it struck him as a very funny name. Brutus lives in Catfish Hill and commutes to Little Liversville, where he is the lackey of the boss of the Veeblefester Corporation, one Rancid T. by name. Brutus works in the outer office—under a forty-watt lightbulb—and wears a green eyeshade and arm garters. Sometimes I'm sorry I didn't name him Jonah, the greatest loser of all time. Brutus's son, Wilberforce, was also given his moniker by Bob Molyneux, who—incidentally—hadn't even been aware of the well-known

college of that name. Wilberforce is a throwback to the Buster Brown type of character with long blond curls, Mary Jane shoes, high collar, and big black bow, but he's a hell-raiser and usually bests his father in most endeavors.

HURD: Would you tell us about some of your methods for keeping the gags flowing and about how you work?

ART SANSOM: Well, I work at home here in Cleveland, and I find that the hours from eight-thirty A.M. till one or two P.M. are the most productive for me. Of course, the gag writing goes on all the time, both in the conscious and the subconscious mind; you're kicking ideas around and you carry them with you. A funny thing— my mind works actively when I'm in the car and driving; I'm sure I'd scare the wits out of the safety patrol if they knew this. My mind is going 60 mph when I'm driving 30 mph. I hate to drive, so I entertain myself by thinking up gags. I try to have the germ of one or two ideas when I pull out of the driveway, and I develop them as I drive along.

In addition, I consider myself fortunate that quite a number of people with creative minds and ideas found their ways to me when I started doing *The Born Loser* and have become friends with whom I get together for lunch and conversation regularly. Most of them happen to be PR people and they're very funny; one of them was a prominent local radio personality who now does some writing for *Laugh-In*. Several times a week I may go into town, have lunch with one of these men, and just informally kick ideas around. We don't sit down primarily to talk gags, but they all take pride that they may be contributing an idea. Sometimes I give them a credit line in the strip, incidentally. These friends constantly call me, though of course in a great many cases there isn't enough pizzazz in the gag suggestion to make it usable as is.

HURD: Will you say something more about your schedule?

ART SANSOM: Well, from Monday through Friday I'm assimilating ideas and trying to develop them. I try to come up with one idea a day, and I keep a pad and pencil by my bedside. Invariably, I will wake up at four A.M. and find that I have come up with the idea I couldn't quite nail during the day. You see, the very last thing before I go to bed, I will look at every gag I've been working on, knowing that, during sleep, my subconscious will work the ideas out. Regularly I will get up, go to the studio, slip a sheet of paper in the typewriter, and put down these thoughts for an hour. I've trained myself to go back to sleep after this early morning session. I wake up again about eight A.M. and am back to the board by eight-thirty. During the week I will have clipped all these typed idea sheets together—possibly there will be ten gags—and then I will sit down on Saturday afternoon and continue through all of Sunday, polishing, rewriting, and getting the words in final form for the strip. On Monday I will rough in the week's six strips in pencil, half of them may have to be done over, more to my liking. I start penciling directly on the illustration board; I don't submit gag roughs to Tom Peoples, our NEA director of comic art. Then on Tuesday I will rough in the Sunday page. Wednesday is set aside for inking the dailies, and Thursday for inking the Sunday pages.

HURD: What are some of the things you strive for in your strip?

Chip and
Art Sansom

ART SANSOM: I strive to make the facial expressions as animated as possible. This is a very important part of punching the gag across. I keep a mirror beside the board and use it to get certain expressions. Some of these expressions I'm still working on, some I already have down pat. I love the double take and the take look to punch the gag. Incidentally, I have loved every minute of *The Born Loser*—it's my vocation, my avocation, and my hobby, and I eat, sleep, drink, and live the strip. I do the whole thing and don't farm any work out. You have to be loose as a goose to do this kind of strip. Personally, I'm glad I made the switch to this technique from being a riveter—Milton Caniff, or perhaps someone else, used this label for the fellow who uses a brush to toss the shadow under one of the rivets on the side of a plane.

HURD: Do you do anything special to replenish your mental reservoir with material for later gag production?

ART SANSOM: I enjoy reading biographies like *Harpo Speaks,* and I'm interested in the life stories of all the professional funnymen. I don't get gags from this

reading but these books are inspirational for me; they keep me thinking funny. Which reminds me—I think an experienced gag writer gets so he reads humor and comedy into most any straight story he comes across. I'm not a great TV viewer, and I tend to stay away from looking at comic sections in the newspapers for two reasons: I'm always afraid I might pick up someone else's ideas, and it's discouraging to see how many real pros are involved in this business of ours. Also I rarely go to the movies.

HURD: Can you say something about your materials?

ART SANSOM: I found early in *The Born Loser* that I no longer liked to work in the medium of ink, pen, and brush. In my illustrative-strip days, by the way, I had used a chisel-end number 2 brush. I would take a number 2, dip it in the ink, and let it dry till it had the consistency of lead. I would then take a very sharp blade and cut off about 1/32 of an inch from the point, so I'd have a square end. That way I could make a hairline holding the brush one way and a broad stroke if I held it another way. I used this for everything but lettering. When I started to ink *The Born Loser* with a pen, it didn't seem to have a professional-enough look, so I evolved the method of using the Japanese-made Pentel pen—with the black felt tip—on coquille board. These pens wear down quickly but they give your work a very professional and smooth look, and I use them for everything, lettering included—everything, that is, except for filling in large areas of black.

HURD: Would you say something about how you got into this business?

ART SANSOM: I've drawn since I was old enough to hold a piece of chalk—my dad bought me a blackboard, which we hung in the kitchen, and I would stand by the hour drawing. I had a regular art class in high school and graduated from Ohio Wesleyan University with a major in Fine Arts. I might add that I didn't particularly dig figure drawing, or making pottery vases, or engaging in crafts. We had a *very* small amount of life drawing because this was a Methodist college. Once, I think, they lured a girl wearing a bathing suit in as a model but that's as close as we got to the real thing. After I started to work at NEA, I started attending a life class once a week—a class that had been organized by several well-known cartoonists in Cleveland. I was disillusioned by the drafting job I referred to earlier—which was all I could get during World War II—and was of course delighted when I was called in by Ernest Lynn of NEA in 1945 to become a staff artist. I think I learned more in one month, just observing Roy Crane, Les Turner, and the others at work, than I did during the four years in fine arts in college.

HURD: Do you want to add any advice for young people trying to enter the field?

ART SANSOM: Try to develop an original style of humor that projects your own personality. Of course we've all been influenced by our favorite cartoonists—I think Claude Smith, who signs his cartoons *Claude,* had possibly more influence on me than anyone else. I can also mention Syverson, Saxon, Barsotti, and others whose work I've liked. Turning out a cartoon is a production: You are the producer, the director, the actor, the writer, the prop man, and the publicity man. Complete dedication is a big reason for any substantial cartooning success. In my own case, I don't need any hobbies. Doing the strip is all I require.

HURD: Are teenagers, young adults, and college students regular readers of newspaper comic strips?

ART SANSOM: Yes. I would say that *Peanuts* has been the greatest motivating force in stirring up the interest of these groups. Incidentally, about 60 percent of my mail comes from adults, and about 40 percent from college students.

The Born Loser: An Update

Chip Sansom

Art's son Chip took over the strip after his dad's death, and we asked him in December of 2002 to continue *The Born Loser* story.

HURD: How did you get started working with your father on *The Born Loser*?

CHIP SANSOM: I began working with Dad in 1977, on a trial basis, strictly as a gag writer. When it worked out better than either of us imagined, Dad hired me as a full-time assistant. I would do whatever odd jobs I could to lighten his workload, such as coloring Sunday pages, filling in blacks, and answering fan mail, in addition to feeding him fresh gag ideas. After it became apparent I was in it for the long haul, Dad began to groom me to eventually take over the strip, teaching me his methods for doing every facet of the job. This apprenticeship lasted until he passed away on July 4, 1991—my fortieth birthday. I have continued to produce *The Born Loser* in his style ever since.

HURD: How do your methods for writing gags differ from those your father mentioned?

CHIP SANSOM: Actually, his methods changed when NEA moved their offices from Cleveland to New York in the 1970s. Working out of his home studio, he no longer had to go downtown everyday, so his conversations over lunch with friends became less frequent. When I came on board, we developed a technique Dad called *snowballing ideas*—one of us would mention the germ of a gag or a humorous situation, and we would bat ideas back and forth until we came up with a usable gag or exhausted all the possibilities. I wish I had a tape recording of some of those sessions. We weren't always successful coming up with ideas, but we always had a ball cracking each other up!

These days, I often snowball ideas with my wife, Brooke, who assists me in some of the same ways I assisted my father. Brooke knows the characters well and has provided me with many funny gags. My

THE BORN LOSER®

by Art & Chip Sansom

UH-OH! THIS COULD BE TROUBLE!

IS THERE A PROBLEM WITH YOUR DESIGN? YOU BET THERE'S A PROBLEM!

WELL, THAT WASN'T SO BAD! I DON'T MIND A LITTLE CONSTRUCTIVE CRITICISM!

THORNAPPLE!

YOU WANTED TO SEE ME, CHIEF? IS THERE A PROBLEM WITH MY NEW TEA COZY DESIGN?

NOW, GO BACK AND FIX IT, PRONTO, OR YOU'RE DEAD MEAT!

I'LL BET THE CHIEF WANTS TO SEE ME ABOUT THE NEW DESIGN I WORKED SO HARD ON! I HOPE HE DOESN'T EXPECT ME TO MAKE ANY REVISIONS TO IT!

IT'S INCOHERENT, INCOMPREHENSIBLE AND INCOMPLETE! IT'S THE MOST WORTHLESS PIECE OF TRIPE I'VE EVER SEEN!

A November 2002 strip by Chip Sansom

nine-year-old daughter, Isabel, is a good source for material, and she gets a kick out of seeing something she said wind up in print. I also have some good friends who enjoy giving me ideas I can work into gags.

HURD: How do you avoid dry spells with your ideas?

CHIP SANSOM: I don't find working at regularly scheduled times to be conducive to writing humorous material. Ideas flow much more naturally for me by observing life twenty-four hours a day, knowing always in the back of my mind that anything I come across could become fodder for the strip. It might be a situation or a phrase, something I read or hear someone say. More often than not, the things I latch on to are not inherently funny, but when I look at them from the perspective of how they might impact Brutus, the humor is fleshed out. When I happen upon one of these ideas, I jot it down on my ever-present note pad or use my cell phone to leave a message on my answering machine—now that's a technique my dad never thought of! When I return to my drawing board, I transfer all these ideas to index cards and attempt to write each as a usable script for a *Born Loser* strip. I place the best ideas on my drawing board for my next week's work. Any incomplete or sub-par gags are put in a card file. On days when I don't have enough ready material, I go through the card file to see if a fresh perspective can make a winner out of one of the bypassed ideas. I also have groupings in the card file for specific holidays and seasonal material.

HURD: When do you sit down at the drawing board?

CHIP SANSOM: I have always been a night owl, and with the inherent distractions of working out of my home, I find my most productive hours are in the evening and late into the night. I do some work every day, but my workdays lengthen as my weekly deadline approaches.

HURD: Do you use any of the same drawing materials your father used?

CHIP SANSOM: When Dad passed away, I used exactly the same materials he used, because that was the way I learned to do the strip. I would probably still be using them today, except that many are no longer manufactured. As these materials became unavailable, I experimented to find what I was most comfortable with. This trial-and-error process often yielded mixed results. After using one brand of pens for a couple of years, I discovered they were the equivalent of using disappearing ink! Today, I use Sakura Micron pens, primarily because of their claim to be archival ink. I only wish their tips were more pliable, like Dad's old felt tips. I use the number 05 pen for lettering and full figures, the number 08 for close-ups, number 1 for bold lines and borders, number 03 for detail lines, and the brush pen for filling in blacks. In place of Dad's coquille board, I use Strathmore Series 500 Bristol board, in three-ply and coarse finish. This board is very consistent and holds up well. I still use my father's technique of making preliminary drawings on tracing paper and refining the artwork on the tracing paper before transferring it to my drawing board, ready to ink.

HURD: Have you changed any of your work techniques owing to the proliferation of computers since your father's death?

CHIP SANSOM: I still hand-draw all my work, using the methods I learned from Dad. However, I use a computer to scan my work and send it, via modem, to my editors at United Media in New York. The saving in time and FedEx fees has more than paid for the cost of my computer system. At this time, I don't foresee using the computer to aid my drawing or lettering. I have considered using it for my Sunday color guides.

HURD: What advice do you have for prospective cartoonists?

CHIP SANSOM: Believe in yourself, never stop honing your craft, and get as much classroom training as possible. I regret that I intentionally avoided taking art courses in school. My father and mother were both such great artists, I felt I would be wasting my time, because I could never measure up. I am sure I missed out on a great deal of knowledge that would make my job easier today. Fortunately, I was blessed to have had the best tutor in the world, my father, to help me make up for that lost time. I owe everything to him. This is why I always sign his name next to mine on every *Born Loser*.

BRANT PARKER AND JOHNNY HART AND THE *WIZARD OF ID*

Story from Issue No. 9, March 1971

In Washington, D.C., I had a good talk with Brant Parker, who lives in nearby Oakton, Virginia. Brant does the drawing for the *Wizard of Id* comic strip and collaborates on the feature with Johnny *(B.C.)* Hart, who supplies the gags. Brant reports that Jack Caprio and Dick Boland are also involved in the production of ideas.

HURD: Would you say something about how you and Johnny Hart first met?

PARKER: Well, around 1947 I was working as a staff artist on the Binghamton, New York, *Press,* and I happened to be judging an art contest for high school students. John was just finishing high school, and I was impressed by the work he had submitted: It was straight illustration, no cartooning, and it was very good. A little later, I met him again, through a friend, and learned that he was very much interested in getting into cartooning but didn't know how to go about it. I had been taking the *N.Y. Cartoon News,* published by the late Don Ulsh, so I gave him a copy of that. In his publication, Don carried a notice that he would write a critique of readers' cartoons if they wanted to send them in, so John got up a bunch of gags and mailed them to Ulsh. Don liked them so well that he offered to act as John's agent in the New York cartoon market. He took John's work around and finally got Hart selling pretty well at the major magazines. Following this, I started sending to Ulsh too, and for two or three years or more we sent ten or fifteen gags (roughs) to him each week.

HURD: How did you two go about coming up with gag ideas?

PARKER: Well, maybe I'd lie on the couch, he'd sprawl out on the floor, and we'd snowball gags, just as we still do. To begin with, we might break things down to *situations* and *gimmicks.* For instance, I might shout out *a huge log* as the first *gimmick,* and John might holler

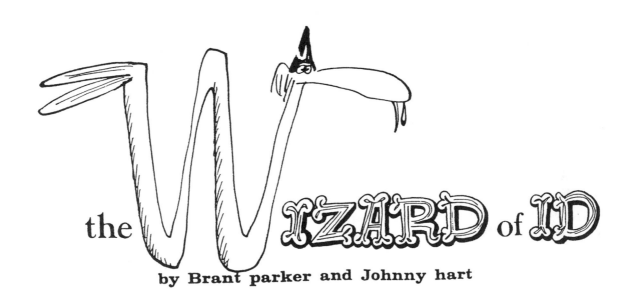

the WIZARD of ID
by Brant parker and Johnny hart

Brant Parker in the Think room, thinking.

back *a hotel* as the situation. Then we'd put the two things together. Maybe two characters have this huge log and they're running with it, about to bash in the door of the hotel, and we take it back and forth from there. If the situation and the gimmick don't jell, we switch to something else. Or on other occasions we'd leaf through magazines—anything that would start us thinking of different things and situations. We'd toss these back and forth all evening, and after we had piled up a batch of gags, we'd flip for the better ones and then we'd each send a pile to Ulsh.

HURD: John went into the air force around 1950 or 1951, didn't he?

PARKER: Yes, he was in Korea for a while and I kept on with the gag cartooning while he was gone. Then I had to go back into the navy, after having been in during World War II. When I got out, I took a technical art job with IBM at Endicott, which is Johnny's home and also where my wife grew up. We did exploded-view drawings of machines, and I learned a good deal about perspective. After Johnny came back from Korea, he got a job in the art department at GE, doing advertising and promotion, because he wasn't selling enough gags to support his wife and himself. Soon after, he decided he wanted to do the caveman thing so he worked up ten or twenty strips, submitted them, and was turned down by four or five syndicates. Finally, the Herald-Tribune Syndicate, which was looking for something new and fresh, bought *B.C.* Four or five years after that, John began to think about doing the strip that became *Wizard of Id,* and he talked it over with Jack Caprio, a boyhood friend who is now with us full-time. He and John had been almost inseparable and they think exactly alike. Caprio at this time was an

engineer with IBM. He does a lot of writing for *B.C.* and some of the art. But Jack just couldn't seem to pull the *Wizard* together—he was having too much trouble with the art—so, at this point John called me at IBM. He and Jack had worked out three or four characters— the King, Rodney, Blanche, and so on. Naturally, these were done in John's style, which was different from what I had been doing for the magazines, but I had to start thinking his way. It goes without saying that I feel natural in it now. I had been doing some newspaper cartooning in Los Angeles and had been with Disney's for several years, but I had never done any comic strip art, so I had to go to a whole new thing.

HURD: As long as you've mentioned what you had previously done in cartooning, will you tell us about your earlier career?

PARKER: I was brought up on the West Coast and my mother was a fashion artist when we lived in Beverly Hills, California. She had quite a few fashion and furniture advertising accounts and worked at home, so I grew up in an art atmosphere. After high school I attended the Otis Art Institute in LA for about twenty-two months, taking a general illustration art course. There was no cartoon course, incidentally. However, I'd always fooled around with cartooning. I think you can learn a lot from copying, and John does too. You can choose the styles and the artists that you like and copy them—even trace. When you do this, a lot of things show up that you'd never see, just looking at the cartoons. You become aware of these details when you trace or copy. If you keep doing this, you become more and more professional and your own style will develop. Anyhow, I had been hanging around the *Los*

Angeles Herald-Express a lot and eventually got a copyboy job and then worked myself into the art department. Pretty soon after that something opened up at the Scripps-Howard *Daily News,* and I went over there to do retouching, maps, and so on.

HURD: World War II came along then, didn't it?

A: Yes, and while I was still in the navy I applied for a job at Walt Disney's. I had heard from somebody on the ship that you could write and get a booklet that explained all about the procedure for applying and the forms to take their test on. There were a number of problems where you had to take one of your own figures, or one of theirs, and draw it doing something that involved leverage—perhaps a character pushing a wheelbarrow, for instance. I got out of the navy, passed the test, and began to go full-time to the Disney school. We put in regular working hours like everyone else, but we went to the school building. There were three or four of us, with an instructor, in each of many offices and they would try us out to see what characters each of us did the best. Each of us sat at a regular animation table. Two or three times a day they'd have classes. They had benches on which you sat and propped your board up—just as in art school—and we drew a great variety of things. We did quick sketching of animals that were put in a little circle cage in the center of the room: sheep, pigs, goats, donkeys, and once we had a small elephant. They'd keep the animals moving, and the emphasis was put on our doing very rapid sketches. Another interesting thing: The models were all cartoony-type people—big fat girls, skinny girls, all types. In so many art schools the models all seem to look the same, but this was never the case at Disney's.

This was my first experience with nude models, too, since we had none of that at the Otis Art Institute. This was around 1945 and 1946.

HURD: Will you say something more about the Disney school?

PARKER: Well, for one thing, they had quotas, which were posted on the board, and you had to keep your rate of production up. How many drawings, and how fast you did them, were noted. I remember that I was especially interested in observing the story-sketch department, where the artists could work in any medium they wanted. The fellows in this department received rough—almost thumbnail—sketches from the story-idea department, and then they worked these sketches up into storyboards, which were put up all around the walls in sequence. A lot of these men worked in pastel colors, some in watercolor. Disney and the directors would come in periodically and look them over, and there would be many changes as time went on. When the storyboards were approved, the drawings went to

animation, where they were split up. Special effects, such as dust or rain or snow, were done by specialists in this field; they rarely had anything to do with figure drawing.

During the couple of years I was there, I finished the school, went through the in-between department, and then went into breakdown—another step along the road to becoming an animator. It was marvelous—a real Fantasia-type experience! I had met my wife in California and, because of her mother's illness, we came back to Endicott, New York, where she had grown up. This brought me up to the point where I got a job as a staff artist on the Binghamton Press and met Johnny Hart, as I mentioned at the beginning of this conversation.

HURD: Would you tell us about your weekly routine?

PARKER: I have a studio in Fairfax, Virginia. Then occasionally I will fly up to Endicott and spend the week, from Monday till Friday, working with our team up there: Johnny Hart, Jack Caprio, Dick Boland, and

In the Think room, developing a gag—from thoughts earlier transcribed on Brant's new IBM portable dictating unit.

myself. I had been going up there about once a month, but during the past October and November I was making the trip every week. When I'm in Endicott, I sit down and talk with John on Monday morning about the gags that are ready to go. Sometimes I may have sent gags for the *Wizard* in, but mostly I'm just concerned with the art. If I do have any gag ideas for the strip, I give them to John and he edits them; it's his editing that is the genius touch. After that I go to my desk with a little pile of 3-by-5 cards—on which the various gags are written—and start to work. The strips have already been cut out of three-ply illustration board, and I start penciling in the cartoons and the lettering on the six dailies for that week. Next I go back and ink in the lettering and the lines around the various panels—that is, when we have an outline around a panel. Finally, I ink the characters, and by this time I'm pretty well warmed up.

You might be interested in the time it usually takes to do these various steps that I've mentioned. I would say that the lettering on each strip takes about ten minutes, the outlining of the panels five minutes, the penciling of the figures half an hour, and the inking half an hour. Allowing for any other problems that may come up, an hour and a half would be about the time I spend on each strip. This would take me into Tuesday on the dailies. Following that, a day and a half or two days would be needed for doing the Sunday page, including the color work. I used to put a transparent overlay on a light board, copy the strip very fast, and then color in the various areas as a guide for the engraver to follow. Nowadays we have a machine that

Cartoon Success Secrets

makes something like a stat—it's a wet process—and I color on that. I then put a drop of a special liquid into my paint water, and it makes the smooth finish of the stat paper completely workable for the color. (*Editor's note:* One such liquid is Braun's Non-Crawl.) I use Maribou watercolors for these Sunday pages.

HURD: What other materials do you use?

PARKER: I think people getting started in the art field are inclined to put too much emphasis on materials, but, for what it's worth, here are a few of mine. I use a regular ordinary number 2 writing pencil, not a special drawing pencil. It's fairly soft. For a time I had been using a plate-finish drawing paper, but I use the medium or kid finish at the present time. I like a very thin pen holder and have been using an Esterbrook 787 oval pen, but it seems they have been discontinued. So we've got an appeal out to art stores everywhere to hang on to any that come into their possession. I use Higgins ink and have used Pelikan, and I like kneaded erasers. The only time I use a brush is to put in solid blacks—a number 2 good-quality camel-hair brush—and a number 8 for my watercoloring.

HURD: What do you do after you finish your Sunday page, when you're up in Endicott?

PARKER: John is doing some Marathon Oil ads and we're also doing TV commercials for them. We've designed *B.C.* giveaway glasses, and these things take up the balance of the week. On the TV commercials, we've done the storyboards, and an animation firm takes it from there.

HURD: When you all have an idea session, how do those work?

PARKER: Well, we might snowball with a tape recorder. Participating would be Dick Boland, who writes gags for *B.C.*—he does no artwork; Jack Caprio, who does ideas and some *B.C.* art; Johnny; and myself. We just pile stuff into the recorder.

HURD: I know you try to stay up with everything that's going on as much as you can. What do you do in this connection?

PARKER: I read *Time* and *Newsweek* and I watch a lot of TV. I love all the shows, and I get a lot out of good situation comedy programs—even the corny ones! The timing they use is very similar to the timing in a comic strip. We often add a panel in the strip just for timing—a necessary pause in the presentation of the gag.

CHARLES SCHULZ AND *PEANUTS*

Story from Issue No. 12, December 1971

Several times, during the early years of *CARTOON-IST PROfiles*, we mentioned to Charles Schulz that the reason we hadn't featured him was simply that the newspapers, magazines, books, and TV networks had kept our readers so well informed about him and his activities that there hadn't been much more to be said. However it seemed fitting, as we prepared issue number 12, completing our third year of publication, to ask him to tell our readers a few things about himself that he hadn't mentioned to any general-interest magazines printed for the public at large: something exclusive for our readers, in other words. We know you will enjoy the response that follows as much as we did.

by Charles M. Schulz

In all the articles that have been written about Charlie Brown and Snoopy and the other things we have been doing, none of the writers has ever mentioned that the one cartoonist who helped most was Walt Ditzen. When he was working for one of the syndicates in Chicago, I dropped in with a batch of samples and he went far out of his way that day and later to give me advice and help that I badly needed. I have always regretted that Walt never got any credit for this where people could hear about it.

Peanuts started as a space-saving comic strip, and although I am sure this helped to sell it and keep it in some of the papers that otherwise might not have given it room, I have always felt guilty about it because I am sure it helped to start a dangerous trend. It is a pity that we somehow cannot cooperate in spite of the tremendous rivalries that exist and produce syndicated material that would be of a standard size. I learned a long time ago that I was going to have to struggle for attention on the comic page when I had the smallest amount of space and others were using black borders and all sorts of dramatic heavy areas to gain attention. One of the best ways, of course, to counteract this was simply to use a little more white space.

Jud has asked me to talk about whatever happens to come to mind, so a couple of other things have occurred to me that are related to the whole problem of trying to maintain our profession in a time when some people seem to think it is struggling for existence. I am not that pessimistic about our medium, but I do think there are many areas that need improving. I think one of the worst things is the system of trying to please readers who subscribe to only the daily or only the Sunday feature. By duplicating Saturday, Sunday, and Monday you punish the reader who follows the strip all the way through. I know that syndicates vary in their approach on this, but I think it is a foolish system; there is enough flexibility in our medium either to run separate stories or not to worry so much about the continuity. I also am convinced that there should be a lot less crime in comic strips. Mystery stories are wonderful and adventure is an absolute necessity, but anything that follows television trends is fatal. In fact, the moment a cartoonist forgets that he is dealing in a different medium and tries instead to duplicate the movie or television screen, he is on the wrong track.

For those of you who may be interested, I have now moved my studio to the Redwood Empire Ice Arena, which my wife and I built three years ago and where Warren Lockhart also has his office. Warren and I have formed a new corporation called Creative Developments, and out of this have come many new ideas for television programs and a very close working relationship with the various licensees who handle our side products. Our major project at the moment is the new movie we are doing with Lee Mendelson and Bill Melendez. It is to be called *Snoopy Come Home,* and I think it will be ten times better than the last movie we made, *A Boy Named Charlie Brown.* We have learned a good deal since we made that one, and we have high hopes that people will really like this new feature. My role is that of writer. I have complete editorial control of the movie and have written all the dialogue and have created every bit of business that you will see on the screen. Fortunately, working with Lee and Bill is very easy, for each of us never encroaches upon the other's area of responsibility. I know what I want in the movie, but I also know my limitations and am perfectly willing to allow the animators to use their imagination where it is demanded for certain scenes.

Something just occurred to me. Due to a misunderstanding in a discussion about my background while riding in an elevator with Carl Rose, I have either been given credit or have been blamed for being a Protestant minister. Sometimes I am referred to as an ex-minister of the Methodist church or a Presbyterian, but actually I have never been anything of the sort. I am strictly a lay theologian and have never pretended to be more than that. The two books that Robert Short wrote were of his own doing and contained ideas and views that were strictly his. I will admit, however, that I have used many scriptural references in *Peanuts* and have always enjoyed doing this. It has opened up a whole new area of thought and has brought in readers from almost every religious denomination, although it has also brought in criticism from those who feel that the Bible should not be quoted in what they call "something as lowly as a comic strip."

I think the *Peanuts* strip itself has changed considerably during the past five years. I am probably using fewer gags than ever before and am depending on the personalities of the characters to carry the strip. I have learned also to trust the faithfulness of my readers, and I certainly never expect to please each one every day. I have learned to take the risk of using ideas that might be regarded as too "in," knowing that those who understand the idea will be flattered and will appreciate it by showing even more attention to the strip than they did before. Probably the most "in" idea I have ever used was

Charles Schulz

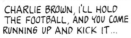

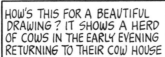

Front view of the Redwood Empire Ice Arena, located at 1667 West Steele Lane, Santa Rosa, California. This is a Swiss-style arena with a full-size hockey rink and permanent seating for four hundred spectators. Peggy Fleming and Joe Garagiola participated in the opening ceremonies in 1969, and Peggy described it as literally the world's most beautiful ice arena. Credit for this goes to Mrs. Schulz—Joyce—who was the guiding hand behind the entire project. There is a special Snoopy gift shop and a wonderfully friendly lunchroom that can handle up to eighty people and is called the Warm Puppy.

the one where Snoopy was pulling the sled up the hill and when Charlie Brown looked down at the sled, he saw that it was named Rosebud. I also love to do things that are really kind of silly, like using terms such as *queensnakes* and *gully cats* but realize that this is very risky because if readers are caught in a mood where they do not appreciate silliness and do not see it in this way, the whole thing is going to collapse, but I am convinced that these risks are worth taking, and I am fortunate in having editors at United Feature Syndicate who are willing to go along with this kind of thing.

I have sent along two photographs, which I hope Jud will print because they show what we do around here when we get a little time off. Naturally, we have a full skating program here at the arena, and we are completely involved with hockey. Therefore, when the ice happens to be empty during the day, we all put on our skates and rush out and have a quick game. Each of you has a standing invitation to drop by any time you are in northern California, but please bring your skates. We will furnish the hockey sticks.

JOHNNY HART AND *B.C.*

Story from Issue No. 26, June 1975

There are so many projects involved in Johnny Hart's cartoon life that covering them all would require a book. We've concentrated here on a conversation we had with him and Jack Caprio, during which he shed a lot of very interesting light on his methods of thinking and his attitude toward life.

John's studio is in his hometown of Endicott, New York, where he writes and draws the *B.C.* comic strip and produces the gags for the *Wizard of Id,* both of which features are distributed by the Field Newspaper Syndicate. Hart has full-time help from Jack Caprio, who works with John on gag ideas and keeps the various projects on which Hart is working at any given time in order. At the time we talked with them, they had nineteen contracts on the fire, aside from these two strips which are high on popularity polls in the United States and around the world.

HURD: Some cartoonists who comment on the social scene try to read everything in sight—newspapers, magazines, books—in order to fill up their idea reservoir. You don't operate that way, do you?

HART: I'm the complete opposite, I guess; I don't even read the newspapers every day. Maybe once or twice every couple of weeks I'll go through the papers, but they depress me. When I *do* make a comment in my strips, the inspiration has come from talking with people about what's going on around us or about things that interest me. And the comment in my case is reduced to its simplest form, which is characteristic of everything I do anyway. I think the comment is better when it's thus reduced to its simplest form and you show the idiocy of it—most things are idiotic anyway.

HURD: Mell Lazarus has said that idea production is a painful process. Do you find it so?

HART: Well, he's pretty intellectual—in fact, most cartoonists are quite a lot more intellectual than I am and much more wordy. I'm hung up with observing human nature in its simplest form. I guess when I look at anything that happens, I take it down to the basic form and wonder what primitive instinct motivated this event in the first place—what caused someone to do or say a given thing. I guess I came by this through inadequacy. I never was terribly bright or a great student and never had the opportunity to go in for advanced schooling.

I think a lot, and I was saying to my wife recently, "If it's possible for a person to think too much, I guess that's what's wrong with me, because I get in some horrible moods a great deal of the time about everything. I get physically and mentally tired from thinking—which causes depression. I wonder about everything. My

Johnny Hart

mind wanders all the time, and I can never fix on any one thing.

HURD: Tell us more.

HART: This thinking amounts to something like daydreaming. A lot of times I hate to sit down and draw—I don't know whether it's laziness or what—but I rather enjoy thinking. I'll spend two or three hours just thinking about nothing or everything, rather than doing my work. I look out the window and maybe I'll see a truck go by with a funny name on it. Automatically I wonder what it's like to be in that business, or who the guy was who painted the name on the truck, or who thought of the name.

HURD: How did you get into this habit?

HART: Originally I started it as an aid to producing ideas. I decided the wrong way to go about thinking up ideas is to lock yourself into just one theme until you come up with something on it. If nothing is working for you on one theme, go to something else or let it snowball in a different direction. You can start with a golf idea and wind up with a dock strike just by letting your mind wander aimlessly until something strikes you. Usually, when something does strike you, it rings a bell and you have a good feeling about it. Then you stay with it a few minutes and something happens. A lot of times an idea is too good to let go. When Jack Caprio and I are having little gag sessions and come up with an idea that's just barely adequate, we'll fool around with it, keep going with it, attack it from different viewpoints, and in practically every case we come up with a much better idea. Our ultimate goal is to make the gag as funny as possible. The most beautiful result you can achieve is to have a hilariously funny idea that also says something or will make somebody think.

Because I started this daydreaming thing years ago, my mind, as I said, wanders all over. I'll be talking with some guy and not listening because he may happen to have a funny mustache or something like that. I'll be watching him talk and thinking about what kind of wax he uses on his mustache, or how long it took him to grow the thing, and then suddenly I'll realize he's talking to me. Then I have to backtrack and figure out what he's said. Some of his remarks are still echoing in my mind and generally I can figure out what he was talking about.

HURD: You've put the words *simplicity* and *cartoony* up on the wall. Would you say something about them?

HART: I guess *simplicity* is self-evident, but *cartoony* was to remind us to exaggerate. If we draw a house we want to draw it to look like a cartoon house, not as a regular draftsman would do it. A tree would be funny with puffy leaves, a dog would always look *unlike* a dog but you'd recognize it as such with its big feet and floppy ears and a nose about the size of a softball—sort of in the John Gallagher or Dick Cavalli style of doing things. And I also related these words to the idea, trying to make the ideas as cartoony and as simple as the drawing style.

HURD: Speaking of *cartoony,* you didn't get into cartooning in high school, did you?

HART: No. I did like the absurdity of the things that Henderson and Partch did, and I was interested in cartooning, but I studied straight drawing during my high school major in art: design, how to use pencil, charcoal, a little bit of oil painting, and so on. Incidentally, I sometimes think that junior and senior high schools are teaching art so well nowadays that a student doesn't always need to take further college or art school training. Every once in a while, when I happen to see an exhibit of work by kids in these grades, I find the stuff so professional—the kind of thing I used to see in magazines when I was coming along. By the way, I think that students who try their hand at all the various kinds of art may find that there's something they like better than strip drawing. In other words, don't set your mind on one particular branch of art until you've sampled a number of them in school.

HURD: Although you said earlier that you aren't a great newspaper reader, I know you have spent a lot of time with books and dictionaries.

HART: Yes. Since I didn't have too much formal education, when I'd read and didn't understand a word, I'd look it up—I always kept a dictionary on my lap underneath whatever I was reading. Here's a funny thing. One day I picked up a book on English usage and punctuation and discovered the semicolon. For the next two weeks after that my strip was littered with semicolons—so much so that I got a call from Harry Welker of the New York Herald Tribune Syndicate. "John?" he said. "Harry Welker."—"Hey, Harry, how the hell are ya?" Then he comes back with "You wanta knock it off with those f—— semicolons?" I knew I'd been doing it, but I couldn't stop.

HURD: After a number of years of doing *B.C.* do you ever find yourself getting bored?

HART: I suppose the drawing end gets tiresome because you've drawn the characters over and over again. But when we come up with a gag where there are lots of wild things happening, or where the characters have strange little facial expressions, I still get as excited as I did the first day I drew them. When we're doing a lot of dialogue stuff, we still try to put extra expression into what the characters are doing. We do use a lot of facial expressions and comic positions of bodies that are rather subtle—they aren't just stock things in which the face is always the same as if it was stamped out. The creative part is the most exciting when Jack and I sit down and have a little gag session. The other afternoon we did two and a half weeks of ideas in an hour.

HURD: Would you tell us about those sessions?

HART: Well, Jack may be upstairs keeping all our projects straight and decide to come down for a Coke. Then maybe I'll say, "Let's do some ideas." He says "OK" and we grab a couple of pads. It takes a few minutes to get into it while we talk about premises and general ideas. We like to work on a theme—the other day it was the publishing business. I told Jack that the other night I was thinking about how everybody in the world is writing a book. This led us to wonder how we could get into this. Readers of *B.C.* know we use a rock as a masthead for our themes—PETER'S DRUG STORE, PETER'S AD AGENCY—and in this case we decided to go with PETER'S PUBLISHING COMPANY. Throughout a couple of weeks of ideas we did, we had people walking up and giving the character manuscripts.

CAPRIO: We both write down every conceivable notion or phrase that you'd use in the publishing business: royalties, galleys, et cetera. Then we go through these lists for funny words such as *rejections* or *advances* that have a double meaning. Maybe there's a pun somewhere there that we can parlay into a gag.

HART: We have other little devices we use—for instance, we straight-line each other. We grab a piece of paper and Jack may write some random sentence like "I never noticed what a funny-looking nose you have" for panel 1. Maybe I'll come up with a line for panel 2: "What do you mean, I've got a funny nose? I've always noticed that your *feet* are very funny looking." Eventually we may come up with a tagline.

Johnny Hart

CAPRIO: Sometimes after someone gives the straight line in the second panel, the gag develops very quickly in your mind—it develops a pattern.

HART: Occasionally we follow this gimmick on the actual daily strip—putting a first balloon in and then trying to follow it up. It's a challenging and fun way to approach idea production because it makes a game of it.

CAPRIO: Later, we may have all the dialogue penciled in, ready to ink, and John may look at it at the last minute and see something we've missed before, a funnier way we could have done the idea.

HART: When you're not locked into things, you can come back and look at a gag as a reader would look at it, and you may see a newer and better tagline.

CAPRIO: Here's another example of this straight-lining method of ours: For panel 1, I wrote, "I've got this great breakfast cereal and still my competitors are outselling me ten to one. What can I do?"

HART: I sat around for a while and then came up with: "Well, for openers you could name them something besides Krappies." We both fell down laughing at this, but because people object to certain words, I changed the line to "I've got this great breakfast cereal shaped like little fishies, with wild colors and flavors." Then we were able to use the funny line because of the fish—crappies.

CAPRIO: John is adventurous in using words—in fact, he might have been the first to use the word *broad* in a strip.

HART: I was rejected for years and years when I used this word, but I just kept putting it in anyway. Of course there's been a change from the old days. Then, *broad* meant *prostitute;* now it just means *girl.*

HURD: Since you work so hard to get just the right words in the strips, does an editor ever change any of them?

HART: Contractually no one is allowed to change any of my work without my approval—and Jack and I do our own censoring. We work hard to put words together, to make them flow, to make them funny, and to give them a poetic sense with a meter and all that.

CAPRIO: The timing in a gag is so important. The gag should flow from panel to panel and certain words should not be repeated, because they draw on the gag and make it a little boring.

HART: We try to say something with fluidity so it has meter and moves gracefully from one panel to the next. At the same time, we try to get all the junk out of it, to bring it down to the most basic way of saying it so we don't become redundant. I've always had sort of a feeling about the way things are said, sort of a poetic feeling—my own idea of what is a classic way of saying something and what isn't. Most of this is directed at the humor end of things. I'm always editing jokes, trying to get them down a little more basically so the surprise comes at the end, so I don't give the gag away in the middle, and so it leads very gracefully and unsuspectingly to a climactic word that cracks you up. I was always interested in simple poetry in school, by the way.

CAPRIO: In the case of something as simple as a single word, John is aware that it has a certain rhythm and rhyme to it. Tell about our problem with the word *cold-cock*, John.

HART: It's a very funny word, found in the dictionary, meaning "hit on the head or knock out," yet it also has sort of a vulgar sense. We put it in a strip, and somebody at some newspaper called and said we couldn't use it. But we did. This was in *Wizard of Id*. They were taking a poll, trying to find a girl whose foot fit in a glass slipper. Someone said, "You can try her sister, she's out in the field plowing. She'll probably get cold-cocked with the plow."

HURD: You've always been knee-deep in humor, haven't you?

HART: Jack and I met in the seventh grade, and we surrounded ourselves with a lot of very funny guys. He and I—and Dick Boland and a whole bunch of other freaky guys—spent all our time trying to be funny—verbally and physically. I've always been a laugher. My father had sort of a sarcastic sense of humor, and my mother was silly—she liked everything that was funny—and she was always laughing. You can see what happened to me as a result of living with these two people all those years. I appreciate all kinds of humor—if a guy falls down a flight of stairs, it's funny—and this appreciation carries up to the subtlest form of humor too. If you spend a lifetime with humor, you begin to see that all things—all the serious things we do in life—are funny. If you really look at them and think about them, they're going to be funny no matter what they are.

CAPRIO: I think we ought to add that previous stories have never explained the basic reason for John's success—*he wants to be a cartoonist more than anything else in the world.* The money to him is still secondary. A lot of good cartoonists simply don't want to do it that much!

BOB THAVES AND *FRANK AND ERNEST*

Story from Issue No. 27, September 1975

Readers seem to agree enthusiastically that the comic strip *Frank and Ernest*, created by Bob Thaves and distributed by the Newspaper Enterprise Association, is one of the funniest ones appearing in newspapers. He and his family live in Manhattan Beach, California. Bob's situation in cartooning is unusual in that he balances a job as an industrial psychologist with the additional work of producing the daily and Sunday *Frank and Ernest* strip. We asked Bob to tell our readers how this came about and to talk about his cartoon career.

HURD: You were exposed to newspapers early in life, weren't you?

THAVES: Yes. My father was a small-town printer who owned, edited, and published several weeklies simultaneously. I was born in Iowa and we later migrated to Minnesota, where I received most of my education.

HURD: That didn't include art training, though, did it?

THAVES: No, but I began early to draw comics, and as a small boy I was fascinated by seeing all kinds of mats of the comics around the newspaper shop. I did the usual drawing for various publications in high school, but I guess I did my first real cartooning at the University of Minnesota. After high school, I went into the army during World War II, and after having walked halfway across Europe in the infantry, I came back to Minnesota and studied industrial psychology at the university.

HURD: I suppose you worked for the well-known humor magazine there, didn't you?

THAVES: Yes, I drew for the *Ski-U-Mah*—and don't ask me where this name came from—it was known affectionately as *Skum*. During my last couple of years at school, I did a more-or-less-daily panel for the student newspaper, *The Minnesota Daily*. I got my bachelor's and master's degrees at Minnesota and then decided to head west with a number of friends who were going to the Los Angeles area. Out here I enrolled at USC in a program leading to my PhD and simultaneously began to do industrial consulting work in psychology to make a living and pay my way through school. During much of this time I was playing around with cartooning, and I began to sell to a lot of the minor markets. As time went on, I continued to do the consulting and also began to sell cartoons fairly regularly. Eventually, I did manage to complete all the course work for my PhD, but by that time I was getting impatient, so I never did take the oral exams or write a thesis. But I've managed all right without a PhD, and my life's probably been happier than if I'd spent an additional couple of years struggling through the academic routine.

HURD: You began to sell some of the major markets, didn't you?

THAVES: Yes—the old *Saturday Evening Post, True, Cosmopolitan, Saturday Review,* et cetera. As the years went by, I continued to combine my two occupations, but when anyone asked me I'd tell them that my principal job was in industrial psychology. I liked the idea of dividing my time between these two activities but I had a family to support. Since magazine work was speculative, I didn't want to jeopardize my consulting by spending too much time on the cartooning, so I began to think in terms of a syndicated comic strip.

I wanted to do a strip where there was fairly wide latitude, because I didn't want to be drawing the same thing day after day. I had in mind some kind of a panel that would be basically sort of a magazine cartoon—where the action could be occurring at any time in history or in any locality so I wouldn't be restrained by a particular setting. Now, I had heard that a successful strip must have characters with very sharply defined personalities

Bob Thaves

with which the reader can identify, and in my naïve way I thought this might conflict with what I wanted to do. But it dawned on me that it's possible to have characters with fairly well-defined basic personalities (or attitudes toward life) who still don't have to be always dressed exactly the same. They don't have to be at the same time in history. So this is what *Frank and Ernest* eventually became. In spite of the changes in setting, and so on, I've kept them basically in character, and I've thrown away cartoons from time to time because Frank and Ernest wouldn't have done a particular thing I'd shown in the gag. Incidentally, I think the syndicated comic strip is almost like the theater: Frank and Ernest are in reality performing from day to day.

HURD: Did you start right out with them as the principal characters?

THAVES: No, my first attempt contained them but there were a number of other people as well. I wanted a long panel, extending the full width of the strip, with something happening at the left side. I had in mind a cast of characters, like a theater repertory company, from which I could pluck the appropriate person each day and have him (at the right side of the panel) reacting to what was going on. I did perhaps fifteen samples with this format but found it was far too complex. However, Frank and Ernest were included in this cast, so I decided to pull them out and give them the starring role.

NATIONAL BANK.

IT'S FOR YOU. YOUR GET-AWAY DRIVER IS CALLING IN SICK.

© 1975 by NEA, Inc. T.M. Reg. U.S. Pat. Off.

THAVES 6/20

HURD: That long panel is fairly unusual in strips, isn't it?

THAVES: Yes. The long panel appealed to me because I've often found myself constrained when doing a magazine cartoon and wishing I could stretch the panel out for more room. And, as you suggest, I knew that the number of long panels available to the reader was very limited—*Miss Peach* and a couple of others. In this connection, I sent a number of samples to various syndicates simultaneously and got a few nibbles, but one rejection included the comment that a long stretched-out single panel would never go in newspapers! I might say that I was awestruck when the strip was picked up by Tom Peoples, director of comic art for the Newspaper Enterprise Association!

HURD: Why did you decide to use large block print for your lettering?

THAVES: I didn't want to do the usual balloon—I feel they're often an intrusion and I also think there's kind of a flavor to the large block print that is perhaps more comic and lighthearted. I felt the lettering should contribute to the tone and feeling of the cartoon, and this isn't the case in the ordinary balloon. In the case of magazines, if the caption is typeset under the panel, nothing is lent artistically to the cartoon. And, too, the block print is an attention-getter on the comic page. So I broke three rules: choosing the long panel, having characters who aren't always in the same surroundings and who change their identities at will, and using the block-print style of lettering.

HURD: Is there any relationship between your background in psychology and your *Frank and Ernest* work?

THAVES: People often assume so but I don't find any relationship between the two—it's as simple as that. I do continue with my consulting, but I spend less than half of the time I used to on it. However, as you can guess, my schedule is still unrealistically heavy.

HURD: I guess you have pretty ideal working conditions, don't you?

THAVES: I think so. I have a wife and two teenage children, and I do my work at home. We built our own house here at Manhattan Beach, so we were able to design it pretty much as we wanted it. Incidentally, ours is one of a number of beach communities that are pretty much all up and down the southern California coast—you hardly know when you're leaving one and entering another. We're about twenty miles from downtown LA, just far enough to get away from the smog. As for our house, I did include an office for myself where I can do the consulting work I bring home—the writing of reports and some analysis of data—and I keep my cartooning records here too. I set up my drawing board in our family room. I've managed to introduce total chaos here because I've gradually spilled out of the little corner I carved for myself originally. Also in the room is a very large loom of my wife's, the children have things they're working on, and there's commonly a surfboard leaning against the wall.

HURD: I know you wanted to say a few things about the tools you use.

THAVES: I had to experiment with various things since I had had no art training, and even today I'm constantly looking for different kinds of techniques and tools. I make regular trips to a large art store in LA once or twice a month and spend half an hour or so wandering around to see what's new. I used to use a Gillott crow-quill pen for my magazine cartoons. It was very fine and flexible, but I found that it was far too slow for *Frank and Ernest* and I made a lot of mistakes using it. So I switched to three Pelikan fountain pens—each with a different nib—and I find these much more workable. I work more rapidly with them and make fewer mistakes. I work on either two- or three-ply Strathmore, the plate finish. Some weeks the three-ply seems to feel better—I don't know why.

HURD: You like to use a lot of shading film, don't you?

THAVES: I'm addicted to it. I use the wide variety of tones and patterns I have on hand liberally. Sometimes I get letters commenting on how much readers like the use of the film in the strip. With a long panel, there's an awful lot of space to fill. I'm aware of the value of white space on occasion, but I'm generally reluctant to leave *all* the extra space white. I rough the strip out very lightly in pencil and then go immediately to a finish in ink. I rarely use a light board, but if I don't like some of a strip and still want to salvage the good parts I've done, I may resort to one. It generally takes a couple of hours to complete a daily, since the heavy block lettering does take time, as does the application of the shading film. The Sunday page may take a full day or more, since there are color guides to be done. And because I got used to thinking in terms of a single panel in my magazine cartoon days, it's harder for me to think in terms of a multipanel Sunday page.

HURD: Do you buy gags from writers?

THAVES: I suppose 25 percent of the gags in *Frank and Ernest* come from gag writers, and I'm always happy to look at submissions. I use the gags in this 25 percent very much as I receive them. Then perhaps another 20 percent of the total number of gags used in the strip are ones I may have been able to convert into something usable from just the seed of a gag that may have been submitted. A fairly large number of the gags I come up with myself seem to surface slowly in my mind—the result of observing and listening. I have some friends who are genuinely funny people. Sometimes I simply make a note of what they say and discover later that the comments I've noted are usable as cartoon ideas. Of course, as many cartoonists do, I will occasionally go back to old cartoon collections, leaf through them, and as a result of immersing myself in these, or of focusing on certain cartoons, I'm able to make a switch—but it's rare.

To continue for a moment on the subject of idea production, I try to take two things that are not ordinarily and logically associated in one's mind and link them in an entirely new and different way. My personal belief is that this is the essence of all creativity. It's necessary to be constantly alert to the possibility of there being something funny in situations you're confronted with. My personal preference is for offbeat gags, where the drawing is an integral part of the joke, so the burden of the humor is not carried entirely by the caption. To illustrate this method of taking two things that aren't ordinarily associated, let's say that Frank and Ernest are standing in a dark room and

FRANK AND ERNEST   by Bob Thaves

INSTEAD OF TONIGHT'S SCHEDULED HORROR MOVIE, WE ARE PRESENTING A POLITICAL REVIEW OF THE FIRST SIX MONTHS OF THIS YEAR.

THAVES

© 1974 by NEA, Inc. T.M. Reg. US. Pat. Off.

holding a flashlight. The flashlight goes out, and you see the beam bending down as water does in a garden hose. Frank says, "Who knows—maybe the battery is getting weak."

As you can guess, I also like gags where the setting is out of the ordinary because I get tired of drawing routine settings such as the living room or the office. I enjoy doing an idea that makes it necessary for me to go to the library to dig out a setting from a remote period or out of medieval history.

HURD: You've said that anyone interested in syndicated cartooning should be very much heartened by one important development in the field in recent years. Would you say something about that?

THAVES: There's an acceptance now of a much greater variety of humor than there used to be—*Doonesbury* is a good example. The opportunity to be innovative is obviously greater than it was a few years ago and includes drawing styles, layout, format, and subject matter. Pages of comics don't look all the same as they did in times past. As an example, you'll notice that *The New Yorker* publishes a much greater variety of cartoons than it did formerly.

HURD: Do you make a special effort to draw cartoons that you think your readers will laugh at?

THAVES: I draw what *I* think is funny and then hope the readers will feel the same.

Jud Hurd's *Frank and Ernest* article reprinted here was originally published almost thirty years ago. The basic concept of the strip has not changed since then: It is still a single panel in strip format with two sustaining characters, oversize block lettering, and a style of humor that has not changed. But the way the strip is produced, handled, and managed, and its graphic "look," have changed substantially.

Today, the computer is a big part of the strip's creation and management. The basic elements of each

FRANK AND ERNEST   by Bob Thaves

strip are still done with a pen (a Sharpie) on paper (Bristol Plate) to produce the "black line." But then the drawing is completed on the computer—adding shading, some secondary elements, and the lettering (done with a font created especially for the strip). All color work for daily and Sunday strips is digital as well. This means there are no complete cartoon "originals." The completed work exists only as a computer file. For me, "originals" are a thing of the past.

Thirty years ago, the strip was transmitted via the post office. Today it is by e-mail: faster, cheaper, and more reliable. Inclusion of our e-mail address in the strip is the principle means of communication with our readers, and that communication has a large simulative effect on the strip.

No organized archiving system existed in the past. The syndicate kept some drawings and I kept some. Some were lost or given away, and no records were kept. Today, our *Frank and Ernest* Web site has a search-able archive of more than four thousand images, and we are continuing to add to it. The site's archive permits easy review and retrieval, as well as other features not described here.

The advent of the computer, along with natural evolution over time, has resulted in a much different "look" in the strip. Some examples are printed here, and a comparison with the ones shown in Jud's original article makes the difference obvious. In general, my style today is much simpler, with less detail, less shading, and fewer elements.

I appreciate very much that Jud chose the *Frank and Ernest* article for inclusion in his book and that he has allowed me to make it current. Thirty years is a long time for a comic strip, and the whole process and end product have changed enormously.

FRANK AND ERNEST   **by Bob Thaves**

THE CLAM BEFORE THE STORM

LOOKS LIKE RAIN--- I'D BETTER CLOSE UP.

THAVES 5-5

MY LATEST INVENTION -- "THE COMEDY CLUB."

THAVES 3-4

UH, OH. MAYBE WE SHOULDN'T HAVE PUT THE POISON IVY SO CLOSE TO THE FIG LEAVES.

EDEN LANDSCAPING DEPT.

2-19

THAVES

BERT'S BURGER BARN

MENU

WE'LL HAVE A HAMBURGER AND A VEGGIE BURGER, PLEASE.

TWO BURGERS-- ONE REGULAR, ONE DE-CALF!

6-30

THAVES

MORT WALKER CONVERSES WITH DIK BROWNE

Story from Issue No. 41, March 1979

Dik Browne was born in New York City in 1917. He attended Cooper Union and began work on the *New York Journal* as a copy boy. He was a staff artist on *Newsweek,* served four years in the army, and became an outstanding advertising artist with Johnstone and Cushing agency. In 1954 he joined forces with Mort Walker to produce the comic strip *Hi and Lois.* Together they also wrote two children's books, *Most* and *Land of Lost Things,* which have been translated and sold all over Europe and South Africa. Dik Browne served two years as president of the National Cartoonists Society, has won their award four times as the best humor strip cartoonist of the year, and has twice won the Reuben award as the outstanding cartoonist in all categories. He has also won the Banshee Silver Lady, the Segar Award, and many other honors. In 1973 he created his own strip, *Hagar the Horrible,* which has now been sold to over a thousand papers. Dik has been married thirty-seven years to Joan Kelly. They have three children and live in Wilton, Connecticut.

MORT: You started *Hagar the Horrible* only six years ago, and already you are in over a thousand papers. To what do you attribute this phenomenal success?

DIK: God only knows. It's an honest strip and it's handled by a good syndicate. But I think everything else beyond that is mystery. If I knew the answer to your question, I'd chop it up, package it, and franchise the thing.

MORT: There have been only four strips so far in the history of the business that have been bought by over a thousand papers. Do you see anything they have in common? (Author's Note: In 2003 there are about twenty strips that appear in one thousand newspapers.)

DIK: Well, let's start by putting *Hagar* to one side. The remaining three, *Blondie, Peanuts,* and *Beetle Bailey,* are all humorous strips. That's the first thing that strikes you. They're all superbly done. The male hero of each strip is somewhat less than normally competent. The women are apt to be a little more intelligent, a little stronger, and this seems to appeal to the American view of the sexes for some reason or other.

MORT: Men can relate to it anyway.

DIK: Perhaps that's it. The women certainly demand it. The other thing that struck me is that the title seems to run to a two-syllable pattern in most of them: *Beetle, Blondie, Peanuts.* There seems to be a two-part rhythm. They don't depend on jokes but on the interrelationship of the characters. They're warm, and they're easy to identify with. One more thing I find interesting about these three strips: They were each created by one man working alone. And these three men all came from the Midwest and were remarkably young at the time.

MORT: Interesting observations.

DIK: I'm not sure about *Blondie* but I wonder, too, whether they have this in common: Weren't they all slow starters? You know, nobody could have predicted the amazing success they were to have in future years. It took them several years to get off the ground. Is that true also of *Blondie?*

MORT: *Blondie* took about five years, I think. It began as a flapper comic strip, then they got married, and then they had children.

DIK: All right. They took a couple of years. I'm sure that *Peanuts* took a little time to get off the ground. I'm not sure that slow growth didn't somehow add a maturity to the strip, give it a chance to mature.

MORT: On-the-job training, anyway.

DIK: I wonder, too, the background of the creators, whether that might not have been a help. You know, coming from America's heartland, maybe closer to the country's mainstream thinking. I don't know, but I thought it was interesting.

MORT: Do you think that in each one the artist has drawn himself? You know, you certainly have in Hagar. Do you think Dagwood Bumstead was like Chic Young?

DIK: Well, I think there must be something there. I'm no theologian, but I believe only God can make something out of nothing. Cartoonists have to depend on themselves. Wasn't it Jimmy Hatlo who used to draw with a mirror propped on his desk? Well, we all have mirrors. Some of them are more conspicuous than others. I don't think anybody could doubt that Al Capp was Li'l Abner. And George McManus must have been Jiggs's double. I see things in *you*, certainly, in *Hi and Lois*, especially in the writing of *Hi and Lois*. You say you're Lieutenant Fuzz, but I see your ideas coming out through all your characters.

MORT: I'm a lot like Beetle Bailey, but as I get older people tell me I'm like General Halftrack.

DIK: I didn't want to say it.

MORT: Even though *Hi and Lois* has always been comfortably successful, I always thought you had another big strip in you. Why did you take nearly twenty years to do it?

DIK: Well, you know, it's true that over the years you urged me many times to try a strip on my own.

MORT: You're like a natural resource. I saw all this great stuff in you and you were wasting it. Not wasting it, but doing special drawings for friends, for instance, for fun instead of making money.

DIK: Well, as you may have guessed after all these years, I'm not a naturally ambitious person. That's not a moral judgment, one way or the other. The world needs ambitious people. I think I'm easily contented, and that's not bad either.

The years I worked on *Hi and Lois* were far from wasted. They were good, happy years. About seven or eight years ago I began to run into eye trouble . . . that's the sort of thing that shakes up a cartoonist. I had to take stock. I had always made good money, but like most guys I had a lot of obligations. I wasn't financially set up for a medical disaster or even retirement. I was fifty-six years old, and the only thing I had ever done successfully was draw funny pictures. So I did the natural thing. I decided to stake out a strip of my own. *Hagar* was the first strip I tried, and I got lucky.

MORT: In real life you are very loquacious and intellectual. But your strip is almost terse when it comes to

Mort Walker

words, and most of the gags are very simple picture jokes that anyone can understand. How do you discipline yourself to do this?

DIK: Well, as far as the simplicity of the thing goes, there is a misconception sometimes in this country that verbosity is wisdom—and we both know that isn't true. As a matter of fact, with the space shortage in the papers today, I think brevity is the better part of wisdom. As to the discipline—well, you just have to do it. You've been an editor and you know that editing down is very important. It's the old wheeze about the guy who wrote he'd like to have written a shorter letter but he didn't have the time so he wrote a long one.

MORT: I just wonder how you keep it from coming out of you.

DIK: Well, to begin with, I believe in simplicity. I think that good ideas are usually simple. Communication is the important thing in the business we're in, so the simpler you can keep it the better. Now there's a personal reason for this, too. As you know, I have suffered eye damage and my vision is not as good as it used to

Dik Browne

be, and because of that I found that I had to give up reading some of my favorite strips. The lettering was too small and the figures were so tiny they were jammed in. So I thought, If I'm going to do a strip, I'm going to do a strip I can read and see. And this meant eliminating a lot of nonessential elements. I found myself bumping up balloons by putting blacks behind them so I could pick out the balloon faster. Using a heavier line in the drawing for the same reason. It defied reduction. I wanted something you could see on the head of a pin.

MORT: I wondered if you'd taken a lesson from Ernie Bushmiller. He's also personally a very intellectual man who has done some great comedy writing for movies and so forth, and *Nancy* is a strip that is so unlike him. He always says, "Dumb it down." He doesn't want to put anything in there that everybody can't understand.

DIK: Well, I agree and I admire Ernie tremendously. As a matter of fact, I'd be less than candid with you if I said he wasn't a great influence on me. I'm very proud of that. I think what he's done is appeal to the univer-

sal. I come from a family that was largely show business, and one of the clichés I remember hearing when I was a kid was, "You don't play to the boxes, see, you play to the balcony." One of my favorite songs is an old English music hall song that goes, "The boy I love is up in the balcony." Well, the boys *I* love are up in the balcony. There are more of them up there, too.

MORT: Your drawing style is also very different in *Hagar* from the style used in *Hi and Lois.*

DIK: I do think the relationship between drawing and the idea is a very tight one. In the drawing technique of *Hi and Lois,* the line is clean and round, and that somehow suits a clean, round, tight, warm family. When you get to somebody as raunchy as Hagar, I like the lines a lot cruder and bolder. Part of that drawing approach comes out of that book you and I did together called *The Land of Lost Things.* In doing that book I did it the same size, no reduction. I found that you get a certain vigor in the line that is perhaps lost when you reduce the thing too much.

MORT: Smooth it out.

DIK: Smooth it out too much and maybe it gets a little plastic. I used to think that was good. But you know one of the things about our business is, there's always change. We both remember when every self-respecting cartoonist did his work with a brush.

MORT: And cross-hatching was out.

DIK: Oh, of course! We had to wait thirty years for Robert Crumb to bring it back in. But you know, there are trends and fads, and I think one of the things that happened in the last ten–twenty years is that many cartoonists have come to realize there is a certain attractiveness in a hand-done quality. An honesty. I think perhaps we can thank the underground cartoonists of the last ten years for that.

MORT: You are Hagar in so many ways: your beard, your little-boy naïveté, your girth. Did you design the character in this way or did it just sort of evolve?

DIK: There may be points of resemblance, but they're purely coincidental. *Hagar* came about this way. I wanted a character who would be instantly identifiable . . . universally recognizable. I didn't want the reader wasting time figuring out who this character was. People are in a hurry these days. Well, a Viking with a horned helmet seemed to fit all my requirements. Better still, everybody likes a Viking. They can

get away with the most atrocious behavior, just because they're Vikings. It seemed a nice change of pace from *Hi and Lois*.

Hagar almost drew himself. Once you draw the horned hat, you need a nose. I made a few false starts here, ended up with something between an orange and a grapefruit. The beard just naturally grew, and just as naturally I made him fat—because thin just ain't funny! If I had anybody in mind when I was starting, it would have been Wallace Beery . . . maybe a bit of Zero Mostel. If you look at me closely, you'll see I bear a stronger resemblance to the late great Ronald Colman.

MORT: Did your own beard come first?

DIK: Oh, yes, my own beard began in a rather modest way some years before Hagar's. It took years of patient care to bring it to its current splendor. Please do not touch.

MORT: I know your horns came later. You showed up with a hat your son Bob made for you out of papier-mâché at Dick Wingert's party. It was still wet.

DIK: I have an impoverished son as you know: Bob, who's always broke and who is very thoughtful. And because he's always broke he's like the French, who became great cooks because they had nothing to eat, so he's always making fantastic presents, and maybe the best present he ever made me was that Viking hat, which I wear to bed now.

MORT: He made you a golf hat with horns on it too.

DIK: No, that one he bought—but the thought was creative.

MORT: How important is a cartoonist's personality to his product?

DIK: It's essential. You can only put into a cartoon what you yourself have. You may have the fanciest studio, or the finest working materials, but whatever value you have walks on two legs every day and gets a headache every night; it's you. That's all. You're your own liability, you're your own treasury, you're self-contained. The last self-contained asset in this country probably is the creative man, especially the cartoonist.

MORT: Do you think, let's say, that a man who had a lousy personality and was universally disliked could do a funny, appealing comic strip?

DIK: Not only could but has, though if you think I'm going to reel off a list of names you're crazy. But to misquote Will Rogers, "I never met a cartoonist I didn't like." I find cartoonists, especially of the bigfoot variety, to be warm, somewhat childlike, a bit naïve, and with all those endearing qualities that I look for in people.

MORT: Maybe that's the reason they have achieved success as cartoonists.

DIK: I will give you Dr. Freud's address and you can call him up.

MORT: Exactly what is a comic strip anyway?

DIK: It could just about be anything that will entertain the readers. On a comic strip page you'll see educational features, adventure, heart-throb, the very funny, the very sophisticated, and the very simple, all with one purpose in mind: to entertain.

MORT: I like to think this is my little space every day where I can do anything I want. I can be funny, I can be satirical, I can make statements, I can even have a heart tug. You know, within humor sometimes you can do all this.

DIK: I talked to Milt Caniff the other day, and he was saying that he felt like a stage producer who designed the scenery, wrote the play, and created the cast; the only thing he doesn't do is sell popcorn. It's a wonderfully self-contained medium, isn't it?

MORT: Do you aim your work at any particular audience?

DIK: Yes. You know, without being a wise guy about it, I aim it at myself. I write to please myself, and I suppose to please my family, because we are all involved in the thing. Aside from my financial reasons for starting the strip, I always dreamed of having a family business, a sort of cottage industry. It's not an original idea, God knows—every commuter in Connecticut has the same daydream—but, you see, the great thing is . . . it worked!

Chris, of course, is one helluva cartoonist. He's drawn *Hi and Lois* from time to time . . . handles the pocket-

books completely. Bob, who plays beautiful country blues under the name of Chance Browne, is our resident designer. My wife, Joan, who always had more faith in me than I had in myself, runs the business side: keeps the books, answers the mail, cooks the food, and supplies the witty one-liners. My daughter, Sally, is still in school at Georgetown, but she helps out with the filing and is a gofer on vacations. It's great, because I think we're even closer as a family because of this business we have going. I rough up all the gags on tracing paper to finished size. Then the family rates them from one to infinity. Sometimes they'll give a gag a one-plus, which means *very good—use this*. I've gotten marks when I caught Joan in the wrong mood as bad as 47, with the added note, *Don't bother me*. The marks keep my head straight.

MORT: But mostly you have to satisfy yourself?

DIK: Yes. In the polls I notice *Hagar* often scores well with men, for instance. But the funny thing is, a good deal of my mail comes from women and children. The women write circuitously; they will say *I'm married to Hagar* or *my father is Hagar*.

MORT: So you don't think you can direct your writing toward a particular audience?

DIK: I think it's deadly. You can't calculate a strip. If you started out to say *I'm going to do a strip that will be for children under ten*, sure as hell you'd get the geriatrics set.

MORT: I remember when we started *Hi & Lois*. I wanted to get away from the henpecked-husband routine. We decided we would have Hi look big and tough—we even gave him a broken nose—and it wasn't long before we fell right into the old trap.

DIK: And Lois was a little on the dumb side, remember that? And very subservient.

MORT: How has *Hagar* been received in foreign countries?

DIK: Very, very well, I'm delighted to say. I don't know how many languages he's in, but if you look at the books back here you see how many translations of Hagar books there are: dozens. *Hagar* is, of course, very popular in Norway, but it's popular in many countries. One of the nice things said to me by a French editor was that it translates very well; a Spanish editor said so too. I think that may go back to the business of fewer words and a simpler style.

MORT: And you do a lot of picture gags, which transcends all language barriers.

DIK: I don't really like to demand a special knowledge of the reader.

MORT: Have you ever had any aspirations to be a fine artist? I say *fine* in quotes.

DIK: When I was very young, I thought I would like to be a sculptor. My father was in the stone business, and I loved the limestone yards where they carved the statues for the buildings in New York and Washington. But it didn't work out. I came of age during the Depression, and we had to trim our sails to the prevailing winds. Unless you were terribly gifted, it was not a good time for fine arts.

MORT: Your mother was in the theater, wasn't she?

DIK: Yes, she was. She was a wardrobe mistress on Broadway, and I grew up around all that.

MORT: Used to hang out and see shows backstage?

DIK: I grew up backstage. I didn't know there was a front of the house! I didn't know there was an audience out there. I thought the actors were onstage performing for their own amusement.

MORT: That probably gave you some feeling for writing and what goes over with an audience, don't you think?

DIK: Possibly. I think our parents create us, don't they?

MORT: Do you think cartooning is an art?

DIK: Oh, absolutely, I think one of the highest arts. The museum is so long overdue. To wait so long to find a sanctuary for the art. It's been a crime. I remember years ago up in Columbia University, being told about the wonderful originals that were lying around gathering dust, crumbling, being lost. Irreplaceable originals. Truly an art form and, incidentally, one of our few great American art forms.

MORT: I was talking to Harry Devlin, and he expressed the opinion that cartooning is still looked down on by galleries and artists. They still don't really appreciate illustrations or cartoons. He thinks it may stem back to the days in England and France when you had to be a gentleman to be exhibited, to be a member of the Academy, and fine art was a gentleman's art, where as cartooning was the art of the masses, vulgar.

DIK: That may be, but, if true, it's a sad commentary on galleries. I can't believe any sane artist would look down on cartooning. It would be like being bigoted against India ink. Any art should be judged solely on quality. Let's face it: A good cartoon is a better thing than a bad painting. The days of the gentleman painter were short indeed . . . and not very productive. Manners have little to do with creativity. One of the few "gentlemen" to make it to the big time was Toulouse-Lautrec, and—surprise! surprise!—he was a cartoonist.

MORT: Do you think what you do, cartooning, is hard work?

DIK: No, of course it isn't. You couldn't pay me, there isn't enough money in the world to make me quit, and it's the same with you. You're going to drop dead one day over the India ink, probably make a terrible mess on the floor.

MORT: I heard a story the other day. Anne Bancroft, who is married to Mel Brooks, came home from the studio after working and sweating all day long. He's in there doing his thing, and she throws herself down and says, "Acting is such hard work!" And he picks up a piece of blank paper from his desk and he says, "*This* is hard."

DIK: Well, I'll tell you I've done both, and I think writing is certainly harder than drawing a bigfoot strip. I think there is a tactile, almost sensual feeling about drawing—it's great, you know—you can really get into it and have fun. Writing, that's a different job.

MORT: Do you get white-paper fever every now and then, when you look at blank paper and can't get an idea?

DIK: Well, I think we all do. Yes, I get it, and I think we all have techniques to deal with it. I've been through as many as anyone. You know, the business of switching or looking up a book of quotes or reading the newspaper. My best is to go to bed. I go to bed with a note pad, and I put the lights as low as I can and still be able to see the pad, and I let the brain go. Incidentally, the best ideas I get are on waking up, I don't know if anybody else has this thing.

MORT: I get a lot of ideas when I wake up early in the morning—about four—when it's quiet.

DIK: Isn't that odd? Sometimes they just pop right into your head. They've been in the back of your mind and just suddenly been released. The six A.M. idea is the jewel. But let me warn you, the three A.M. idea is a rattlesnake. I checked this with my son Chris. We have both had the same experience. You wake up in the middle of the night and you write this gag down and you're laughing your head off—you say, God! I've written the funniest gag in the world! Then you wake up the next morning and look at it and just giggle a little bit, and by afternoon you're looking at it and saying, "I don't understand what was so funny about that."

MORT: You know one thing I often wondered in leaning back in my Barcalounger or lying on a couch—this is where I work on my ideas—I wonder whether or not just the physical thing of lying down and having the blood in your brain instead of in your feet helps you think of ideas.

DIK: I think it's terribly important to relax. I've gotten into a little mysticism or something. I draw a black dot on a white page and I just look at it and I try to put my brain almost to sleep: you know, half think about what I'm thinking about but not *think* about it. And my God it works, you know, it seems to break the logjam somewhere, as if you're focusing on something.

MORT: As long as the little black dot doesn't start crawling up the page, you're all right.

Was there any particular *Hagar* strip that brought an unusual response from your readers?

DIK: Yes, there was one. It's about a lawyer who was named after our mutual attorney, Coyer the lawyer. Well, lawyers all over the country, from Governor Connolly to Judge Sirica, saw this as one of the few positive gags ever written about a lawyer. It seems every time a kid graduates from law school his parents give him a copy of this thing.

MORT: Do you sell copies?

DIK: Oh, yeah, we sell copies. What we do is, we ask the person to send fifteen dollars to the Milt Gross

Fund [the NCS fund for cartoonists in need] or to the museum, and it's surprising it's still going on to this day. We still get requests for it.

MORT: You did an update on it just recently, didn't you?

DIK: Yes, but as a matter of fact I don't think we received a single request for that one. I thought it was a funny gag.

MORT: I thought it was too, as good as the first one, but as you said before, you can't manufacture it. If you direct an idea in a certain way in order to appeal to lawyers, it probably won't.

DIK: You're absolutely right.

MORT: You've resisted using *Hagar* as a forum for your social and political beliefs. Why?

DIK: That's not my cup of tea. I have no political axes and damn little wisdom to spare. I sell giggles. My hat is off to those who can do it, but it's a chancy thing. More cartoonists have come a cropper by pushing a political slant than any other single thing. Wasn't it Sam Goldwyn who said, "Messages are for Western Union"?

MORT: Yes.

DIK: Now, that's philosophy! Incidentally, what happened to *relevant*? Do you remember? Relevant came right after *new generation* and just before *viable*.

MORT: Poor box office, probably. I used to go to the movies when they were doing relevant stuff and I'd come out feeling like I'd been to a lecture.

DIK: Well, unfortunately, ideas are much like fashions. Yesterday's viable idea looks pretty dumb today.

MORT: Of course, I think whenever you draw you're making some kind of a comment. I love Al Capp's re-mark. He said, "Every time you draw a dog, you're making a statement on dogs." I think we're making statements on the army in *Beetle Bailey*, we're just not forcing it. It sort of flows out. Life is relevant. Marriage is relevant. Work is relevant.

DIK: Relatives are relevant.

MORT: But not more than once a year. Do you have a philosophy of humor?

DIK: Do I have a philosophy of humor? Philosophy is a heavy word, but I have some ideas, all right. Suppose we talk about comedy. Comedy may be an art, but it is not a science. It's a little hard to define and it's very hard to make rules about it—Rules that last. People laugh at different things at different times. If you don't believe this, just ask any stand-up comedian. The gag that killed them last night lays an egg today. There are some generalities that I buy. There is the difference between humor and wit. Though they sometimes blend and merge, they represent two distinct approaches to comedy. Now I've got to quote this for you, this comes from the *Merriam-Webster's Collegiate Dictionary:* "Humor is that quality which appeals to a sense of the ludicrous or absurdly incongruous." I think that's legitimate. Humor is apt to be good-natured and even compassionate. If I could pick one symbol for humor, it would be Charlie Chaplin's little tramp. For me, he's the ultimate humorous character. Mark Twain had a quote on everything. Here's what he said about humor: "Everything human is pathetic. The secret source of Humor itself is not joy but sorrow. There is no humor in heaven." Do you know why? Because there's no sorrow in heaven, so you don't need humor. Everybody just walks around saying "Hello, hello."

Cartoon Success Secrets

MORT: But not laughing, just smiling.

DIK: Just smiling. It doesn't hurt that much. They don't have to laugh anymore. OK? There's an old Irish saying, "What never made you laugh will never make you cry." It's usually applied to children. But if you just turn that saying around, you may have the secret well of humor. Wit, on the other hand, is aggressive. It's defined, once again by the dictionary, as "the power to evoke laughter by remakrs showing verbal felicity or ingenuity." You once said, and I thought it was very apt, "Wit needs a target." That's true. It does.

MORT: And a sharp point.

DIK: If I had to pick somebody to symbolize wit, as opposed to Charlie Chaplin, it would be Oscar Wilde. Now, everybody laughs, you know. I'm not saying it isn't funny; of course it is, it's a legitimate form of comedy. But you're picking on somebody. You know, you got to zing 'em, that's what wit's all about.

MORT: OK. So love is mixed in with humor?

DIK: Oh, absolutely. And then another thing. By its very nature, wit is verbal. Not visual. It's verbal. It's a remark you make. And because of translation difficulties, I think it's less universal than humor. In cartooning, when wit is used in cartooning, it depends less on drawing than humor does. You remember the old magazines where they would have the witty sayings underneath the drawings? As a matter of fact, some magazines still do it. The relationship between the drawing and the witty remark is very slight. You could use the same man and woman every week, just putting new witty remarks underneath.

Harry Hershfield was one of our wittiest brains. I'm not positive about this, but I'm pretty sure he became a full-time writer when he decided he could use the space better by filling it with words instead of drawings. The cartoons weren't doing anything. It was the words that were important.

MORT: My mentor John Bailey, cartoon editor of the *Saturday Evening Post,* used to say, "If you can cover up the drawing and get a laugh out of the punch line, you don't need the cartoon."

DIK: I think that's a perfect example. There's one more thing about humor. There seems to be a relationship between humor and drawing that's natural. In the leading strips it's all of a piece. The drawing is part of the writing; the writing is part of the drawing. We are not going to go into the subdivisions: satire, all the rest; you can spend a lifetime. I'm almost embarrassed by going over humor this analytically. It's sort of like performing an autopsy on a girl you love.

MORT: I usually go around quoting Leo Rosten, who said, "Humor is the affectionate insight into the affairs of man."

DIK: Well, I agree and I appreciate that quote, and I think Leo Rosten probably knows more about humor than anybody in America—present company excepted.

MORT: As long as we're quoting—this has nothing to do with the conversation, it's just to show off a little bit—one of my favorite quotes from Mark Twain is, "He had a peanut for lunch; therefore you could not say that he was full of drink without seriously transcending the truth." If you analyze that a little bit, there's sympathy in it.

DIK: There is. Well, you know, you're right. Because there's compassion in it, isn't there?

MORT: If you were the feature editor of a newspaper and could choose fifteen strips for your comic page, what would they be? You can leave ours out if you want.

DIK: We damn well better leave ours out.

MORT: Pick fifteen other ones.

DIK: Well, I'll give you that list, but first I must take leave of my senses.

MORT: I always thought it would be fun.

DIK: Do you? Do you really? OK, Mort. I have a dentist who doesn't give novocaine; you'd probably find him hilarious. Leave one name out and you're dead. The surest way to get on an enemy list is to *make* a list. But I will say this: I would like to see a better balance of straight strips and comic strips. Not just for the straight strips but for the healthful comic section as a whole. I think they are such an important element. Even to the point where I'd like to see them get a little more space than they have. I think it's difficult for them to do the job they do so beautifully in the same space that a bigfoot strip has. I think it's logical and I may be a traitor, but I think it would be good for the health of the business as a whole if they get a bit more space.

MORT: Jules Feiffer made an impassioned plea at a Newspaper Comics Council meeting. He just reminded all the editors and cartoonists there that graphics have become a tremendously important part of some of the

more successful magazines and publications today, such as big books, coffee table books, *New York* magazine, *Esquire,* other magazines that really employ graphics. And here the newspapers, which have the opportunity to use their graphics in a better way, are minimizing them, reducing them to a size people over fifty can't even read anymore.

You wouldn't even care to mention maybe some of your favorite strips?

DIK: Well, I'd rather not, because if you leave one out you've lost a friend. I love them all. If you'd like, I could tell you the strips that influenced me, or that I grew up admiring. Yeah. I don't mind that, because they're such a mixed bag. One of them was Ed Wheelan: *Minute Movies.* Oh, God, I loved his *Minute Movies.* Nell Brinkley was a heck of a penwoman, and I loved her drawing. The original strip that knocked me flat was Milt Caniff's

Terry and the Pirates. It was a sunburst the first time I saw a Sunday page by him.

MORT: My heart used to pound even when I'd see his signature. I didn't know there was such glamour.

DIK: You're right. Impact. Russell Patterson, in another way. Tom Henderson—fantastically funny. But those were just some. There were many more.

MORT: Just briefly tell me a little bit about your working schedule, what kind of a day you put in, what kind of a week.

DIK: Well, I get up about seven and I'm usually down at work about eight. I'll hit the Barcalounger in late afternoon and doze off for an hour. I find that somehow when I'm not playing golf or looking at television, most of my time is spent drawing or writing or thinking these days.

MORT: Do you have a particular day to do your writing, or do you just do it anytime?

DIK: No, I like to get started with the writing on Monday. Monday's my day for sending work in, getting started on the writing, getting the week off good.

MORT: How many ideas do you try to write in a day, for instance?

DIK: Oh, I *try* to write a hundred.

MORT: How many *do* you write?

DIK: I probably write thirty gags a week. I probably draw up something like eighteen to twenty. I select six dailies and a Sunday that got good marks from the family. I try to balance my gags: a picture gag, some including Helga and Lucky Eddie, et cetera. When I've got my batch ready, I—or Chris or Bob—light-box it on Strathmore with pencil, and it's ready to finish. Sometimes I skip this step and ink right on the light box.

Dick Hodgins, Jr., a neighbor and buddy whose lettering I admire almost as much as his fantastic artwork, is kind enough to letter *Hagar* for me. He also does a lot of artwork on our European books.

Hi & Lois is handled much the same way, except that the talented Frank Johnson does the basic inking on the strip, I finish it and send it to New York, where Fred Schwartz letters it.

MORT: What have you learned about yourself in the last six years?

DIK: Well, like most people, that I'm capable of more work than I thought. I used to manage to fill up a week just drawing *Hi & Lois*. Now a regular flood of strips, books, and God only knows what moves through the cellar every week.

MORT: With your tremendous success, have there been any differences in your life?

DIK: Of course. I've got an edge of financial security, and that's a real good feeling. There's more work, of course, but that's a pleasure—and I get a kick out of the publicity. This week has been a gasser. *Hagar* made *People* magazine, we got a call from the mayor of Milwaukee, and to top it off, *Hagar* made the *New York Times* Sunday crossword puzzle.

Vive la différence!

Zeke Zekley on George McManus and *Bringing Up Father*

Story from Issue No. 44, December 1979

In the thirties, when your editor worked in animation and in the comic strip field in Hollywood, he used to visit George McManus and his assistant, Zeke Zekley, from time to time at their studio. In 1979, for the first time in many years, we met Zeke again and asked him to reminisce about the creator of *Bringing Up Father* for our readers.

HURD: How did you and George McManus get together?

ZEKLEY: It was fascinating the way my long association with George started. George was my idol when I was a kid, and the margins of most of my schoolbooks were evidence that I was influenced a great deal by him. (My mother, incidentally, saved these schoolbook cartoons and gave them to me some years afterward.) One day in 1935 when I first came out to California—dead broke—I was sitting in a restaurant watching a friend of mine, also an artist, who was table-hopping, doing sketches for tips. Both of us were keeping our heads above water that way. At one point my friend came over to me and mentioned that George McManus's brother was sitting a few tables away, and with just the mention of this name I started doodling on the tablecloth. Later, when I was standing out in front of the restaurant on Hollywood Boulevard waiting for my friend to finish, a waiter came after me, holding this tablecloth, and asked, "Did you do this?" I thought, My God, I'm going to have to pay for the tablecloth! I was too nervous to lie, so I said, "Yes, I did." He took me back into the restaurant and introduced me to Charlie McManus, who was interested in my doodles and who said that his brother George would probably like to talk to me. He arranged a meeting, which led to our twenty-year association and a father-and-son relationship that continued till George's death in 1954.

To begin with, I ruled the lines for the *Bringing Up Father* pages, did the lettering, and filled in the blacks. Eventually I got to draw a lamp, and sometimes a character. Then, when I got a little bolder, I'd suggest ideas, and when they started flowing I became a collabora-

BringingUp Father

© K.F.S.

By GEO McMANUS

tor, rather than just an assistant. He was a generous man and appreciated what I did, and in return I took a tremendous load off his shoulders. More and more of the work developed around me, and it came to the point where our styles merged to such a degree that we couldn't tell who did what. There would be times when George would ask, "Did you draw these spats?" and I'd have to say, "No, you did!"

Once in 1938, when George was in South America, he penciled a few weeks of stuff very roughly and put it in the mail, but because I had to make a trip to Detroit at that point, some of his stuff reached me and some never did. So on my way back to California, I drew some substitute strips on the road in motels and piece-mealed them to the syndicate in New York. This was the first time I substituted some of my work for his.

HURD: Say something more about what it was like to work with him.

ZEKLEY: I memorized most every *House & Garden* and architectural magazine I could put my hands on, stored away a lot of this, and later introduced a tremendous amount of intricate background work into the strip. I often wonder how it was that I didn't leave my eyeballs on the drawing table. When I look at a Sunday page as it was in those days—you had a top part, a *Rosie's Beau,* a *Snookums,* and *Bringing Up Father* (first twelve panels, later reduced to eight)—and realize that we did these plus six daily strips, I don't know how we did it or sometimes how *I* did it. Today it wouldn't be possible!

HURD: When I'd drop into your studio in the Corinne Griffith Building on Sunset Strip from time to time,

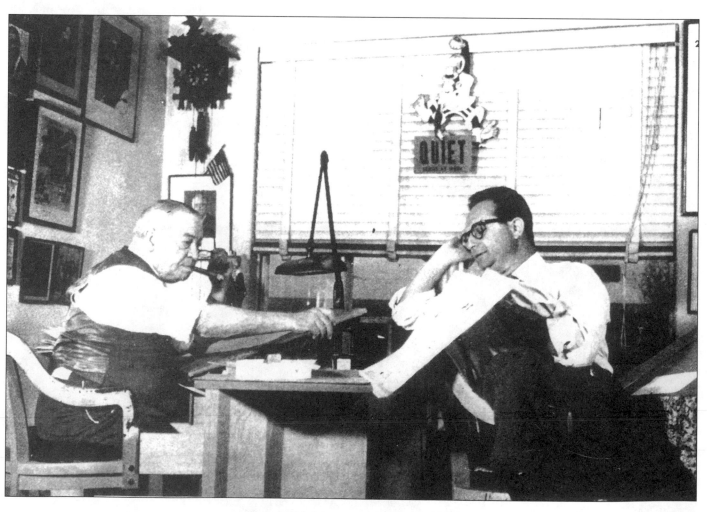

George McManus and Zeke Zekley

Zeke Zekley on George McManus and *Bringing Up Father*

I'd see you at your board, sitting in front of McManus at his board. Did you toss ideas back and forth?

ZEKLEY: Sure. Occasionally he'd holler out, in despair, "Have *you* any ideas? I haven't got any!" I'd come back with, "What if Jiggs is doing this?" "No, I've done that!" Then I'd say, "You've *thought* of it but you haven't *done* it." We'd go through this routine and I'd have to convince him that he'd been with the strip so long before I came with it that I didn't even remember what he'd done then. Further, that a previous generation had either forgotten those long-ago strips or had never seen them in the first place. So if we drew some of these ideas again, they would be new, they would be fresh.

As far as the drawing was concerned, I think that everybody in those days who wanted to be a cartoonist liked filling empty space with cross-hatching or shading without any real meaning. From George, I learned

that black and a simple white line was very effective. I think he must have been influenced at one time by the Japanese, who place a high value on clean lines and solid blacks. I know he was influenced by Charles Dana Gibson in handling girls' hairstyles.

HURD: What was your daily routine like?

ZEKLEY: Every evening after we left the studio, he and I would go somewhere to eat, and after I got married we'd send the car and have my wife join us, so for the first five or six years of our married life she never knew what the inside of a kitchen looked like. George's wife was in ill health, he maintained her in their home with several people to look after her, and he lived separately in an apartment. They had no children. He was the godfather of both of my children, incidentally.

George was one of the dearest men in the world, and I love recalling the many foolish things we'd do. For

Left: Jud Hurd and George McManus in 1950
Above: Claudia Hurd and Jiggs's creator, 1950

Cartoon Success Secrets

George McManus receives the Silver Lady Award in Beverly Hills in 1952. Left to right: *L.A. Examiner* columnist Vincent X. Flaherty, Zeke Zekley, Tiny Naylor, Jimmy Durante, George, and Jack Dempsey. In the background is an enlarged *Collier's* cover announcing a three-part McManus story, "Jiggs and I."

instance, before air-conditioning was installed in buildings everywhere, we worked near the open windows, and since it was California and there were a lot of flowers, every so often bees would invade our office. When this happened, George would run across the room and lock himself in the closet, leaving me to fend off the bees.

We worked so close to the windows that passersby who knew what was going on would frequently wave and get a return salute from us. One of these was Frank—*Moon Mullins*—Willard, who had a crazy routine. He and his assistant, Ferd Johnson, would work for forty-eight straight hours (or fifty-six, whatever it took) without sleep, get out their whole week's work, and then collapse. We'd be coming in for breakfast at Armstrong & Schroeder's here in Beverly Hills just as Frank and Ferd, with about three days' growth of beard, would be having dinner at eight o'clock in the morning. After that they'd go home, take a shower, hit the golf course, catch up on their sleep, and then repeat the same routine over again. We kept regular office hours—we were at the office at eight-thirty or nine and quit about four—but we worked seven days a week.

Frank Willard didn't drive a car, but on days when he wasn't working he'd sometimes have his chauffeur,

Albert, drive him by our office in his long Cadillac limousine. Wearing a white straw sailor hat, he'd lean out of the back with his feet up on the front seat and yell, "Work, you SOBs!" The *Saturday Evening Post* once ran a two- or three-part series about Frank called "The Magnificent Roughneck," and this description certainly suited him to a T.

HURD: Let's hear some more McManus stories, Zeke.

ZEKLEY: Well, we had our weekly fire in the office. George, as you know, smoked anywhere from twenty-five to forty cigars a day (which habit made Ripley's *Believe It or Not* any number of times), and every time he'd light up he'd throw the old one in the wastebasket or toss in a match that wasn't completely out. He was seated behind me, and once in a while he'd very quietly inch his foot up toward me and then start

fanning the smoke my way, leaving it to me to drown the wastebasket fire. Sometimes when we'd been working too hard, the pranks would start with rubber bands and paper wads in the back of the neck. He brought a squirt gun, I followed suit the next day, we barricaded ourselves and so on, just to break up the routine. A certain amount of the tedium and monotony got to us occasionally, and horseplay seemed to be our remedy. George could recite almost entire routines from old vaudeville acts, because he went back a long way. His father was the manager of a theater in St. Louis, where George actually got the inspiration for *Bringing Up Father* from a play called *The Rising Generation*. And having known people from the Ziegfeld days—and so many top stars—he had loads of nostal-

gic stories to tell. I was twenty when I broke in with George, who was fifty-one at the time, and though he was many years my senior, I never thought of him as an old man because he was so young at heart. There was a reserve about him but there was also this wonderful never-lost boyhood of practical jokes he delighted in. I remember one year when he went up to San Francisco to a summer encampment of the Bohemian Club, whose membership consisted of doctors, lawyers, politicians, and other successful men from all walks of life. They lived in tents among the giant redwoods for a week, putting on their own shows every night, complete with orchestra, and George would do a lot of the decorations.

Jay Maeder and Garry Trudeau on Problems Cartoonists Face

Story from Issue No. 46, June 1980

After receiving this note from Garry Trudeau, we talked with *Miami Herald* staff writer Jay Maeder, who very generously granted us permission to reprint pertinent parts of a long story of his that appeared in the paper on September 23, 1979. We found it very interesting.

by Jay Maeder

The comic strip business is a vast entertainment industry whose doings are not ordinarily the stuff of every-day conversation. You hear about the comics business chiefly when it is congratulating itself on the occasion of a watershed anniversary—Popeye, star of *Thimble Theatre,* turned fifty this year; *Gasoline Alley* hit sixty—or when some very famous feature is retired after a long and respectable run.

News is made when Lucy pledges at last to hold the football in place for Charlie Brown. News is made when *Doonesbury*'s Joanie Caucus is admitted to law school. News is made when *Mary Worth* finally does the unwed-mother story.

Behind the scenes there is a nuts-and-bolts business whose modern realities are seldom reported beyond the trade press but which have everything to do with why your favorite features are, or aren't, run by your hometown newspaper. They have everything to do with why your newspaper is running fewer strips than it was a decade ago and why it is running them measurably smaller. They have come to have everything to do with the very aesthetics of the medium.

The modern realities are that (1) newspapers are regularly going out of business these days and (2) the remaining papers face increasingly staggering newsprint costs that make a page of comics an expensive luxury for many an editor.

In a buyer's market, the seller is unwilling to offend. And syndicate resistance was minimal when, in the early seventies, the newsprint-crunched newspapers began to demand that smaller strips be provided.

Smaller strips meant the syndicates had to go to their cartoonists and demand fewer panels, less background detail, larger dialogue balloons with fewer words in them. Those conditions effectively limit the cartoonist's ability to build a gag or to construct a cogent dramatic narrative. Today, editors complain to syndicate executives that the comics somehow don't seem to be as good as they used to be.

Daily strips have already been reduced in size about as much as they can possibly be—let it be recorded, incidentally, that *Miami Herald* readers enjoy much larger daily comics than readers of many other papers—but resourceful new methods of reducing Sunday comics seem to be devised every week; running five or six features per page is no longer uncommon.

Doonesbury's Garry Trudeau has lately become the first cartoonist to officially resist the newspapers' widespread modern practice of reducing their daily and Sunday strips to barely readable sizes. Universal Press Syndicate, which distributes *Doonesbury,* has announced a new contract stipulation that flatly prohibits client papers from reducing the strip beyond a specified point. Such a demand is unheard of in the comic strip business. In addition, Trudeau is stipulating that papers must run his strip on the comics page and not, as some do, on the editorial page. Universal unhappily expects to lose papers, and executives at other syndicates are horrified—not because it's inherently a bad idea, but because *it is not the way things have always been done.*

Form dictates substance: Virtually across the board, cartoonists are obliged to incorporate throwaway panels into their Sunday strips so a paper can leave out as much as half the feature if that's what it cares to do.

```
DOONESBURY

Dear Jud:

The Miami HERALD recently ran a piece about
    the problems that cartoonists are
facing today, and what what we are trying
to do at UPS to remedy them.

I think it would make interesting reading
for your cartoonist subscribers. Perhaps
you could get the reprint rights?

All best,

Garry Trudeau
```

"The customer is always right," says Bill Yates, comics editor at King Features Syndicate. "You can't sell cornflakes and tell people how to eat them."

The new *Doonesbury* contract marks the first modern-times occasion that anyone has ever told the customer how he must eat his cornflakes. It's a measure of the syndicate's prevailing timidity that Garry Trudeau's action to preserve the integrity of his creative product is universally viewed as dangerous. It's dangerous, of course, because it might work, and then other cartoonists might make the same demand.

Yates, as it happens, is a former working cartoonist himself, and old sympathies run deep despite the temperance expected of a syndicate editor. In an unguarded moment he allows himself to say out loud what everyone really thinks. "Sometimes when I read the newspaper and I see the comics reduced down to such postage-stamp size, and I hear that they don't have the space, I look through that paper and I see all sorts of garbage, fillers, little factual tidbits that nobody gives

a damn about, stories about something that happened in Bangor, Maine, or something. I can't see how they make such a fuss about a comic strip."

Editors, actually, love to fuss with their comic strips. Editors commission surveys and attend seminars and address one another and give one another awards. "The comics pages, after all, are virtually the only ones in the newspaper where we can, without compromising our own or our newspaper's integrity, give the reader precisely what he or she wants," Tom Wark of the *Philadelphia Inquirer* said in remarks before the Newspaper Comics Council last spring. "Our job as editors is to find out as certainly as our resources permit what the readers *do* want."

Accordingly, at the newspapers' level, the science of "comic strip management" has supplanted the old-fashioned seat-of-the-pants strip-buying habits editors indulged in when newsprint was cheap.

Three distinct "reader clusters" are identified. One group, chiefly older readers, gravitates to dramatic

Garry Trudeau

serials such as *Brenda Starr* or *Rex Morgan*. A second group likes the "sophisticated" humor strips of *Doonesbury* or *B.C.*; a third prefers "light" humor, those one-shot chuckles that one digests, passes over, and forgets in a few seconds. Reader surveys and data-processing techniques are employed to help editors select a proportionate number of features for each group.

Adjustments are made for this and that factor. If a strip, for example, rates low with the overall readership, it may be a candidate for early cancellation—unless it happens to rate fairly well with some specific demographic group the newspaper has targeted, in which case it will probably stay.

What goes—and something surely will, if an editor plans to pick up a new feature for which he or she has decided there is otherwise no room—will be that strip whose disappearance will infuriate the fewest number of nontargeted readers. Theoretically, all this makes everyone happy.

The system is workable enough when the issue is deciding what existing strip to drop but patently useless when the issue is deciding which new one to take on. Some newspapers query their readers about what new strips they'd like to see, a practice that is well intentioned but fatally flawed—the readers, of course, have no idea what features are available. Someone who has never heard of *Star Hawks* is not likely to ask his local paper to carry it. Nor will he ask for vintage strips that the syndicates years ago stopped trying aggressively to sell because editors didn't want to buy them because there was no reader demand for them because the readers didn't know they were still around because editors hadn't bought them because the syndicates weren't selling them.

At the syndicates' level, in turn, the name of the game is developing material that is not necessarily what anyone thinks the public might enjoy but what is most likely to be bought by editors concerned with managing their reader clusters.

The editor who cannot buy *Beetle Bailey* or *Hagar the Horrible*, either because they cost too much or because another area paper holds territorial exclusivity, can buy *Boner's Ark* or *Sam and Silo*, also products of the prolific Mort Walker–Dik Browne shop and done in the same gentle style.

The editor who cannot buy *B.C.* can buy *Crock*. If *Peanuts* is not available, *Fred Basset* certainly is, assuming the editor thinks *Peanuts* is about a dog who talks to himself. The editor who can't buy *Blondie* or *Hi and Lois* has a choice of any number of other middle-class suburban strips where husbands rush to catch buses and wives stay home and burst into tears when the pork chops burn.

Gil Kane, who draws *Star Hawks*, has a number of thoughts about comic strips:

"It is possible for newspaper strips to be individual and intelligent and provocative and still be very, very popular if there are editors who want that sort of material and recognize it and promote it. Editors get what they ask for.

"Most businesses look for new ways. They have creative heads, they have all sorts of things to keep from standardizing their product. When they're too standardized and refuse to be competitive, they end up like Chrysler. I mean, European cars have their own market and they deserve it."

Doonesbury, a brash rule-breaker of a strip, was widely perceived as a bad risk when the then-fledgling Universal released it nine years ago. "Look, I think you have to be motivated by profit," Kane says. "That's the only thing. But since every syndicate in the world is using a single standard and competing for a single market, look how intelligent it was for Universal to set up a separate standard and immediately supersede all the other syndicates.

"The point," he says, "is that if originality and an individualized point of view will make money, then I say that *it is viable to be original.*"

Dean Young and *Blondie*

Story from Issue No. 46, June 1980

When the son of the creator of a very long-running top comic strip takes over the writing of that feature and, along with his cartoonist partner, maintains the strip's high-ranking position, that's certainly a unique feat. Since that is exactly what Dean Young, son of Chic Young, the man who created *Blondie* for King Features Syndicate in 1930, has done, we talked with Dean to find out how it happened.

YOUNG: When my dad passed away in 1973, *Blondie* was appearing in 1,600 newspapers, but we lost 300 of them soon after the announcement of his death was made, and sometime after that we lost 200 more. These cancellations were the beginning of a period of transition for me because, although I knew how to write for my dad and knew exactly what *he* wanted, suddenly he was gone. I was still trying to write *Blondie* for him, but he wasn't here and it just wasn't working out. That's when I decided to write the strip in a manner that would make me comfortable by reflecting my own type of humor. Humor is a very private thing. My dad had his kind and I have mine. That's when all the good things started to happen. We got back all our newspapers, gained some more, and we are now in almost 1,900 newspapers.

HURD: Can you give an example of this different approach?

YOUNG: On one occasion I did a page where Blondie wants Dagwood to have his hair styled. He is very

much against it because he likes his hair the way it is and always has been. She literally drags him into one of these hairstyling places, where they proceed to spray forty cans of lacquer onto his hair. They have his cowlicks all slicked down, so they aren't sticking up, and he goes home hating it. The family likes his hair and keeps telling him it looks good, and the kids say it's cool. He goes to bed, still grumpy, and Blondie says, "You'll get used to it, you'll like it, you'll see!" Meanwhile she goes to sleep as Dagwood is still grumbling: "I hate it, I can't stand it anymore!" He goes into the bathroom, and you see him shampooing with his hair all lathered up. In the last panel he's back in bed with all his hair sticking straight up in the air just as if a vacuum cleaner has sucked it up on end. He looks at the reader, saying, "Boy, it sure feels good to be *me* again!"

This is an example of a strip my father would not have done, and I think it was a very funny strip. He wouldn't have done it because his humor was probably more traditional in scope. I suppose mine is more contemporary—I guess that's the only way to explain it. This kind of material is maybe a little foreign to the flavor he liked to project.

HURD: When did you first begin to work with your dad on the strip?

YOUNG: I can remember when I brought my first Sunday page to him. I had roughed in the dialogue in twelve panels, and I added some explanations while he was looking at it. Then, as he crumpled it up and tossed it into the wastebasket, he said, "That's not too bad. Why don't you go in there and try another one." I was probably about twenty-five at the time.

HURD: What sort of training had you had before this?

YOUNG: I graduated from LaGrange College, in Georgia, with a degree in business administration and had ideas of owning my own advertising agency. I became an account executive for an agency in Miami, worked there for a couple of years, and then became a sales promotion executive for the southern division of a large grocery chain for about a year and a half. I would come over in the company plane from time to time to do promotions on the West Coast of Florida and, of course, would stay with my folks in Clearwater Beach. On one of these trips my dad detected that I wasn't really thrilled with my work, so he suggested, "Why don't you come over and write for me." Immediately I

Chic Young

in the final typewritten form, which I send to Jim, I also describe each panel: what's happening, what the characters are doing, where they're facing, and so forth. Jim puts his Midas embellishment on my cold typewriting and turns everything into a warm, living, breathing commodity called *Blondie*.

HURD: I notice that a *Blondie* Sunday page always consists of more panels than the average comics Sunday page. You don't fill the space with panels involving huge close-ups and so on. Why is this?

YOUNG: My thinking is that the *Blondie* Sunday page is a kind of unique concept in that it offers a short story to the reader. Each Sunday we really try to tell what essentially is a short story in those twelve panels. In contrast, some other Sunday pages seem like extended dailies. I'm not knocking that way of doing things, just trying to clarify what *we're* trying to do. I need those twelve panels to tell the story.

HURD: Can you think of any reactions you've had from readers lately?

YOUNG: People ask me, "Where are the puppies? I haven't seen them around lately." I explain that the pup-

said OK, went back and packed my stuff, and worked for him for ten years before his death.

HURD: Does your collaboration with Jim Raymond, the brother of Alex Raymond of *Flash Gordon* and *Rip Kirby* fame, work easily?

YOUNG: It certainly does. Jim is a great cartoonist. He knows exactly what I'm thinking and what I'm talking about in the scripts I send to him, as far as the gags are concerned. He's a consummate cartoonist in my opinion, we have a very warm and harmonious relationship, and we work well together because we have a great deal of respect for each other. Jim has a home in Michigan but he also has one on Great Harbor Cay, one of the chain of the Berry Islands in the Bahamas, so he travels with the birds. We talk on the phone frequently and see each other from time to time, but when we do get together, we're more apt to be talking about golf, spearfishing, or tennis than about *Blondie*.

First of all I write the dialogue, because I'm thinking already of the picture I have in mind. After I have this rough dialogue done, I'll go back and polish it. Then

Jim Raymond

pies are still around, they're there; you just don't see them. They're nomadic in nature and they like to roam around the neighborhood, but Daisy is a more domesticated type of dog so you do see her. Besides that, it's very hard to draw those five little puppies in one panel.

HURD: What did you think of the *Blondie* movies, of which there were I think twenty-eight between 1938 and 1951?

YOUNG: I think that when they were done they were funny, and I still think a lot of that stuff is funny . . . although the humor then was more slapstick than humor is today. I think we've upgraded our humor in the respect that it is more sophisticated now, just as the readers are. But don't get me wrong. If slapstick is done right, it can be extremely funny.

HURD: Would you say something about your schedule, as far as writing *Blondie* is concerned?

YOUNG: I do my dailies first, spending maybe two and a half days and one night on them, and then the rest of the week, plus another night, on the Sunday page. I

like to vary the situations in accordance with Dagwood's workweek. I'll try to have one daily that is involved with him at the office, maybe I'll throw in another at the lunch counter, then one where he's with Blondie on some domestic matter at home. Naturally, I won't have two dailies concerned with a door-to-door salesman back to back. Most of the time I establish the situation first, and then I let the characters bounce off and react against one another until they do something I think is funny. It's hard to explain, but I attribute the final result to a dominant gene that my dad gave me.

HURD: What do you do when you have one of those days when it's hard to come up with ideas?

YOUNG: I may go through strips that have been done in the past because they can activate the machinery in your mind and stimulate you in new directions. I may use a different form of an idea that I run across in this way. Something happens in your mind that triggers a different version.

MORE ON JOHNNY HART

Story from Issue No. 48, December 1980

HURD: Johnny, back in June 1975, in Issue No. 26 of *CARTOONIST PROfiles,* you said a lot about how you and Jack and Dick come up with ideas for *B.C.* and *Wizard of Id*, so we won't go over that again. But here's something all cartoonists would like to know: What do you think have been the factors that have made you one of the very most successful cartoonists ever—with the word *genius* having often been mentioned? I'm not flattering you when I say that. Was it your genes, or extra hard work, or what?

HART: You said you weren't flattering me, but that sounds like the biggest buttering-up job I've heard in a long time. Seriously, you've told me in the past that I'm a soul-searching kind of guy and I *do* look back and try to figure out why I am where I am, or am as successful as I have been.

HURD: I want to inject the comment here, for the benefit of our readers, that it was I who tried to get you to analyze your cartooning success and not you who started the subject.

HART: I do know one thing—when I look back—that one way or another I intended to be successful. I think this feeling started when I got out of the service and decided I didn't know how to do anything but draw. I had a pretty good sense of humor and I had studied other cartoonists because of my fascination with the magazine cartoon. And of course my friend Brant Parker just happened to pop into my life somehow, by marrying a girl who lived in my hometown. As you recall, he judged a high school art show and liked my work, which was terrible. But he saw something in it. Brant has an eye for talent, a very unusual man who can see deep beneath the surface. (Obviously he can, or he wouldn't have picked *me* out.) He made it a point to meet me and talk with me, and we became good friends. The drawings of mine in the art contest weren't cartoons, but Brant looks carefully at drawings, how lines get down on paper, and he seems to be able to tell whether a person has it or doesn't have it. He notices the technique, or an underlying potential of technique, and probably analyzes drawings in the same way handwriting experts analyze handwriting. In my case he may have said to himself, "This guy has an innate talent or instinct and doesn't even know it." In any event, for whatever reason, whether it be fate or whatever, why did Brant come to Endicott, why did he pick me out, why did he sit me down for a single evening, turn my whole life around, and make me want to become a magazine cartoonist? He convinced me in one evening that I should do this.

There's an unexplainable magic between Brant and me, and it developed, I think, the first time we ever met. For whatever reason, Brant thinks everything I say is funny—I know it's not that funny, because I say the same things to a lot of other people without their breaking up—but he has the kind of laugh that turns me on and I actually start *saying* funny things. I become like a stand-up comic and do this to him all the time on the phone.

Johnny Hart

I spend one minute on the phone saying something and four minutes waiting for him to stop laughing.

One night we were down at the studio when I started doing bits, he started laughing, and suddenly things that normally don't come into my mind made me sound like Don Rickles doing a stand-up bit. Normally I'm a slow talker, but suddenly I was spouting all this crazy stuff—and I didn't even realize how funny it was when I was saying it. Brant got to laughing so hard he lost his breath and started whimpering and making funny little sounds. He was sitting on a set of steps that led down to a little landing by the back door, and he got laughing so hard he slid all the way down the steps and was lying on his back on the landing in complete hysterics. Well, this is the kind of rapport we've always had.

I remember the things he told me that first night, back around 1950 when I was nineteen, that convinced me to become a magazine cartoonist. My favorite cartoonist in the whole world was Virgil Partch, who was the hottest thing in magazine cartoons at the time. So Brant, in an effort to sway me to become a magazine cartoonist and having found that I liked Partch, sat me down and started drawing. He started analyzing Partch's cartoons, his thick and thin lines, and so on. Brant said, "You notice that the back of the arm is an L-shape and the inside of the arm is a curve? That he often opposes two straight lines with a circular line, and he can draw an entire character with a single unbroken line?

Can you imagine how I felt at that point? I'm nineteen years old, listening to this inside stuff about my

cartooning hero. I'm talking with Brant Parker, a guy who's been working with Walt Disney for years, and who worked with Virgil Partch at Disney's, and I knew then there was just no other way I could go in life than to become a magazine cartoonist. Another thing Brant told me that night: "Whenever you draw anything, always make it cartoony." He gave me two important words: *simple* and *cartoony*.

The next step along the way for me was a total fascination with Dick Cavalli's work. He drew every character with a deadpan expression, saying all these terribly funny things. His people were always stiff-backed, with their noses straight out, eyes half closed, making incredibly funny remarks. Everything Cavalli did would just lay me out, so I began to copy him. Then I discovered John Gallagher, with his crazy-looking people and animals, a cartoonist with an unbelievable sense of humor. So you see I learned this style of humor that all the cartoonists at that time were using, selecting the ones as models that I thought were the funniest. I

copied them, and after a while my own style began to evolve. I copied the special elements in the work of these cartoonists that appealed to me.

HURD: I think you've said that you might have been an actor if things had worked out differently.

HART: I actually had a couple of avenues to take—I might have been a comedian or an actor. Drawing came very easy to me. Movies were a big, big thing in my life, and probably, if I'd had my preference, I would like to have been an actor or a comedian. I enjoyed standing up in front of audiences when I was younger and I did my share of that. In high school Jack and I used to sing together onstage and do comic bits. When I went into the service, we got together a group of people for a jazz group. I wrote parodies. I got with a bunch of guys who were good dancers, and they taught me soft-shoe. I used to write and arrange all these comic bits, and eventually we went overseas and formed an entertainment group that toured Korea, entertaining troops from all branches of the service. Back in Georgia, at the

NCO Club, I had performed with Chuck Mantelli—who taught me photography, incidentally. Chuck, who became one of my great buddies, went on to be the first photographer ever to win the Eastman Trophy three times.

Ironically, my youngest daughter has just graduated from the Boston Museum of Fine Arts and is a pho-tographer herself. It's funny how you're making me think of all these things.

HURD: Which have you found it easier to do, John, sit alone doing gags or bounce gags back and forth with someone else?

HART: Originally I worked alone, of course, and I discovered that I was capable of producing pretty good

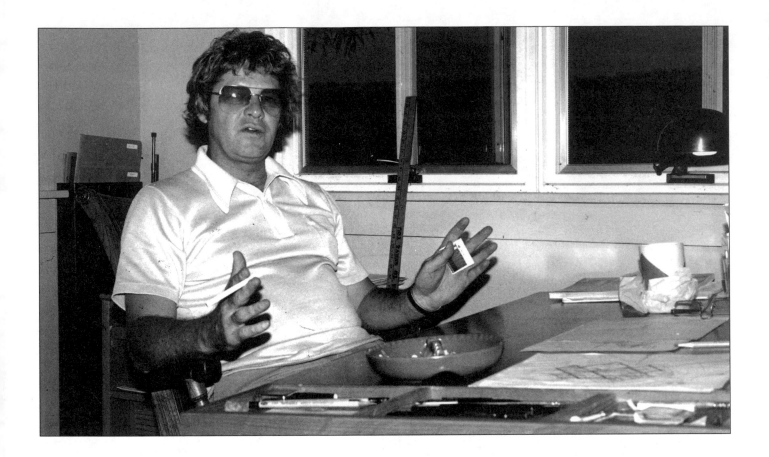

stuff. I like to work alone, where there isn't anyone else around—I can work really well. Years ago I found a method of thinking up gags that's ruined my life in a way, and that's to let my mind wander. You start off, for instance, thinking of a guy on a desert island, and you wind up with somebody trying to make a broad in a penthouse. The mental process just drifts from one thing to another: A bottle floats up on the shore of this desert island; nothing seems to come to your mind with that . . . there's a note in the bottle from an extortionist . . . or the bottle becomes a bottle in somebody's penthouse with this guy trying to make out with a broad . . . things just keep snowballing.

As you know, I'm fascinated with words and I wonder just how this term *snowballing*, which is used by a lot of gagmen, got started. I suppose some writer dropped a snowball at the top of a hill, watched it start rolling down the hill, continuing to build and build, and decided that this was similar to the way he and another cartoonist were building their gags.

You enjoy the creativity of your own mind and, with mental rambling, being able to make something out of

essentially nothing. You just go from one thing to another. I found out rather early that if you stop somewhere along the line, fascinated by one thought, and spend twenty minutes trying to get a gag out of it, you've defeated yourself. But as long as your mind keeps rolling along, something will hit, and from somewhere—maybe out of the ether—*bang!* A tagline comes in! It's almost like God sent it down: "Here's a tagline for you—*zot!*" You write it down, and while you're writing your mind is wandering off somewhere else.

In my case, I actually trained myself to make my mind wander. Now that's fine when you're working alone, but when you're out among a bunch of people and somebody's talking to you, it can be embarrassing. Maybe they say a word to you and it triggers a thought, and your mind starts working in all directions. Suddenly the guy finishes what he's been talking to you about and he says, "What do you think? Does that make any sense to you?" You wake up with "Oh, yeah!" But you're back on the desert island, and he just told you how to make some money on the stock market. Some cartoonists like to lie down quietly somewhere when

Cartoon Success Secrets

they're trying to think up ideas, but when I'm up against a deadline, pacing back and forth seems to speed up the mental rambling process for me.

HURD: You've often mentioned that you're fascinated with words.

HART: I like words to have meter, and for them to be poetic yet simple, I like to put the most important thing I can say in the fewest possible words. I haven't got a very good vocabulary so I have to work hard at this. If I can say a funny line in four words, that a normal person would take twenty-seven words to express, I've accomplished my purpose. I'm shooting for this shorter line, which will quite possibly be funnier than the longer version—and certainly easier for the reader to pick up. Simplicity is the name of the game.

HURD: I remember Brant Parker told you always to make your drawings *cartoony*.

HART: He said, "If you want to draw a house, you don't make it like a real house. Your cartoon house is very

tall, has a big peaked roof, with a door, a window, and a big high, funny-looking skinny chimney." You need only to look at anything Brant Parker draws to realize what *cartoony* means. In my estimation, he's the absolute master of this kind of drawing. I don't think anybody tops him—and I'm not saying this because he and I are friends. I think all young cartoonists who want to learn how to draw should look to the *Wizard* or *Goosemyer* as examples of how to do it. I give him incredible things to draw, such as a blacksmith in his shop—and he groans, because drawing blacksmiths is one of his pet peeves—but there isn't another cartoonist in the world who, with just a few little items, can get across the idea of such a shop better than Brant does. He gets tremendous mood in the drawing—you know just what kind of a place it is—and he's accomplished it with great simplicity.

As I've said, *cartoony* and *simplicity* became very important words to me, and I extended them into every phase of what I do, including words. I do love words. I even wanted to be a poet. I don't like to bore people with a lot of words, or a lot of lines in my drawings. I like to say something clever and *funny*. If I had my way, every strip I did would produce a reaction so that on a given evening I could say to myself, "Right now there are this many million people lying down on their living room floors, gripping their sides with hysterical laughter, because they have just read the strip!" I like to hear people laugh.

. HURD: With your various projects under way—such as the *Wizard* live-action movie, an animation special to be produced in Canada, the building of your new studio, and so on—what's your schedule like, John?

HART: I always considered it a curse that I have always been totally unscheduled. I don't think you could pick out two days in my life on which I have done the same thing at the same time. As a matter of fact, I think I fight it. I wander around aimlessly, doing whatever I need to do at the moment. I admire scheduled people, such as you or Jack Caprio, and wish I were more like you both, and I suppose you wish you were more like I am. There's frustration in all of us. Take Jack, for instance: I could clock his arrival at the studio, same time every morning—he'd hang up his hat and coat, first of all. Then maybe there'd be some glasses in the sink—he'd wash out all the glasses, put all the stuff up in the cupboard, go up the steps and into his room, check out his desk, and so on. This would be part of his routine every day. Then take my case. I may come in at eight o'clock or two-thirty in the afternoon. I have no idea when I'm going to show up. I may have been up all night watching a movie or reading a book.

Story from Issue No. 49, March 1981

Here is the second half of our conversation with Johnny Hart, creator of *B.C.* and *Wizard of Id*.

HURD: John, I asked you earlier whether you preferred creating gags all by yourself or if you'd rather work with others. You talked about some of your methods when working alone, but you didn't have a chance to tell our readers about writing gags in collaboration with other gagmen.

HART: Working alone is fine—I can do that and it's fun—but working with other people is like working

"There are three things which are real: God, human folly, and laughter. Since the first two pass our comprehension, we must do what we can with the third."

—The Ramayama as told by Aubrey Menen, 1954

**My name is Johnny Hart.
I do what I can with the third.**

with an audience. If I have one person like Jack Caprio, I will bounce an idea off him, and if it cracks him up I have a reaction. He represents 5,000 people in an audience who laugh! Just for a change of pace, several of us who work on ideas for the strips used to hole up occasionally in a local hotel for a day-long gag session. I'd rent a suite for Jack, Brant, Dick Boland, and myself and have hors d'oeuvres and a bunch of drinks sent up. The suite at the Sheraton in Binghamton had about six rooms in it—with a living room as big as this boathouse we're in now. We'd wander around, pace back

and forth, and turn out something like a month's work during our day-long stay. Jack and I might be doing ideas and Brant, who doesn't write gags himself, would say, "How about if you did this . . . ?" He never came up with the tagline, but he felt the flow of ideas that Jack and I were tossing back and forth, he could picture the drawings that would be called for, and he would suggest things to us and we'd say, "That's *it!*" He has an uncanny knack for being able to do this. If he'd been in the movie business, he would have been one of the greatest directors.

These sessions were absolutely beautiful, no matter where we held them—in the studio, in a hotel, or wherever. The ideas seemed to be better, come quicker, and be much more positive under the conditions I've just described. We deal with words, and maybe one of us would say, "Okay, the tagline is *So, if you're so great, why didn't you do this?* Then one of the other guys would pitch in with "We don't need the word *so* on the front." Then back and forth we'd go. "That's right, we don't need it—take the *so* out." "We don't need *why* either: *If you're so great, do this.* We'd boil all these gags down. The input is tremendous when you bounce things off one another this way, *plus* there's another great advantage. When you say something funny, and it's really funny, you *know* it's funny because everybody reacts. If one of us comes up with a really great tagline, and everybody just falls down, laughing like crazy, this beats the hell out of sitting in a room alone, saying to yourself, "I'm pretty sure that's good—aah, I *know* it's good, I'll use it." The bouncing is the best. There may be some

More on Johnny Hart

153

cartoonists who are so egotistical that they say, "I do all the gags myself; I don't work with anybody else." But I'm not one of them. I believe in working with other people. I believe in testing myself on other people. The final product is what's important. I want to be sure the gag is funny.

HURD: Haven't you said in the past that Sparky Schulz was your inspiration for doing *B.C.*?

HART: That's right. I was in the art department at GE here in town and had been selling magazine cartoons. *Peanuts* had been running for about eight years nationally, but it hadn't appeared in our local paper until the time I'm speaking of. I found that everything he did was funny—really classy; his stuff was like magazine cartoons in comic strip form. This turned me on, since I'd never realized you could do things that funny in comic strip form. One night as I was leaving the GE plant, I hollered out, "Well, I'm going home tonight and create a nationally famous comic strip." One of the guys in the outfit was a frustrated gag-writer-car-

toonist type who had been doing some gags for me and knew I'd submitted many caveman gags to the magazines. As I was going out the door, he yelled, "Why don't you do one on cavemen? You can't sell them anyplace else!" He knew I loved to do caveman gags because they're so stupid and cartoony and simple. I had done all kinds but never *sold* one.

So I went home, had supper, sat down at the drawing board, and created this little triangular character. I think the first gag had to do with an egg, and since I didn't know what to call the strip, I gave it the title *Suck Egg*. How's that for a scoop? About a month later I had a batch of samples of *B.C.*, which I put together in a little booklet with a spiral binding. I bound them in the booklet so a syndicate would have to read them in a particular order. I then submitted *B.C.* to several syndicates before the old New York Herald Tribune Syndicate bought it.

HURD: How did Jack Caprio and you happen to start working together?

HART: Jack and I met in the school hallway in the seventh grade. There was this big long wide hall. He was going one way, I was going the other, we were both wearing corduroys, and each of us was *wiff-wiff*ing his way down the hall. As we approached each other, we both stopped, looked at each other, and started laughing at the sound. We exchanged names, shook hands, and we've been friends since that moment.

HURD: You've certainly been fortunate in being able to establish a great rapport with the people you've worked with over the years. Your folks were also an important factor in your development as a cartoonist, weren't they?

HART: Yes. And by the way, you're getting me to talk about developments I've never analyzed in this way before—which is good.

Mom and Dad always had good senses of humor and they were aware of what was funny all the time. I guess I chose my friends with this in mind. In the early part of my life I was really hung up on sports and wanted to be an athlete. Then I began to meet people like Jack Caprio and discovered that what was really important to me was a sense of humor. Evidently I got that from my mom and dad. They didn't talk like normal people; everything they said was a funny line. My dad would pull little practical jokes on my mom and they'd both come out with subtle little needling lines all the time.

Without realizing it, I must have been pretty good at selecting friends with a really good, nice, clean sense of humor. Jack became my friend, Brant became my friend, a guy named Curly became my friend, and there were others, of course, down the line. Each of these people has a particular sense of humor, often somewhat different from the next fellow's. If we all had a really dumb sense of humor—if we all liked dirty jokes, for instance—that would be stupid. But this way, one guy would lean toward the visual type of humor; Jack was always a great story man—he would create stories and act them out—while Curly was always the satirical one with great comments and a tremendous insight into life.

So I was surrounded by friends who together could formulate a very well-rounded sense of humor. Maybe I acted as sort of a catalyst. I learned from each of them, and, as I brought them together as friends, they each learned from everybody else. If you have two people you like because you get along well with them, and there are two *other* people you get along well with, you can introduce those four people together, and they're going to like each other because you become the catalyst. Of course, if the first two people are dodos and you like them for that, and the other two people are high-class snobs and you like them for that, you're probably not going to bring these pairs together. Or you might bring them together just for laughs, to see how well they get along.

What must have brought the groups I was with together was our love of humor. Often of an evening a bunch of us would sit on a three-foot wall in front of the local cemetery (when I look back, I think we were dull but brilliant at the same time). We'd sit on the wall and do nothing but make up stories and create gags. We did that every night for about two years. Then, about a hundred steps away, was a coffee shop, where we'd sit in a booth, drink coffee, tell jokes, and laugh. These guys were incredibly creative. We even created our own language so nobody could tell what we were talking about. It was a distortion of words.

HURD: What do you tell young people who come to you and say they want to be cartoonists?

HART: I tell them they have to have *total* desire. This encompasses the fact that they must be able to accept rejection and just keep going. I've never known of anybody who couldn't accept rejection that ever made it in our business. These people usually say, "Editors are a bunch of fools!" and then they quit trying and get a job in a garage or someplace. You have to want cartooning success more than anything else. I got rejected and rejected and rejected, but I kept on going.

Rejection should inspire you. Some of the work that young cartoonists send me is really bad, but then I think back to how bad *my* work was when I started. I still have some of that stuff in trunks. If I were an editor and somebody sent me these old cartoons of mine, I'd throw them in the garbage! So there's a process you have to go through to get better and better, and it's called *practice*. I never tell anybody that his or her work

is bad and they should get out of the business. Sometimes it might be better if I did that, because the young cartoonist might rise up and say, "Well, I'll show *him*!" I usually tell them the things I've just mentioned—and if they're not willing to abide by these rules, they should forget about cartooning.

When you draw a character, you have to believe that this character actually lives and exists. If you believe that, it comes across to readers. They don't think of the character as one-dimensional, on a piece of paper, but multidimensional, as in real life. When I draw *B.C.* I don't see him as a bunch of lines, I see him as a many-dimensional character in my own mind. All successful cartoonists know and believe this. These funny little lines on a piece of paper are actual people and they actually exist. The reader looks at them and believes it because you believe it.

I found over the years that *I* don't actually put the words in a character's mouth, the character does. It's almost like I know where I'm going with a character, and that character talks to *me*. I may say, "Naw, that line's not good enough. *This* is a better line." And so on. It sounds really strange but it's true. If you just put down any old line or joke, you know the character wouldn't say that. And when a character says something, I give him or her an expression that goes with those particular lines. These words come out because that's the kind of person this is—with a distinct personality. As far as I'm concerned, this is an actual living little being.

It's been fun, in doing the storyboards for this animated special we're working on, to go from the comic page to animation and to actually *prove* that these characters are multidimensional and can turn around and do many things. You have to think of them as actual people. If you're just trying to make some money by putting a few lines on paper, you might get six newspapers but the public will see through you. Either the characters live or they don't. When I look at the comics, there are certain ones that are real to me and others that are not. When I'm drawing characters, I think about what they're doing and saying, and somehow the "thick and thins" of my lines give the characters an extra dimension. Your mind has to be fully involved with what you're doing at the time you're doing it.

HANK KETCHAM AND
DENNIS THE MENACE

Story from Issue No. 49, March 1981

With the celebration of the thirtieth birthday of Hank Ketcham's famed *Dennis the Menace* panel, we got on the phone with Hank and asked him to reminisce about the past and the present. Following are some of the things he talked about.

Jud, when you asked me to give you some thoughts on *Dennis the Menace,* I was reminded that it was exactly thirty years ago that I created him—right here, not far from where I am today—in Carmel, California. Recently I got a note from Mort Walker, telling me about the birthday celebration for *Beetle Bailey*'s thirtieth, which means that Beetle and Dennis are the same age—both kids, I guess. So there are still a few survivors from the old magazine days, a bunch of us who would be around every Wednesday on Madison Avenue, going to see Gurney Williams at *Collier's,* Marione at the *Saturday Evening Post,* Lawrence Lariar at *Liberty,* dropping stuff off at *The New Yorker* as a ritual, and so on. Kirk Stiles and Ed Nofziger were among those going around, as well as Chuck Saxon, Mort, Stan Hunt, and others.

Looking back at some of my old stuff that people paid money for makes me shudder. If I got samples from youngsters like that, I'd tell them to go back to school to learn to draw and get some more experience. I guess what I *didn't* do was use the eraser often enough. Now I find my drawing board is full of eraser crumblings for every drawing I put out. I certainly didn't find them in the old days!

I was doing a lot of experimenting then, too, working with all kinds of different techniques, being inspired first by one, then another. Noel Sickles was a big inspiration to a lot of us. I remember Bud would come over to my place when I was living in Connecticut, give me encouragement, and suggest that I improvise and experiment with the pen, turn it over and draw on the back side, try to break it and see how far I could stress it. He opened my eyes to many little things that were very helpful, and certainly stimulating at the time. I think most young people coming up do look to the older cartoonists for some sort of guidance, and if they're fortunate enough to meet them, they are probably throwing the same kinds of questions at them that I did when I was their age, wondering what kind of paper they use, what tools, and so on.

Hank Ketcham

I used to like to hang around with my colleagues and chew the fat and talk shop. Now, even though I live in sort of a colony of artists and cartoonists—with Eldon Dedini and Gus Arriola as two of the very heavyweight types—we don't talk shop, even though we're good friends. I guess by the time we get through the day, we're kind of tired of *thinking* shop and don't want to talk it any further. And I've found that, as time goes by and my responsibilities seem to broaden, I spend more time in the studio and less time in the outer world. I've become a hermit of sorts, and I think it's a trap that most of us fall into; we become sort of hidden, away as it were, and our social life is at a minimum. Does that indicate that we like to associate with the people we manufacture from ink better than the ones who are running around in flesh and blood? We can always erase them, of course, if we don't get along with them. It's just that we enjoy what we're doing, and if we do have deadlines, we want to meet them, and there's a certain amount of research work to be done.

We can jolly well find enough to do to put in an eight-hour day, and that's why I like to have my working place as comfortable as I can, with all the necessary gadgets like music machines, a fireplace, a rug, a coffee

DENNIS the MENACE

"THAT'S *TWO TREES IN A ROW* YOU HIT, DAD!
YOU'RE GETTIN' BETTER 'N *BETTER!*"

DENNIS the MENACE

"READ ME THE PART BETWEEN 'DEAR SANTA' AND
'VERY TRULY YOURS' AGAIN...I MIGHTA FORGOT SOMETHIN'."

machine, pretty pictures, and camera gear. It's kind of fun to sit up here, put on the thinking cap, and do some reading as well as the drawing.

I have a couple of youngsters—Scott, three and a half, and Dania, almost eight—and they come up here once in a while and invade the place for my bowl of candy, which I keep here on the coffee table. And of course they like to look at all the comic magazines, play with the guitar, try the bugle, and generally raise hell. They have about thirty seconds before I blow my stack and whisk them out of here. Actually, they're pretty good and don't bug me too much. They know this is Daddy's workshop and it's best to leave him alone—otherwise, smoke and fire comes bellowing out of his mouth.

Going back to cartooning for a moment, I'm delighted that CARTOONIST PROfiles has become kind of a textbook for the educational community. It certainly deserves it. You've put in a lot of hours, hard work, and good thinking in getting it launched, and I'm pleased that it's doing so well.

One of the nice things about being a cartoonist (with the exception of the political cartoonist, who is usually with a paper in a particular city) is that we can pretty much move to any spot we choose. (As long as there is an airplane nearby to take our drawings to the marketplace.) I guess I figured that out many years ago when I moved to Europe and stayed there for eighteen years. It worked beautifully, too—I had a lovely penthouse studio overlooking Lake Geneva, with an international airline ten minutes from the front door, and excellent telephone and cable connections. I never missed a deadline, and everything worked beautifully. If the dollar hadn't weakened so badly and the franc hadn't remained so strong, I might still be there. But it got to be so darned expensive, and the kids were getting to an age where I wanted them to get to know their own country a little bit. Dania spoke French fluently when she came here, but now she pretends not to know a word of it because naturally her peers only speak English. I guess we'll have to send them back for a couple of

"THE SUSPECT *WAS* IN CUSTODY... BUT HE HAD TO GO TO THE BATHROOM, SO WE LET HIM GO."

DENNIS the MENACE

"WHY CAN'T YA JUST **SHAKE HANDS** AND MAKE UP?"

years of high school or college. But the move back to the United States was actually beneficial for me. Of course, it's been a culture shock too. When I first came back, everything seemed to me to be so inexpensive and reasonable, yet everyone around me was complaining about how terribly expensive everything was. But of course I'd been dealing with the Swiss franc. Now I've been back long enough to realize that, yes, it is bloody expensive. So I just have to pedal faster and charge more, I guess. Being here and being exposed to TV on a regular basis made me much more aware of the American scene, and a little bit more current on favorite words and expressions that are being used. And the general conveniences are so superior to anything they have abroad that it's a real treat to be in America again. I'm very pleased, and my whole family is of course just as enthusiastic—especially living out here on the Monterey Peninsula, where there are no extremes in weather, and where there are gorgeous sights and smells and no pollution. And there's a golf course about three hundred yards away, so it's really la crème de la crème!

As far as the feature is concerned, I've had a bunch of writers working with me for years. I sit as an editor here and collect the material I think will work best. One man alone gets to the bottom of the barrel in a hurry and starts recycling a lot of things. But if you have half-a-dozen people all thinking about your product, you get a nice spectrum of ideas. I'm sure people realize that Bob Hope didn't come up with his own ideas all the time. My main writer is a man on my staff. Each of the six submits ideas to him, and then he refines the submissions and sends them on to me.

Dennis keeps going right along; he seems to wind up at the top of most readership polls, which is encouraging. We're preparing a musical comedy for Broadway featuring Dennis, with a talented group of colleagues. Joe Raposo, who was musical director of *Sesame Street,* is the composer, and Hal David, president of ASCAP and former collaborator with Burt Bacharach, has written some beautiful tunes ("Raindrops Keep Fallin' on My Head" and "Do You Know the Way to San Jose?").

I'm writing a lot of the rough structure of the book, but we really haven't zeroed in on a writer yet. I would hope now that we'd get the musical on the boards in the fall and it would be a thirtieth anniversary present to Dennis's poor old dad. We have all the finances worked out, so green lights are flashing. Considering the success of *Annie,* I think *Dennis* should have an enormous success because of the added humor that will be there. But this musical comedy stuff is really an awesome challenge. You don't realize it until you get into it. So it's a new adventure for old Henry and I'm licking my chops.

One of the things I'd like to see develop is a couple of youngsters who might be serious about drawing *Dennis* and taking over some of the responsibilities here. That means I'd have to go into a big training program with them, equipping them to do the job. But I can't go on doing the strip forever, and there are a few other things I'd like to do besides *Dennis*—after all, I have put in my years with him and I think I could train someone to interpret him successfully.

So, Jud, if you have your ear to the ground, you might pass the word and ask likely people to drop me a note at P.O. Box 800, Pebble Beach, California 93953 with some samples of their work. As you know, we have a successful comic book operation which has been going for about twenty-five years. Fred Toole has been writing them and Bill Williams has been doing the drawings. We've just signed a new arrangement with the Marvel Comics Group, and I know we'll be needing some extra help in that direction. Bob Bugg, who does a valiant job on the Sunday page and is a neighbor of yours in Connecticut, doesn't need any help, but one of these days he might want to lay his brush down, in deference to some other chores, so I'd like to have someone at the ready for the Sunday page. You could be a great deal of help to me, Jud, if you would look over the field with your practiced eye and perhaps nudge one or two potential candidates. It could be a young lady, for that matter—why haven't there been more women and minorities in this business? It's a perfect setup—no muscle needed and the field is wide open! They don't have to play golf—that's not a prerequisite, although we have plenty of athletic facilities in the area. Actually, when they get under my thumb they won't have too much time for fun and games until they get their wheels on the track so they're producing something.

I suppose readers are interested in how a cartoonist spends his day. I built my studio above my double garage, which is about thirty yards from the back door.

"SHE FORGETS I BEEN *LOOKIN'* FOR COOKIES JUST AS LONG AS SHE'S BEEN *HIDIN'* THEM!"

"I KNOW WHERE WE CAN CATCH A COUPLE OF SWELL HAMBURGERS."

It has a cathedral ceiling—like a barn, really, with exposed beams—with cork and wooden walls, a big fireplace, a bathroom, a photocopier, and a paper cutter—something I've wanted ever since I was in the second grade. I'm up here at eight-thirty A.M. or before, every morning, at which time Dottie, my secretary, arrives. She stays until twelve-thirty, during which time we do a lot of letter writing, filing, phone answering, and bill paying. Then I go down to the house and fix a salad or a sandwich and a glass of milk and come up here to do a little reading. I pretty much have the afternoon to myself to get into my drawing—roughs or finishes. Every once in a while I do take the afternoon off and go out and whack the golf ball at Cypress Point or Pebble Beach. I follow this schedule during the week, and sometimes also on Saturday, depending on the pressure. And yet people still wonder how a little five-year-old kid keeps a grown man busy every day of the week for eight hours! I don't know either, but he *does* and I'm still smiling. Dennis is fun to be with and I enjoy him. But, as I've said, there are a lot of other things I'd like to start getting my teeth into, and hiring a couple of assistants and setting up a cartoon school out here will be an awe-inspiring, time-consuming chore. I'm game if I can find a couple of others who are game as well. With a little good planning for built-in succession, this feature could go on as *Blondie* has done.

I do travel still when time permits. We visited our friends in Europe last May and had a marvelous time as usual. And I expect to go back in late November for an examination of the Bordeaux wine country, with a couple of experts, to learn more about Château Lafite-Rothschild and a few of the other great houses up there. I have an interest in a Bordeaux winery up in the Médoc, and I'll be visiting that as well. So you see we cartoonists don't spend all our time drawing pictures! But the deadlines *do* keep you close to home and of course the kids' school starts next week. It's good for me, having the youngsters around, because my eyes and ears are reopened, and I'm much more aware now of all of the props and accoutrements of kids, and of the various phases that they go through—which is a nice refresher course.

"BOY! WHEN IT MELTS FASTER THAN I CAN EAT IT... THAT'S **HOT**!"

"I'VE HAD HIM UP TO **HERE**!"

"YOU *COULDN'T* HAVE ME UP TO THERE, 'CAUSE I'M ONLY DOWN TO **HERE**!"

Hank's son Dennis was about four years old at the time of this 1951 Carmel, California, photo.

DENNIS the MENACE

"WHAT *FOR*? YOU ALREADY KNOW WHAT I LOOK LIKE ... AND NOBODY ELSE *CARES*!"

"HOW SWEET IT IS, JOEY... I GOT A DOG, A CAT, A MOM AN'A DAD AND MARGARET ISN'T TALKIN' TO ME!"

BILL WATTERSON AND *CALVIN AND HOBBES*

Story from Issue No. 68, December 1985

by Bill Watterson

As the new kid in town, I am somewhat hesitant to offer my experience as a guide for cartoonists. It is only within the last few months that people have stopped referring to me as a washout and a drain on society. Nevertheless, I have picked up some knowledge along the road, and what I don't know for certain I'm willing to invent. Here are some of the lessons I've learned.

If you want to sell a comic strip, just become an editorial cartoonist, get syndicated, and win the Pulitzer at least once. I would guess that about half the strips on the local comics page are drawn by people who have done this. The other half are done by Mort Walker. After graduating from Kenyon College, I was offered the job of editorial cartoonist for the *Cincinnati Post*. I was well on my way to my first Pulitzer when, three months later, the editor suggested I update my résumé and get it in the mail. Getting fired meant I had to sell my strip the old-fashioned way. It took me five years, and for this delay I will never forgive my editor. Here is some advice: Never buy a Porsche on credit.

My first comic strip submission was a sort of outer space parody. I drew several weeks' worth of the strip and simultaneously mailed it to about five syndicates.

For the kid in each of us, and for each of us who has been a kid…

Calvin and Hobbes brings back all the wonder of being a child. With warm wit, sharp insight and amusing art, cartoonist Bill Watterson creates the world of Calvin, the type of six-year-old boy we are all familiar with, and Hobbes, his tiger friend, companion and confidant, who, to some, is stuffed, but to Calvin is real.

I figured whichever called me first would be the lucky one. As it turned out, the syndicates sent the strip back so fast I can only assume they went to considerable expense. Most syndicates sent a standard rejection slip, but a few editors took the time out from their busy schedules to write me a personal note. The most succinct one said, *God, no!* but not everyone has such a gift for invective, and the others had to resort to time-worn vulgarities. I took their generous advice to heart and abandoned the strip.

MOM, CAN I DRIVE ON THE WAY BACK?

OF COURSE NOT, CALVIN.

CAN I JUST STEER THEN? I PROMISE I WON'T CRASH.

NO, CALVIN.

CAN I WORK THE GAS AND BRAKES WHILE **YOU** STEER?

NO, CALVIN.

YOU NEVER LET ME DO ANYTHING.

SO DAD, WHAT DO I DO WHEN I CATCH A TIGER?

BRING IT HOME AND STUFF IT, CALVIN! CAN'T YOU SEE I'M BUSY?

SHEESH.

NO, REALLY, I COULDN'T EAT ANOTHER BITE!

WHAT'S ALL THIS NOISE? YOU'RE SUPPOSED TO BE ASLEEP!

IT WAS HOBBES, DAD! HE WAS JUMPING ON THE BED! HONEST!

"HOBBES" WAS **NOT** JUMPING ON THE BED! NOW GO TO SLEEP!

YOU WERE **TOO** JUMPING ON THE BED!

WELL, **YOU** WERE THE ONE PLAYING THE CYMBALS!!

HERE WE FIND A THRIVING CITY: BRAND NEN BUILDINGS, A BUSTLING ECONOMY.

A SCENIC THOROUGHFARE WINDS THROUGH THIS HAPPY MUNICIPALITY. HERE, A FARMER DRIVES HIS LIVESTOCK TO MARKET.

TRAGICALLY, THIS SERENE METROPOLIS LIES DIRECTLY BENEATH THE HOOVER DAM...

The next few years were spent scrutinizing a few of the newer strips and trying to fathom what the syndicates were looking for. I recognized that many strips were reflecting some of the country's social changes (women in the comics, for example, stopped throwing rolling pins and became lawyers), and I worked to make my comic strips more "eighties oriented." The topical strips I did then are an acute embarrassment to me now, and I've found as I go that I have less and less tolerance for trendy strips. It may be a matter of personal taste, but it seems to me that most of these are narrowly conceived and lacking in heart and are often just crass attempts to cash in on anything popular. No doubt some hack is at this moment polishing up a strip about a Vietnam-vet rock star with a computer. Anyway, I was fortunate in that nobody gave my work a second glance and these dismal efforts were quickly relegated to their deserving oblivion. It took me a while, but I finally learned this lesson: Draw what comes most naturally to you.

This had never dawned on me until a syndicate suggested I draw up a strip focusing on what had been two

minor characters in one of my earlier submissions: a small boy with a rampant imagination and his stuffed-toy tiger. These were the two silliest characters of the strip, and the ones I had obviously had the most fun with. So I began working on *Calvin and Hobbes*. I found I was immediately comfortable with their personalities, and they often seemed to write their own material. I would just stick Calvin in the bathtub or in his tree fort, and he'd usually say something funny. In the past, my characters all seemed to be straight men waiting for me to make a joke. I should have fired them long before I did. Calvin and Hobbes were a pleasure to work with, however, and the syndicate gave me lots of help and encouragement all the way, up until they decided not to take it.

I sent the strip to two other syndicates and received two more rejection slips for my new scrapbook. (I figured out that there was no sure formula for success when one syndicate wanted me to eliminate characters and the other recommended I add some.) Finally, I sent my strip to Universal Press Syndicate, where Lee Salem had the shrewd perspicacity to offer me a contract. I

Bill Watterson

© 1985 Universal Press Syndicate

WATTERSON

had the shrewd perspicacity to sign it, and the result is that *Calvin and Hobbes* will see print.

Of course, launching a comic strip does not guarantee me a lifetime of steady income. Universal Press is gambling on this strip, and if it bombs I'll be back to robbing the elderly of their welfare checks before the year is out. Thus it is with great humility that I offer the following observations about successful cartooning.

There are no secret tricks to becoming good. A great comic strip just comes down to strong characters, consistent humor, and some minor ability to convey ideas through pictures. After that it's all lipstick and rouge. When one studies the best comic strips (*Peanuts, Pogo,* and *Doonesbury,* to name a few), it's quickly apparent that their creators not only care about their characters but have gotten inside their characters' heads. When the cartoonist really understands his or her characters, they become sympathetic and likable, even when (like Lucy) they are not always the best intentioned. The reader recognizes the characters' motivations and thought processes and identifies with them. The characters become "real." In short, when the artist communicates a character's integrity and warmth, readers will respond to it. This is what cartooning is all about, but it is not something one can explain how to do.

The important thing is that the cartoonist treat the strip seriously, as an art form. Obviously the idea is to make money with it, but a comic strip is more than a sales commodity. A strip will never contribute anything beyond the cynical lining of a few pockets if it owes its genesis to a research committee's analysis of what pap a fifteen-year-old will digest or to a marketing division's brainstorm of how to get free advertising from some product line. A comic strip that is not the result of an artist's own unique sensibility debases the art. If you want to pander, go into advertising. (I did, and there are worse ways to make a living.) A comic strip has the potential to do more than just sell cute car deodorizers. Like a good novel, a comic strip can let people see the world through new eyes and thus enrich their lives. Considering how little time most people spend reading comics, that's not bad.

Ultimately, it doesn't matter what the strip is about, how it's drawn, or how many words or characters it has. If the writing is good enough, the artist can break almost any rule in the book. The best strips, and the ones that last the longest, are usually done by those who aren't content to roll out a gag a day and hit the golf course but by those who challenge themselves and the medium year after year. I believe that quality inevitably succeeds. There is always room at the top. It is my hope that I can develop *Calvin and Hobbes* into a strip that will encourage and excite others in the way many strips have done for me. There is not a job in the world I'd rather be doing.

MORE FROM HANK KETCHAM

Story from Issue No. 70, June 1986

On March 12, 1986, Hank Ketcham—and the whole world—celebrated the thirty-fifth anniversary of his famed *Dennis the Menace*. With this event in mind, we asked Hank to reminisce a bit for our readers and to share with them a few of his thoughts about the profession as he experienced it over the years.

by Hank Ketcham

When I lived just around the corner from you on Meeker Road, when radio was king, when dozens of weekly magazines eagerly sought cartoons to fill their back pages, some paying as much as $60 a drawing, we were enjoying a more simple life. I thrilled at the contemplation of my weekly excursions into the Big City and the relaxed reunion with fellow cartooners assembled in hallways and reception rooms awaiting their séance with the humor editor. Guys like Don Ulsh, Gus Lundberg, Graham Hunter, Tom Henderson, Ed Nofziger, Ben Roth, and Salo and Ross. George Wolfe and Henry Boltinoff, a pair of genuine jokers. Quiet Stan Hunt, Mischa Richter, Greg D'Alessio, and Hilda Terry, some in line to see Editor Chuck Saxon at *Modern*

An All-American Classic

Dennis the Menace

HANK KETCHAM

REPRODUCTION OF FIRST WEEK
DENNIS THE MENACE
By Hank Ketcham
AVAILABLE IN TWO-COLUMN SIZE

For Release Week of March 12, 1951

"YOU DIDN'T CATCH US! WE RAN OUTA GAS!"

" .... AND THE DARN ANTS KEPT CARRYING THEM AWAY, CRUMB BY CRUMB, UNTIL THEY WERE ALL GONE. THAT'S MY OPINION."

"I'M MAKING A LIST OF PEOPLE TO BITE WHEN MY TEETH GROW BACK IN."

"SURELY THERE'S SOMEBODY I CAN TAKE A POKE AT FOR YOU!"

1986

DENNIS THE MENACE

"IF IT WASN'T FOR MR. WILSON, THERE'D BE A BIG, EMPTY SPACE IN THE WORLD."

DENNIS THE MENACE

"WHY **CAN'T** I CALL YOU GEORGE? YOU DON'T CALL ME MR. MITCHELL!"

DENNIS THE MENACE

"GOT ANYTHING YA WANT DUG UP, OR BURIED OR SPREAD AROUND?"

DENNIS THE MENACE

"TO THE REAR.... **MARCH**!"

How much longer, Lord?

Hank explains the above drawing, which he did especially for
CARTOONIST PROfiles, this way: "I've been getting more grumpy
as the years tick by and often yearn for freedom. Time to travel,
to write, to golf, to develop other properties, to goof off."

Screen or Mort Walker at *1000 Jokes.* And a bunch of regulars whose names I can't recall.

And the lunch at the Pen & Pencil or Danny's was always an invitation to a Lost Weekend.

I seemed to have particularly good luck with Marion Derrickson, Gurney Williams, and John Bailey. John Kennedy was always able to dig up an advertising job, and the return trip on the squeaky New Haven & Hartford was usually blurry.

In the spring of 1950 I toured Shriners Children's Hospital in San Francisco with a bunch of our colleagues and chatted with Allen Saunders about syndicated cartoons. He had two recommendations: Avoid a panel format because it was too easy for a paper to drop and do not, under any circumstances, develop a property featuring children. So much for the expert's advice.

The panel approach was, of course a natural for anyone who was brought up on magazine cartooning. I simply thought in those terms; breaking a joke into three parts merely weakened the gag, in my estimation. Except for special cases of timing, I still feel the same. Besides, I don't care for the clutter of balloons; I much prefer to have all the space to myself, thank you.

Kennedy trotted over to see Bob Hall with my penciled roughs in October of 1950. Bob had just started the Post-Hall Syndicate and was looking for new material. He wanted to see two more weeks of samples before offering me a contract. *Dennis* made his debut on March 12, 1951, and I have been happily in chains

Cartoon Success Secrets

ever since. Well, happily may be an overstatement. As a matter of fact, I've been getting more grumpy as the years tick by. But baby needs a new pair of shoes. . . .

The shrinking-space syndrome annoys the hell out of me. Whatever happened to managing editors and publishers with taste, foresight, logic, and guts? Are newspapers now controlled by accountants, lawyers, and greedy stockholders, interested only in the bottom line? Most of these newspaper executives wail and moan about the loss of revenue to television, yet they badly mishandle and play down the features that TV cannot supply. Garry Trudeau should be applauded for taking a strong stand for the space he feels necessary to properly display his feature. This should have triggered some further thinking on the part of editors across the land, to consider the plight of other features suffering from the shrinks. The profession doesn't appear inviting to talented artists and writers under present circumstances. Talking heads will survive, but exciting graphics are already down the tube. It is still not too late to revive the patient.

You see? I told you I was getting grumpy.

I would like to see the National Cartoonists Society with more relevance, more teeth, and fewer "honors." I feel that the ranks should be enlarged with the admission of gag writers from all corners of the industry. These talented people who prefer cash to credit are the very backbone of humor. We would be honored to welcome these folks into our fold.

On the other hand, writers, even more than artists, are loners. Terribly independent creatures, often anti-social, seldom venturing from their habitat, and certainly not joiners. So it may be almost impossible to attract this breed of cat to join with kindred spirits in the breaking of bread and the splashing of wine. Come to think of it, I don't feel comfortable with more than eight or ten in the room.

You have become a much needed and, I know, much appreciated catalyst of the cartoon profession, Jud, and to you many thanks and applause of congratulations are in order. Please keep up the outstanding good work.

Mark Russell, the outrageously funny political satirist, told a gathering in Monterey last week that he didn't believe my short hero was only five years old. He said Dennis was sharing a split-level condo in Fort Lauderdale with the Gerber baby.

Cordially,

Hank
3-13-86

JIM DAVIS AND GARFIELD

Story from Issue No. 71, September 1986

During the three-day sessions surrounding the 1986 National Cartoonists Society Reuben Awards Dinner in Washington, D.C., your editor had a chance to sit down with Jim Davis for shoptalk that the two of us had been trying to make time for, without success. Jim's myriad activities in the preceding years had always prevented it, so that it was with a good deal of pleasure that we finally sat down to talk. Jim describes the years during which he was trying to come up with a successful comic strip and the thinking and preparation that went into making *Garfield* the great success that it has become.

HURD: What makes *Garfield* different from other cartoon cats, Jim?

DAVIS: When I created *Garfield,* I suppose the logical thing would have been to sketch cats or use cat references to design the character. But I purposely didn't look at any cats. I felt that what I saw in my mind as a cartoon cat would be funnier and truer to Garfield's nature than any cat I could possibly have copied. I took the characteristics of a cat and incorporated them in cartoon form, rather than take the physical attributes of a real cat and try to resolve them into a cartoon character. Over the years he's become more the cartoon version of a cat than a real cat, in that there's been a Darwinian evolution of his features to better facilitate the gags. His eyes are larger for more expression, his ears are smaller because they didn't seem to play much of a part. His body is a little less cumbersome than it used to be and his limbs are a little longer, the better to help him reach a pie on a shelf or to kick Odie. In order to make him a better performer, he has changed without any conscious thought on my part, and he's much more pliable than he used to be.

HURD: Obviously some of the positions he gets his limbs in are much funnier than the anatomically correct positions of a real cat.

DAVIS: He is the only cat in the world with an opposable thumb. This helps him drink coffee in the morning. While he is a cat, he steps outside of what we feel would traditionally be a cat's duties, to do those things that I feel cats would do if they could. He will have a cup of coffee in the morning—cats would if they could because I think they're a coffee-drinking type of animal. There's been a tendency to dress up some cartoon cats in different kinds of outfits and put them into widely divergent situations for the sake of a gag. I've always treated *Garfield* as a real cat, in that I don't dress him up in a lot of funny costumes. As a real cat, he'll lie in a sunbeam, he'll knock things off a shelf, he'll hate dogs. In other respects he will do those things that border on his human instincts. I've treated him as a human in a cat suit. But that's not untrue of the way many people feel about cats—people attribute human thoughts and feelings to cats anyway, because they're so laid back. You assume that they understand what you are saying.

HURD: Did you have lots of cats around in places you've lived, or did you often think of having a cat as a principal cartoon character, or did you become aware early on of the current cat phenomenon?

DAVIS: I had worked for five years on a comic strip called *Gnorm Gnat* because I thought bugs were funny and lent themselves well to good comedic personalities: Gnorm would be nice, Spider would be bad, the Bookworm would be smart, and so on. I even had a fruit fly named Freddy, and as everyone knows, the fruit-fly life span is only a few weeks. Since he only had two weeks to live, he always complained about his insurance premiums, and he especially liked to buy things on time. After years of trying to get *Gnorm* syndicated, I was told by one editor that the art and the gags were good but nobody could identify with bugs. Fortunately, I never sold it, or I'd be stuck with a bug strip.

HURD: Were you working on this when you were assisting Tom K. Ryan on *Tumbleweeds*?

DAVIS: Yes, I was. I started with Tom in November of 1969 and worked for him for nine years, and it was during this time that I tried *Gnorm Ghat*. In fact, by virtue of doing Tom's backgrounds, borders, and balloons, I picked up the discipline it took to maintain a syndicated feature, so this gave me the courage to start pursuing the idea of a strip of my own. After the *Gnorm Ghat* debacle, I took a long hard look at the comics. I saw a lot of dogs doing very well: Snoopy, Marmaduke, Belvedere—you name him. But there didn't seem to be any cats at that time (I was unaware that *Heathcliff* had preceded *Garfield* by some five years).

I knew and loved cats. I grew up on a farm near Fairmount, Indiana, which is better known as the hometown of James Dean. We had about twenty-five cats, on and off, in order to keep the mouse and rat population down. I might add that the cat population fluctuates widely with the amount of machinery that's used around a farm. Our cats were strong, independent

Jim Davis and *Garfield*

types that could survive on their own and they were good mousers. While they contributed to the catness of *Garfield,* they didn't directly contribute to his basic personality. Garfield, suffice it to say, wouldn't survive very long on his own out in the wild. He would like the outdoors better if it were inside.

HURD: This might be a good place to ask you to describe some of his characteristics.

DAVIS: He has most of the human failings—he's fat, lazy, cynical, selfish, and generally endearing. Those qualities, for some reason, are lovable in an animal; he would be disgusting as a human being. In fact, when I took that long hard look at the comics, I decided I wanted to work with an animal because they provide so much more latitude for humor than a human character does. By virtue of being a cat, Garfield is not black or white, male or female, young or old. I didn't lean toward an animal character in order to be able to make any social or political comments; rather, I thought I'd be free to move in and out of more fantastic situa-

tions than I could with a human character. My experience with cats taught me an awful lot: They have an almost mystical appeal, they do many things instinctively, they seem to have an extra sense that gives them a better grasp of the environment than we human beings do. They seem to be above it all. For this reason, I could plug a lot of traits into Garfield that maybe I couldn't into a dog, a mouse, a rabbit, or a squirrel.

After looking at the comics, and seeing dogs doing very well, I felt that if there were that many dog lovers out there supporting a dog feature, surely there were cat lovers who would love to see a cat feature. I had no idea that there were so many cat lovers out there. Cats were becoming very popular, through Heathcliff and through Kliban's book, though I hadn't seen either of these works at the time. In fact, had I seen them, I might have changed Garfield's color from orange, just to give him a more distinctive appearance.

When I created *Garfield,* I decided to take a cat's body and go through a mental exercise in the creation

Cartoon Success Secrets

of his personality. I said to myself, Given the fact that, in my opinion, cats have more of their primal instincts intact than any other domesticated animal, what would a human being be like in an animal's body with all those primal instincts still there? I felt this would be a character out for his own creature comforts, out after the basic needs in life—food, shelter, love—and not apologizing for them. It also occurred to me that such a character would be fun to do because we live in a time where we're made to feel guilty about feeling this way—about overeating, oversleeping, and not exercising. At that time, in 1976, *All in the Family* was very popular, and Archie Bunker would say awful things and get laughs. Of course that kind of a character, the crusty old curmudgeon with a heart of gold, has always been popular. I wanted to be syndicated, to do a strip, and there was the temptation to do a cute cat, à la the "cat calendar." But I decided to do a cat with texture, with the chance that he might not be as appealing initially but would have better staying power in the long run; this cat would be true to my sense of humor too.

Initially, I think there was a little bit of resistance to Garfield. The editor of a Swedish publication indicated, for instance, that Garfield rarely smiled, so in the initial months of the strip I gave him more of a smirk. Another editor called saying he'd seen the sales kit and didn't like Garfield. I said, "And Garfield doesn't like you either!" but he bought the feature and has been a loyal supporter ever since. I learned early on that if I tapped into what really gored people each day—not the big things, the little things—people identified with the feature because, more often than not, when readers laugh at a strip it's not because it's funny but because they're saying, "Isn't that true!" Long after readers have forgotten a gag, they remember the personality, the strength of character.

HURD: To digress for a few moments, tell us what was involved in selling your strip.

DAVIS: I decided to submit it to one syndicate at a

time. I figured that since I'd gone that long without being syndicated (I was thirty-two years old and had been trying about eight years), I'd only submit it to the larger syndicates one at a time. Maybe I was arrogant, but after eight years I dreaded the thought of having two syndicates take the strip at the same time. I had enough rejection slips to paper my bedroom. I guess I hoped to get comments from the first syndicate I tried, comments that would help me sharpen the strip up for submission to the next syndicate on my list. Each time you send a feature to a syndicate, I feel it should

with Tom Ryan and *Tumbleweeds*. At that time *Garfield* had no stripes, and Lew recommended that I add them. He was also a big believer in the strength of the personality of the characters and encouraged me not only to turn Garfield every which way in an art sense but also to examine him from every angle in a personality sense. In other words, he forced me to look closely at Garfield's personality, not just his humor. The stripes, he thought, would give him more display. I worked in pen with a fine line back then, and had very sketchy backgrounds, and stripes gave *Garfield* a little more

be your best effort. If you shotgun all the syndicates at once, I think you lose your credibility. You go from making an honest attempt to get syndicated to being someone who feels the urgency of just getting something on paper.

United Features held *Garfield* for about four months, as I recall, and then Lew Little, who was with the syndicate at the time, called and expressed interest. I had known Lew over the years, through his association

impact on the comics page. United Features Syndicate took the strip.

With the comics getting smaller these days, we've obviously had to simplify. I feel that drawing a comic strip is like telling a joke. I like to work in three frames because to me the natural timing of a joke is *bom-bom-t'da!* If the eye can flow through a strip smoothly and not be stopped by having to read a lot of words or look at some clever twist in the angle of the artwork, the

Jim Davis

reader is more apt to laugh once he gets to the punch line. To me, the eye has to flow through the gag. The timing of a strip gag is not the same as the timing of a spoken gag. A good gag in a comic strip cannot just be read—you have to have a fine balance between the words and the images. If the joke stands on its own, there's no use in drawing it. Of course, a good sight gag—a good pantomime gag—is worth a lot. I feel you should do something with a comic strip that you can't do in any other medium.

To begin with, Garfield had very tiny eyes and a big cumbersome body, and he was more or less a lump on John's tabouret. Only those who read the first strip would know that John is a cartoonist. I made him a cartoonist because it always bugged me that nobody ever knew what Ozzie Nelson did for a living. I gave John a job but chose to delay developing it.

When I first began, I considered calling the strip *John*—about a single guy who had a cat. But every time I started to write a gag, Garfield would come up with the punch line. He wrestled the spotlight away from John, so I talked with Lew Little, and with Tom Ryan, about the problem I was having. They urged me to go with the instincts of the writing and give the strip to the cat. I saw the wisdom of their comments, and because I wanted to work with an animal anyway I let Garfield take the show. He keeps taking a bigger piece of it—in one sense I feel I've created a monster—but the editors and the readers expect things of Garfield so some choices are out of my hands. He is so real in my imagination—his personality is so well established—that I know how he'll react in a given situation. Not how *I* would react to it, nor how I might have *him* react to it, but how he *actually* would react. I feel a responsibility to make each gag, each day, stand on its own.

HURD: You're bringing more people into the strip now, aren't you, Jim?

DAVIS: Yes—and that's for art support. When *Garfield* started becoming popular, the syndicate came to me with the proposition of licensing. By virtue of my experience as a commercial artist, and with Tom Ryan, I felt comfortable getting involved with the licensing myself, actually doing the artwork for the coffee mugs and the T-shirts. As Garfield's popularity grew, the demand for my art time also grew, so I hired an artist. Even before this I had an assistant—Valette Hildebrand.

HURD: When was the first Garfield published?

DAVIS: June 19, 1978. When we initially signed the contract for *Garfield,* we were going to hold him and develop him for about a year and get a good backlog of strips. As people were looking at the strips, it occurred to us that not only did we feel the feature was ready to go but we felt a certain sense of urgency as far as the cat idea was concerned. It would have hurt if someone else had come out with a cat feature before *Garfield.* It's one of the things you think about for eight years. The moment it jells you can't wait to get it published.

From the very beginning, Valette had helped on the lettering and the blacking in of the strips. She has now taken over the brushwork on the strip, as well as the lettering. As the licensing program grew, I kept hiring artists one at a time, thinking each one was the last person I'd ever need. About five years ago we moved out of Muncie, Indiana, into the country. Before this I'd been working in the family room of my home, but there were four of us and things were starting to get crowded. I finally took a step to fulfill a lifelong dream of mine to move back to the country—but this time on my own terms (I wouldn't have to do chores anymore). We bought thirty acres of woods and meadow about four miles outside of Muncie. The property already had two small buildings on it—one a little ranch house that we remodeled into a studio, figuring it was more room than we'd ever need; the other house is Valette's home—and we eventually built on the property. As the staff grew, we remodeled the garage and made it into an office, and then there were more additions. Then I built another studio right behind it for myself. Now we're getting ready to add a second story to the old studio because we have twenty-six employees. All this was born out of our determination to do absolutely the best art possible for the licensing program, true to Garfield's personality and true to the product in each case. I should add that the purpose of having all these people was to free up my time to concentrate on the

comic strip. Never during the course of the licensing program has the comic strip taken a backseat. Not only is it the one legitimate reason for the entire program, it's by far the most important and the best thing I do.

I now have two assistants: Valette and Gary Barker, who does the penciling. I still write all the gags for both features. When I write, I also see the gag at the same time, so I do a thumbnail sketch. I design the strip, working on a 6-by-9-inch pad of paper with a fine-tip pen, and I have templates in the pad for the daily and Sunday strip. After this I give the thumbnail sketches and gags to Gary, who does the penciling on the cartoon board in blue line so we don't have to do any erasing. His penciling comes back to me for touch-up before it goes to Valette for inking. Gary, quite frankly, is a better artist than I am, so I don't have to do very much work on that end of things. After Valette's inking, the strips come back to me for checking, I sign them, date them, and send them out. This system allows me to concentrate on writing: I write the strips, I contribute to creating the licensing program, and I also write the TV shows. I'm a writer. I'm a good enough artist that I can get the feeling and flow of the gags, and I know how to structure and design a strip. But with all the responsibilities and distractions that can come in an industry like this, I've tried to focus on my strengths.

HURD: Jim, would you say something about your thought processes when you're trying to come up with gags?

DAVIS: For me, the gag writing takes an awful lot of mental preparation. First of all, I should say up front that I do use different methods of writing gags, but there is one standard way I use the most. I'll get to that way in a moment.

About 5 percent of the time I'll use a different method; it depends on how busy or how tired I am. Of course, the perfect gag-writing situation is to be very well rested and have a very high energy level, but sometimes when I'm closer to deadline, I'll pull in a friend or two and kick ideas back and forth. Ron Tuthill, who's a very funny guy, may get together with Valette and Kim, my secretary, and this group is very good about feeding me situations to spark the punch lines that then start coming to me.

However, 95 percent of my gag writing is done alone, with me sitting in my library at home. I rely on coffee and cigarettes, getting the heart pounding very hard, and I build my energy level way up. The closest thing I can compare my mood to is a working meditation. I concentrate so hard on the character that eventually I can see him in my mind's eye. Garfield is there—he is moving about—and I consciously place him in a situation. What he does to the situation seems to be of his own volition. I literally watch a television set in my head—this is the closest thing I can compare this process to. I watch Garfield interact with the other characters, I pursue the situation until he does something funny, and then I back up three frames and cut it off. This may be a little oversimplified, but it is essentially the way my thought processes work. A good gag will make me laugh in the same manner that, I hope, a newspaper reader will laugh. If it tickles me, something translates through. One of my philosophies of cartooning, especially when encouraging hopeful cartoonists, is that they should have fun doing the gags. If you have fun doing them, people will have fun reading them. If the gags are created in the proper atmosphere, if you are in a good mood when you create them, people will react the same way.

Early morning is my best time for doing gags, since I'm more rested, but I have no specific schedule for gag writing. If I've had sufficient sleep the previous night and can keep my energy up during the following day, I can write late at night or anytime during the day, as long as I'm alone. If there are any real distractions around me, any extraneous noise, sometimes I'll put on some music like the Modern Jazz Quartet, which is good to write to. There's no particular humor in their music but all the other sounds are blocked out. Once I start writing, it takes so much energy that I can't maintain a good level of creativity for more than four hours. By then I'm washed out. It's an emotional workout.

HURD: Do you ever wake up in the night and jot down an idea that has just come to you?

DAVIS: Nothing funny ever occurs to me unless I'm concentrating on it very hard. I've never been able to observe a situation or have a gag pop into my mind during the night. I have to go in search of gag ideas. I once likened it to walking into a dark closet, taking gags off the shelf, and bringing them out.

In the early days of *Garfield*, I never knew how big the closet was. It worried me when people asked if I was ever afraid of running out of ideas, but then I thought of the great cartoonists, like Sparky Schulz and Mort Walker, who have been having fresh ideas for thirty-five years. I felt that if they could stay so funny, day in and day out, there certainly would be a wealth of material to address over the years.

DEAN YOUNG AND STAN DRAKE ON *BLONDIE*

Story from Issue No. 72, December 1986

For the past couple of years, Stan Drake, who has been drawing the *Juliet Jones* comic strip for thirty-three years, has taken on the additional heavy responsibility of drawing the top-rated *Blondie*, which is syndicated to more than two thousand newspapers. *Blondie,* of course, was created in 1930 by Chic Young, the father of Dean Young, who has been writing the strip very successfully since his dad's death in 1973. Since Stan Drake's studio and *CARTOONIST PROfiles* are both in Westport, Connecticut, your editor sat down with Stan to talk about *Blondie* at some length.

Since Dean Young happened to be in Vermont at the time, it was necessary for us to talk with him by phone about Stan's new chores and about how the strip continues to be contemporary. First, our conversation with Dean Young and then the long sessions with Stan Drake.

Dean Young

HURD: Dean, during the conversation I've just had about *Blondie* with Stan here in Westport, he spoke enthusiastically about the pleasure of working with you on the feature.

YOUNG: I feel the same way about him, you know. We've got a really good relationship going; we're good teammates. I'm delighted to have someone with world-class ability in the person of Stan drawing *Blondie*. The graphics are looking great—certainly in the style we want them!

We pretty much try to stay contemporary. We keep *Blondie* in updated clothes, and all the furniture, cars, and props in the comic strip are pretty much up to date so they can relate to the world and our society. The long-running traditional gags that have to do with Dagwood's personality and his character, such as eating and sleeping and all the things he's notorious for, are going to be used from time to time because they're part of his nature. They lend themselves so well

® BLONDIE

A portrait of Dagwood Bumstead by Stan Drake

to the gags and the choices that we want to set up for the Bumsteads.

HURD: Cartoonists are generally impressed that the strip seems fresh after all these years!

YOUNG: Because it's fifty-six years old, we have to avoid becoming an anachronism, and I work at that. I think in contemporary terms of my own life, the way things are going for me, and I try to relate this to the comic strip. I like to deal mainly with domestic situations, and I primarily stick with eating, sleeping, raising children, and making money—these are my four mainstays. I go through these categories and try to have all my setups and situations come from these four primary concerns.

These days I often do ideas that will appeal to more feminist-type women. I don't want Blondie just stuck at home by gags limiting her to that setting alone. I want Blondie to be a complete woman, and I want readers to respect her not only for her ability to maintain a home but also for her own mind and her own

Stan Drake

A portrait of Blondie by Stan Drake

Dean Young

person. If readers admire a character's personality, and the way he or she is, they feel affection for that character—which I feel is very important. Your characters have to be respected and loved because that's what this comic strip business is all about. When readers like a set of characters and then see them running around in all sorts of funny antics, that provides an added dimension.

HURD: In view of the changing lifestyles today, does Dagwood do things differently now from what he did in the past?

YOUNG: Yes. A lot of the changes in the way he acts nowadays have to do with his relationships to women. I'm careful to see that he doesn't do things that might make a segment of women readers unhappy or upset. I just want to entertain the largest audience I can get to with wholesome and clean humor. I don't want to make

any group or persons unhappy with the way *Blondie* characters behave. I want to make friends, not enemies. This was my dad's formula, and the advice he passed on to me in this connection has worked very well.

HURD: Stan mentioned the Qwip system that you and he use. Would you say something about that?

YOUNG: We use this on every set of strips. I send him the scripts and then when he gets his "pencils" done

he'll put them in the Qwip machine in Westport and I can see them instantaneously on my machine in Florida. Then, if there are any things we want to talk about, we can get together on the telephone. But by and large, there are not too many things we need to discuss on these occasions. I've got a Qwip machine up here in Vermont and one in Florida, so Stan and I can send graphics all up and down the East Coast. The telephone people hook a Qwip into your phone system. You make a phone call, put the phone down, and the Qwip computer transmits *Blondie* as Stan has drawn it.

HURD: Does one buy such a machine? Are they expensive?

YOUNG: I think they cost about $2,800 and I believe are made by Exxon.

HURD: Are some of the situations that Dagwood gets into the same as those you've experienced yourself?

YOUNG: I guess you could say I'm his alter ego. I think I'm pretty Dagwoodian! I think and do things like he does, but I hope I pull them off with a little more finesse and am not as often the victim of circumstances. I hope I don't get inexplicably caught in the web of Bumsteadian plans that have gone astray as he does.

HURD: I imagine that you feel a lot of the success of the strip has been due to the fact that your dad, Chic Young, and you have pretty much thought of yourselves as everyday family characters.

YOUNG: I think that says it pretty well.

Stan Drake

HURD: How difficult was it for you, Stan, to shift from the beautiful illustrative style you displayed in *Juliet Jones* for so many years to the *Blondie* style we're going to talk about today?

DRAKE: Strangely enough, I really am a cartoonist—I had to work hard at drawing straight illustrative-type stuff. I started out with Johnstone and Cushing (the advertising cartoon firm) right after the war and my bent was really toward the semifunny stuff. But I learned how to do *Juliet Jones* because they wanted an illustrative strip. I had to work hard at becoming an illustrator. Being funny with my pencil actually is the real me!

HURD: I've forgotten whether you had any formal art training.

DRAKE: Yes, I had a couple of seasons at the Art Students League before World War II. Life drawing was the main part of what I got there, although I did work with John McNulty and learned a little bit about arrangements and perspectives. When I got into advertising, an art director told me, "If you want to make out in this business, you must learn how to draw pretty girls and handsome men." So I bought copies of *Vogue, Harpers Bazaar,* and *Mademoiselle,* and when I got home, I'd place some vellum over the heads of the pretty girls in the magazines; I must have traced seven or eight hundred heads in this way. Every night I'd practice drawing pretty girls and handsome guys, and finally I got to the point where I knew what made a face pretty and what the proportions were. Soon I was drawing them without having to trace them.

HURD: What about that great pen-and-ink technique you demonstrated in *Juliet Jones*?

DRAKE: This was an advertising style I developed. You couldn't sell brushwork to advertising agencies as you could to the comic books. Because the old comic books were all brushwork, this style made your work look dated and had a comic-book look. The advertising agencies wanted a modern style, so I practiced with a pen and came up with a sort of avant-garde, trendy look for my work. When I took *Juliet* up to King Features, the strip was done in the style I'd been using in advertising.

HURD: To digress for a moment, had most of your advertising work been with Johnstone and Cushing?

DRAKE: Yes. Then, when I left them, Harold Kitelson and I formed the Drake-Kitelson Studio, where we specialized in line art. In those days hundreds and thousands of black-and-white spots were used in advertising. Today you hardly see any of them there because of the various clip-art services supplying spots on every conceivable subject.

HURD: Now let's get into our topic for today—about what was involved when you got the job of drawing *Blondie.*

DRAKE: First of all, I had to copy; I had to make my drawings look like the ones done by Jim Raymond, who in my opinion was a genius. In a situation like this, you're forging another man's handwriting. Jim would do folds a certain way, he would have characters walk in a specific way, and his little expressions are all gems. It was really tough to follow this exacting prescription; it took me a year to become comfortable with the strip. In the beginning, of course, I had to get the strip out using a combination of a light box, enlarger, and copy machine. This was fine if I just had Dagwood standing there, but suppose he and Blondie were climbing up a mountain and Dagwood was hanging from a tree. Let's assume that Jim Raymond had never drawn him in that position, so, as in hundreds and hundreds of other instances, I had to make up his action. And it was necessary to have him hanging the way Jim would have had him hanging. And the expressions would have to be apropos of the situation, not just a dead likeness of Dagwood. I really had to get these characters in my fingers. It took a year, maybe more.

HURD: Do you have a big file of past proofs of the strip?

DRAKE: When Dean Young decided to go with me as the artist, he had King Features get together ten years of proof sheets—the years from 1969 to 1979. In the beginning, of course, these were of inestimable value because, although I had loved *Blondie,* I had never considered ever having to turn it out myself. I can probably do a drawing as well as anyone right from scratch—one drawing—but suddenly I was faced with a deadline every week. There was a Sunday page consisting of twelve panels, with sometimes as many as sixty people in that one Sunday page, and no close-ups: every character shown head to toe! Each panel 3⅝ inches wide, with the heads of Blondie and Dagwood about half an inch high, and within this tiny area I had to get expressions and make them look like they were done by Jim Raymond. I was convinced after a month or so that this had to be the toughest strip to do.

HURD: I know your feelings about the status of *Blondie* in the comic-strip world gave you the determination to lick these tough problems you've spoken about.

DRAKE: Yes, I guess one has to say, in all fairness, that *Peanuts* and *Blondie* have shared the number-one spot in newspapers all across the country. As far as King can tell, both *Blondie* and *Peanuts* appear in over two thousand newspapers. Just think, Jud, fifty-six years ago this strip was created, and here it is—still number one. It's an incredible thing!

I can't say enough about Dean Young and his ability to stay with the strip and keep it fresh after all these years. He does a remarkable job.

HURD: Juggling two strips—*Juliet Jones,* which you've been doing for the past thirty-three years and now *Blondie*—is a herculean task.

DRAKE: I'm working ten to twelve hours a day—sometimes fifteen—seven days a week, Christmas, New Year's, holidays. One of the big problems in getting help is that if you get a guy who's good, he's busy. And if you're getting someone who's learning, you might as well do it yourself during the time you might be teaching this person.

HURD: What help do you have on *Blondie*?

DRAKE: Dean has a longtime friend down in Florida, Denis Lebrun, who letters *Blondie*. And when I send him the strips with the characters drawn in, he inks in the backgrounds—the outside of the house, the living room, scenes like that—and saves me a lot of work in that way. But the figures, the layouts, the conception, and the action—these are up to me and I ink them myself, of course. Denis does a great job and he's a fantastic assistant.

HURD: Does Dean Young have any criticisms about the way you're drawing the strip?

DRAKE: Well, in the beginning, Dean's phone bill must have been $4,000 a month, calling Connecticut and saying, "The button is too big, the button is too small, do this, do that." But I want to go on record as saying that every time he called, he was right! I just hadn't seen it. He knows the strip so well he just took it for granted that I would too. But I was a beginner, really, as far as *Blondie* was concerned. I really lucked out with Dean Young's personality, because he might have been a tough guy to work with and I would have had to put up with it. But it turns out that he's one of the best guys you'd ever want to meet—kind, patient, generous.

It's been fortunate that I've been able to adapt and go back to the action and the little fun stuff that I love and forget all the folds and all the shading I had to learn in the illustrative game over the years. What I'm doing in *Blondie* is what I always wanted to do.

When we started, Dean took a gamble and I took a gamble, because I didn't know if I could really do the strip the way it should be done. It was a real challenge. I said to myself, I'm going to do this, I'm going to learn how to do it right, but it sure was tougher than I expected. And the fact that Dean seems to be pleased with what I'm doing means the world to me because I've tried so hard for that guy. I knew the limb he was out on with me and I wasn't going to let him down. I'm still finding my stuff looking better than what I see on my proof sheets of six months ago. I'm not saying that I've got it yet.

HURD: I've heard comments that Blondie seems a bit sexier than she used to in the old days.

DRAKE: Yes, we've had conversations about that. Dean himself reminded me that in the beginning she was a flapper—very tall and slender—a pretty chorus-girl type. This was why Dagwood Bumstead's father disinherited him—because he was marrying a flapper. After that she because a housewife. I agreed with Dean that Blondie should be a housewife, yes, but why not a gorgeous, well-built, sexy housewife? What's wrong with that? We don't want her to get dowdy-looking and dumpy; she's got to love Dagwood so much it's funny. Part of the humor is that this beautiful girl loves this guy who looks sometimes like Mickey Mouse with those big eyes.

I sent Dean two drawings, about eight inches high, portraits of Blondie and Dagwood, just the heads, as if I were a portrait painter. I painted them with all the shadows and all the nuances of a real portrait. I did Dagwood first, and then Blondie came out as this gorgeous blonde. I made her hair, with the little curls, into real hair, with every twist and turn, making it look silken. Her eyes were gorgeous in the portrait and she is a real woman. Blondie in the strip is a caricature of a real person, but Dagwood is a cartoon; when I finished his portrait, he looked like an alien from the planet Zerk. He's got these huge eyes, so what you have is a real woman married to a cartoon, because no way, with that hair and those eyes, can you make him look like a real person.

Dean says, "I like her in slacks." It used to be that she always had a dress on and he has tried to update this and that. The strip nowadays doesn't have the look of the thirties—she has more than that one dress she always used to wear. Now she has a different dress every day, and she's got the latest clothes. Dean has even sent me catalogs of women's fashions to put on Blondie and to keep her "today." When Dean mentioned the slacks, I said, "OK, but her legs are pretty and we like to see them too. Today's slacks are pipe stems—they don't have the flaired bottoms that used to look so cute—and if we put her in slacks, there's no zap. True, women don't go around the house in high heels, they wear little flats with their slacks." So I said, "Dean, what do you want? Do you want her to be sexy or to be real?" He said, "Let's forget 'real.'" So I guess he wants her to look real jazzy. Dean is the final word on the strip; I'll do anything he wants. I make some suggestions occasionally, but he's the final judge.

HURD: Do you recall any other corrections that Dean made when you first tackled the strip?

DRAKE: Yes, in some instances the bottom of Dagwood's neck comes down to a V shape, and in other instances it's rounded. Dean sent me a little sketch with the comment, "I prefer the rounded bottom and not the V-shaped neck."

So I went back through the proofs and found that Jim Raymond drew Dagwood about six different ways over a period of ten years. There's a whole sequence of a year or two of the V neck. And then all of a sudden, for some reason or other, the rounded neck appears.

HURD: Have you reached a point now where, if you have to draw the mailman approaching the Bumstead house, you can do him without referring to any proofs?

DRAKE: Yes. I've realized, after working with the strip for a while, that every character walks the same way. They all stand the same way. They have different clothes and their faces are different. The women stand the same way, whether it's Tootsie or Blondie or a girl they meet on the street. Dagwood walks the same way as Herb Woodley walks. Kids walk the same way.

Chic Young created this whole thing and has got to go down in history as one of the geniuses of the industry. His eyes began to bother him about 1950, and Jim Raymond actually did most of the drawing from 1950 on. Raymond's name didn't get on the strip, I think, until about 1972 or 1973. Raymond subtly got away from the wild slapstick look of the early days, and he and Dean both calmed the strip down and tried to keep it up-to-date without being unbelievable. For instance, a car racing from the scene couldn't have all four wheels off the ground with nuts and bolts flying in all directions, which is the way it used to be done. Dean took the cuffs off Dagwood's pants and now they're just rounded off on the bottom because no one wears cuffs anymore.

HURD: Does Dagwood have frequent changes of costume as Blondie does these days?

DRAKE: Dagwood has a V-neck sweater, a cardigan, a jacket, a black suit, and that's about it. He always wears black pants.

HURD: I know you've said that to draw *Blondie* you can't just be a cartoonist with a bigfoot style, because you're drawing the actions of real people.

DRAKE: When they sit down at the table, or on a chair, you'd be amazed at all the little hand gestures and facial expressions. Dagwood must have four hundred facial expressions, each one indicated by just a little tilt of the eyebrow, and his mouth is so expressive. It's just endless!

Hurt: Let's go back for just a minute, Stan. When you started to develop an illustrative style years ago, what pen were you using?

DRAKE: A Gillott 290. I cultivated it and grew to love it. I took great pride in learning how to master it, and the first twenty years of *Juliet Jones* were done with a 290. But something happened to the metal in that pen and the ink wouldn't flow no matter what you did. I find it very difficult to handle, so I use a Hunt 102 now.

HURD: I want to pin down the date when you started to draw *Blondie*.

DRAKE: I was given the go-ahead signal on August 8, 1984, but I had been working on it—trying to learn how to do it—for a couple of months before that. *Juliet Jones* was released for publication on March 9, 1953.

HURD: I understand that you're now doing the Sunday page in nine panels instead of the traditional twelve panels that *Blondie* had religiously adhered to.

DRAKE: There's an important point here: We can pick up a lot of papers using nine panels who cannot carry the strip in quarter-page size. As you know, each page of many Sunday comic sections consists of four quarter-page comics, one above the other. And *Blondie*, of course, would fit into this arrangement with the nine-panel format.

I do want to add one more thing, Jud. You obviously feel it's important to include what we've talked about today in your magazine. As chronicler of the world of cartoons you have done a magnificent job over the years with *CARTOONIST PROfiles*, and I'm proud to be part of it. I really enjoy this profession—the guys in it are the nicest bunch of people that I've ever met—ingenuous, real, unaffected, terrific. I guess I've enjoyed this because I realize that the backbiting in some other lines of work is awful. But there's none of that in our business.

MIKE PETERS AND
MOTHER GOOSE & GRIMM

Story from Issue No. 77, March 1988

Mike Peters says he's able to juggle so many cartoon assignments successfully only because his wife, Marian, handles the business side of his activities. Peters creates the *Mother Goose & Grimm* comic strip for Tribune Media Services, and his editorial cartoons for the *Dayton Daily News* are distributed by United Feature Syndicate to many newspapers. In December 1987 he received the Elzie Segar Award from the National Cartoonists Society. This award, given annually to a cartoonist who shows exceptional ability in comic ideas, was founded to perpetuate the memory of E. C. "Elzie" Segar, the creator of *Popeye*. Mike was also named to the 1987 Esquire Register, "an honor roll of men and women whose accomplishments, values, and dreams reflect America at its best," and scheduled to be featured on the nationally syndicated television show *Headlines on Trial* in January 1988. Peters is also a regular guest every two weeks on a news program in Japan, similar to *Today,* where he discusses current political issues.

by Mike Peters

In doing the *Mother Goose & Grimm* strip, I've learned more about myself than about cartooning. I've been discovering that no matter what you think you can do, you can double or triple your output if you put your mind to it. For the past several years I've been living almost two lives—it amazes me when I look at all the work I've done just on the strips. None of that work would have happened if I had not forced myself to get it out.

For many years I was knocking out editorial cartoons, not thinking that I also had the energy—or the creativity—to invent a whole other world and do it every day. That's staggering. When you double your output, you learn that your limit is not what you thought it was. Whereas I used to spend a whole day just on my editorial cartoon, I discovered that I could do both it and my strip in the same amount of time. Nowadays it takes me about an hour and a half to do a cartoon. I always thought that when you doubled your output, your creativity would dim in all areas, like putting too many plugs into a light socket. What I found was that the *Mother Goose* strip enhances my excitement for the editorial cartoon and vice versa.

Here's an example. Formerly, if I hit a blank wall while working on an editorial cartoon, I would just get up from my drawing board, walk around, have a cup of

Mike Peters

coffee, come back, sit down, tear my hair out, and keep looking at that blank sheet of paper until I finally came up with an idea I liked. The time I spent from when I first got up from the board till I got a good idea was a negative period when nothing was being produced. On the other hand, when I'm doing both editorial and strip work, if I hit a blank wall on the editorial cartoon, I get up from the board, move to another chair (just to get away physically from the board), and start thinking about the strip. Whether I've had a mental block while doing the editorial cartoon or have come up against a stone wall while thinking of strip ideas, I'm usually fresh when I jump to the other side of my cartoon life. This really amazes me! It means all that negative noncreative time I just mentioned has now become creative time.

When I first started doing *Mother Goose & Grimm,* I could not believe I was putting myself in a situation where I would have to produce a comic strip *every day*— or for the rest of the life of the strip, at least. I thought, My God, am I losing my mind? How can I do that? Lying in bed at two in the morning, I would think, I've got to do an editorial cartoon and a strip tomorrow, then an editorial cartoon and a strip the next day, then both of them a third day, and another, and another, and on and on. I began mentally to add the numbers up. I figured that a Sunday page is equivalent to three strips, so I'd be picturing nine *Mother Goose & Grimm* strips and five editorial cartoons a week! How could I ever do it? I called up my friend Doug Marlette, who as you know does the *Kudzu* strip for Tribune Media Services. When I told him about these cartoon nightmares of mine, he said, "Look. Think of it like brushing your teeth. You don't lie in bed thinking, Gee, I've got to brush my teeth twice today and twice tomorrow and twice the next day—that's six times I've got to brush my teeth between now and Wednesday—how am I ever going to do that? You just get up and brush your teeth. That's how you should view doing your cartoons. Just get up and do them—get them out of the way."

Well, that really helped. Another thing Doug suggested was what he called "priming the pump." He said, "Every day find half an hour or an hour to sit down with your drawing pad without putting any pressure on yourself to come up with an idea. If you make little blips on the pad, or write down little marks,

that's great, but if you don't write down anything that's all right too, because you're that much closer to having some ideas tomorrow. Just sit down and try to create without feeling that you have to come up with ideas at this particular sitting." I usually put something on the pad, no matter how short a time I may be sitting there. Something goes through my head. It may not be very good but at least it's something—it's a blip, an electrical impulse, and that's what I'm looking for. That's what Doug Marlette meant by priming the pump. You may sit there all day pumping and pumping with nothing coming up, but eventually something will appear out of that pump. The work you're doing now is going to pay off.

One of the things that bothers me about a lot of strips, and also about a lot of editorial cartoons, is that you can tell after reading a bunch of them that the creators are not pleasing themselves. On the other hand, you can easily identify the strip in which it's obvious that the idea and its execution really made the creator laugh. That cartoonist was really entertaining himself or herself.

As I looked through the comic pages, I often found myself getting depressed. But if I saw something that's really great, I'd say, "Why didn't I think of that? Is that a beautiful idea! Boy, so-and-so is really cracking today!" Then, if I saw the other side of the coin and looked at some strips that were really awful, I'd think, "Those people are cartoonists, and I'm a cartoonist. Am I that bad?" In the past I was always comparing myself to everybody else. I'd wonder, How do I fare against so-and-so? How does the editorial cartoon look on the page? How does *Mother Goose & Grimm* compare with everybody else's strip? I was always getting depressed, one way or the other. Oh, gee, he's so much better than I am! Why is that body of work so depressingly mediocre? Will I be mediocre?

Well, nowadays I just don't look. The only thing I know for sure is that if you please yourself, that's about the highest compliment there is. If you actually make yourself laugh, if you actually entertain yourself, you're hot, you're cracking, you're doing what a creator should be doing. I don't do *Mother Goose & Grimm* or my editorial cartoon for the public. Sure, I would love for the public to jump up and down and turn cartwheels and have thousands of people around the

mike PETERS

Grimmy's evolution

Cartoon Success Secrets

country saying, "Boy, that Mike Peters strip is really funny today!" But in the first place I can't believe that would happen, and second I'll never see people reading my strip because we cartoonists resemble childlike hermits who stay by ourselves at our little drawing boards drawing cartoons to try and please ourselves as we did when we were ten-year-olds. It's ironic, but cartooning is one of the few jobs where you do what you did when you were a kid but now you get paid for it!

If you're not pleasing yourself, you can't assume you're pleasing the public out there. So this is what I try to aim for. If I don't enjoy what I'm doing, or if I'm getting bored by it, there's a pretty good chance I will be boring the public too. So what I probably work hardest at is to try to entertain myself, to wait till I come up with something that actually makes me chuckle.

The editorial cartoonist side of me has a very easy time. It's almost like sitting on the side of a river with your hook out. All you have to do is just wait there for an idea to strike. You're waiting for something you care about to hit you. In picking a topic for an editorial cartoon, I can't just look at the front page and think, Well, that's a big story so I'll draw about it, because sometimes I don't care about that big story. Let's say it's about the deficit. Well, of course I feel sorry about the deficit—I really feel bad that we're spending money we don't have—but I surely don't feel emotional about it. Often, though, when I do a cartoon against the NRA, the National Rifle Association, or one in favor of the ERA, for women's rights, I really feel passionately about the subject. On these occasions I believe I'm absolutely right and the people who are against me are absolutely wrong. Now, out of ten cartoons I do on these two subjects that I feel passion for, maybe three of them will be really effective; the other seven will not be as strong as my feelings are for the subject. But if I pick a subject I care nothing about just because it's on the front page, my average will be ten out of ten that are not effective. If I don't feel anything about the subject, I can't expect the readers of my editorial cartoon to feel anything either.

I read the papers, watch CNN, have C-Span on my TV as audible wallpaper, and keep a notebook in which only topics that I have some feeling for are listed. Then maybe I'll spend one or two hours coming up with what I think is a pretty good idea. A lot of my creating is discarding. I come up with lots of ideas—I brainstorm with myself all the time. But I also spend a lot of time drawing a cartoon, looking at it, and saying *no!*, drawing another one and saying *no!*, and so on. Finally—BINGO! Something will strike me as being particularly good. That's the one I'll use.

I often think of how to explain to someone the process of brainstorming with yourself. Picture a wheel with spokes and put a topic at the hub of the wheel—let's say the ERA, the Equal Rights Amendment. I know what I feel about the ERA. I think the amendment ought to pass. For instance, I think it's outrageous that even today there are women who cannot get insurance at the same rate at which a man can get insurance. So I draw a wheel with ERA at the hub, and all around the wheel on the spokes I'll write words relating to women, and there might be twenty-five or thirty spokes. I'll just brainstorm, putting down anything I can think of about women: Eve, Mona Lisa, Alice in Wonderland, Cinderella, Snow White, Marie Antoinette, Joan of Arc, Betsy Ross. After I've come up with a number of words like these, I stand back and start letting my eyes make connections—ERA versus Betsy Ross, ERA versus Snow White, ERA versus Alice in Wonderland. I brainstorm and eventually something pops. Having done this so often, I'm not scared by a blank piece of paper anymore.

The creation of my editorial cartoons is a different process from the one involved in doing the comic strip. The editorial cartoons all come from without—things I see happening all around me—national topics, social problems, whatever. I read and I watch, and ideas come to me. The strip, on the other hand, involves, I think, a totally different part of my brain. It's all very personal; all the ideas for *Mother Goose* come from within. I usually have my pad with me, and I think about what I've done that particular day: What did I learn, what did I see, but mainly what did I feel?

I knew I wanted to do a strip, I knew I wanted to be able to draw cartoons at home so I could be with my family more than when I was working down at the *Dayton Daily News* office every single day. (Nowadays I work at home and do both my editorial cartoon and the strip in my own little office.) I didn't know what the strip was going to be about, but I got out all my favorite editorial cartoons, laid them on the floor, and looked at them. A great way to find out where you're going is by seeing where you've been. So looking at these editorial cartoons told me (1) that I loved drawing animals and (2) that I loved doing fantasy. So I decided to put these two enthusiasms together. Mother Goose and the Brothers Grimm were always very important in my early life. I'd owned dogs, and I'd always wanted to use a crazy little dog in a cartoon, a dog that would act exactly as dogs do—not walk on its hind legs but chase cars, have fleas, eat out of trash cans, and drink out of toilets. . . . Incidentally, the first time I had the dog drink out of a toilet, I lost Pittsburgh. The whole city of Pittsburgh dropped me; it was a crushing blow. Some lady started a campaign against this outrageous drawing of mine, and when the syndicate contacted her by mail and asked her why she was so exercised about this, she replied, "We can't have a picture like this in the paper, because if other dogs see it—well, you know what will happen!" The whole thing was crazy. So I don't see any reason why little Grimm shouldn't be drinking out of toilets, because real dogs do. (I was hoping that would be the title of my next *Mother Goose & Grimm* book but my publisher turned me down.)

About six months into the strip, I learned that I was the dog, Grimm, which I hadn't realized before. Here's how I found out: I have this thing about corn chips—Fritos. If someone is eating Fritos in my vicinity, I find myself going over and wolfing down any stray bits that may be left. But in order to avoid killing myself with all the grease and salt, I devised a new scheme. I would go to the vending machine at the newspaper, buy one of those bags of Fritos, take a mouthful of chips, crumple up the bag with most of the Fritos still inside, and throw it away in the trash can so I couldn't finish it. Well, one day my wife, Marian, found me halfway down the trash can, digging these little crumbs out with my finger, and she said, "My gosh, that's the dog! You're Grimm!" I realized that I am, and that's when the character started coming together for me. I stopped drawing just dog things, started thinking of Michael things—my fears, my desires, whatever—and projected them onto the dog. That made it a lot easier for me to draw him because now I understand him.

My work habits have changed since I started the strip. When I was just doing the editorial cartoon, I'd go to the office around eight A.M. and stay till five, by which time I'd have a cartoon done. But now that I work at home, I find that cartoons and life have merged. I'm able to see my kids off to school. About seven A.M. I'm often sitting at my drawing board, going over subjects

that I think would make good editorial cartoons. I usually finish the editorial cartoon by ten. Marian generally rushes it down to the paper. (I might have taken an hour or so the night before, going over topics and possible ideas, letting them jell while I'm asleep—which for some reason works. The mind is an amazing tool. Often when I do this, I wake up much closer to an idea than if I'd started the editorial cartoon at six A.M. from scratch. Your brain works in the middle of the night, sifting through different things—it's really fascinating.)

After finishing the editorial cartoon, I take a shower and, refreshed, I begin the other side of my day. Strips take me about an hour to draw. It may take me a half hour to come up with a sketch that I like. I pick and choose a lot. Sketchwise I may do one cartoon five or six or seven times before I get a sketch I enjoy. The inking of the strip is fairly easy—I turn on TV and get lost in whatever I'm watching as I ink. I feel I get my best ideas early in the morning, so if I sometimes get done with my editorial cartoon at night, that's great, because it means that at seven-thirty or eight A.M. I can start thinking of strip ideas. This is often pretty productive because maybe by ten I've got some blips down on the paper. I enjoy drawing. If work is enjoyable, it's going to seem natural, and if it's natural, it's me.

It's interesting how certain cartoonists are so involved with style. They talk about people having an Oliphant style, a MacNelly style, a Tony Auth style, or a Doug Marlette style. The problem with that is that you can put so much emphasis on the style of the cartoon that you don't pay enough attention to what the cartoon says or to how funny it is. A lot of cartoonists keep drawings by other cartoonists nearby because they're fascinated by the styles of these other people. When they think of an idea, they can picture it being done in a certain kind of style, so they pull out those cartoons and look at them—this helps them, it's an aid. But how wrong this is! If you're a cartoonist, and you're worried about style, the most courageous thing you can do is to get rid of all cartoons by other people. Throw them out of the house—you're like an alcoholic if you don't. I should know; I went through fifty different styles during the first ten years of my career.

At this point, your editor spoke up.

"Maybe we should add, Mike, that during their early learning period all successful cartoonists have been influenced by the work of other cartoonists they've admired. They've studied how their heroes achieved certain effects, learning from each of them. What you're saying here is that a cartoonist *who has reached the point of doing cartoons for publication* should forget about the other guy's style and trust his or her own instincts."

I find that I work best by setting little deadlines for myself if I've overloaded my work schedule. I'll tell myself that I'll have one strip finished by ten A.M., or perhaps some preliminary work on a book of cartoons done by two P.M., and I just plod along meeting all the little deadlines.

Another thing: You've got to trust your own instincts when you've got a number of cartoon irons in the fire—an editorial cartoon, a strip, maybe a book. You don't have time to test your ideas out on a number of people in the office, say, as many of us have done. Don't try to see the world through someone else's eyes and don't try to *be* someone else. If your idea seems right to you or makes you laugh, go with it.

A lot of my cartoonist friends and I have teamed up with our wives, and our wives have become business managers while we remain the creators. I couldn't get my part done if Marian were not on the phone three or four hours a day, talking with my respective syndicates (United Feature Syndicate for the editorial cartoons and Tribune Media Services for *Mother Goose & Grimm*), with merchandisers, with the people who are doing my calendars, with those who are doing the next *Mother Goose & Grimm* book, and with the *Greater Buffalo Press* about the coloring of the Sunday page. Many wives have taken over the really hard work of negotiating, the calling and prodding that leaves us cartoonists the time to create. I would never be able to manage all the cartooning I do without this very considerable help from my wife.

Before I sign off, Jud, I have to tell your readers one more story. In high school, back in St. Louis, I neglected my studies terribly because I was drawing cartoons all the time—in the margins of my schoolbooks, on my notebooks, everywhere. As a result I barely graduated—only because my teachers were good Christians, I guess. Anyhow, two or three years ago my high school invited me to visit and receive an award for my newspaper cartooning. While I was back home, I happened to look over an old yearbook. One of my teachers had written by my photo, *Dear Mr. Peters—you'd better grow up real soon because you can't always be drawing cartoons!*

SCOTT ADAMS AND *DILBERT*

Story from Issue No. 84, December 1989

We asked Scott Adams to tell us how his lifetime obsession with cartooning carried him to the point where he could combine the production of his daily and Sunday United Feature comic strip *Dilbert* with a nine-to-five job as a financial man in the engineering department of Pacific Bell.

by Scott Adams

Some of my earliest childhood memories are of drawing cartoons. I don't remember any time when I didn't want to be a cartoonist. Many of my likes and dislikes have changed over the years, but my obsession with cartooning has been constant.

My mother always told me I could do anything I wanted when I grew up. Cartooning would be great fun, I thought, but how many people actually make money at it? I'm a practical guy. I decided to go to college, major in economics, get a thankless job with some soulless corporation, and live out my days in anonymity and quiet despair. (Well, it seemed like a good idea at the time.)

But in my first year of college I decided to indulge my cartooning fantasy in a limited way by taking a drawing class.

Scott Adams

The class seemed to go pretty well. I was always the first to finish our drawing assignments, so I figured I must be the best artist in the group. An easy *A,* I thought.

Then one day my instructor showed me the "correct" way to draw a maple tree, in stark contrast to my simple cartoon renderings. Since I was never wrong in those days, I took exception and pointed out that my cartoon tree was much better than her artsy little tree with all the squiggles and shading.

I got the lowest grade in the class. And I learned that cartoons are not art, at least not to everybody. Discouraged, I hung up my pencil and tried to put cartooning out of my mind.

Fate and My Carburetor

One day in senior year my car broke down on a new highway halfway between Syracuse and Oneonta, New York. It was the dead of night and dead winter. No coat, no traffic, no civilization for miles. It was about zero degrees and nothing but snow as far as the eye could see. I jogged a few miles trying to delay frostbite. Limbs numb, teeth chattering, too cold to swear out

DILBERT™

He's a genius inventor (if you consider his pocket lint converter a great invention). Dilbert and Dogbert. A man and his dog, simply unique.

loud, I promised myself that if I lived I would sell my traitorous car for a one-way ticket to California and never see another snowflake as long as I lived. (I do stuff like that.)

Later that night, just before frostbite purchased my miserable life, I was rescued by a traveling shoe salesman who was bored enough to pick up a vibrating blue hitchhiker. A few months later I finished school and sold my car to my sister in exchange for a one-way ticket to the West Coast. I took a job at a big bank and set about the business of crushing little people on my way to the top.

But cartoons kept oozing out of my fingers, sometimes during business meetings, always while I was on the phone. A dumpy-looking character with glasses began appearing in my business presentations and on my office blackboard. I wasn't conscious of creating him; he just evolved.

The cartoon dumpy guy gained popularity around the office. Several people suggested that I try cartooning professionally, but I didn't know where to begin. At this point, fate stepped in.

One day I came home just as a Public Television show called *Funny Business* was ending. I caught enough to see that it was part of a series about cartooning, so I wrote to the host of the show, cartoonist Jack Cassady, and asked how a person becomes a cartoonist. To my surprise, Jack wrote back, going into detail about art materials, books to buy, and how to submit art to publishers. He said he liked my work, from the samples I had sent, and advised me not to be discouraged by the flood of rejections I was likely to get at first.

Following Jack's advice I bought a copy of the 1986 *Artist's Market* and found out what conventions to follow and where to mail my cartoons. I sent off several of my best single-panel cartoons to some magazines and waited for the money to start rolling in. Unfortunately, only rejections arrived. Ignoring Jack's advice, I hung up my pencil and turned my thoughts away from cartooning again.

I finished my MBA during the evening at Berkeley and got a new job at Pacific Bell as a financial guy in the engineering department. The little dumpy guy with glasses came with me and rapidly gained popularity in my new office. Everybody thought they knew who he was, not surprisingly, since he was transforming into a composite of the engineers I worked with.

He needed a name, so I solicited suggestions from coworkers. One struck: Dilbert. Dilbert asked for a dog, so I gave him Dogbert. Yes, both of them talk to me.

Fate wasn't through with me yet. One day a letter came. It was from Jack Cassady. He said he had been looking through his files and came upon the cartoons I sent him a year before, and he wrote just to tell me that my work was good and he hoped I hadn't gotten discouraged by rejections.

How did he know? His encouragement was enough to make me take my pencil out of storage and set a new goal: to be published someplace, anyplace, sometime before I died. I decided to draw a cartoon a day for the rest of my life, and if nobody ever published them I would just fill the attic and leave them as my legacy.

One day a friend suggested that I enter Dilbert and Dogbert in a "People Who Look Like Their Dogs" contest in the Sunday *San Francisco Chronicle/Examiner*. Although the contest was intended for photographs, I sent my cartoons. Dilbert and Dogbert placed in the top five and, in the most unlikely way, accomplished my objective of being published.

Delirious from my success, I decided to try for the ultimate cartoon goal: syndication. I reasoned that being rejected by a cartoon syndicate would carry more prestige than being rejected by magazines. I had my pride to consider.

I worked up about fifty cartoon strips, attached a cover letter and description of the characters, made eight copies, and bound them in cheap plastic covers. Nothing fancy, just clean and simple. I mailed copies to the major syndicates listed in my 1988 edition of *Artist's Market* and waited.

In a few weeks an editor of one of the syndicates called and expressed interest. I was ecstatic. Then he suggested that maybe I should take an art course. I didn't tell him about the tree incident in college.

Later I got a message on my answering machine from a syndicate I didn't recognize. I didn't remember sending a package to a United Media. Probably some little company trying to make a name for itself, I thought. Might as well call back and humor them. I reached United Media's comic editor, Sarah Gillespie.

Sarah said she liked Dilbert and asked if I was interested in a development contract. Playing it cool, I said I would be willing to discuss it. Then I asked the question that will haunt me forever. "Do you handle any cartoons I might be familiar with?" "Yes," Sarah said. "We handle *Peanuts* and *Garfield*."

To her credit, she did not add, Maybe you've heard of them. Realizing now that my negotiating position was somewhat compromised, I asked her to mail me the contract. United Media turned out to be the parent company for United Feature Syndicate, Inc., to whom I had mailed my cartoons.

Although I was an experienced negotiator at my day job, I was far too emotionally involved to negotiate this contract. I needed an expert. I might not get a second chance.

So I called the San Francisco Comic Art Museum and asked Barry Gantt, the director, if he was aware of any local attorneys with syndication contract experience. Barry suggested talking to the museum's attorney, Jeff O'Connell. Jeff was familiar with the industry and experienced in its dealings.

I arranged a meeting with Jeff to discuss working together. Frankly, I had no way to tell in advance a good lawyer from a bad one. But I got a good gut feel from Jeff, and his high level of interest in this area, coupled with his experience, gave me the confidence to proceed.

Then the agony began. The logistics of negotiating a complicated contract by mail and phone proved to be quite frustrating. Although we were not far apart on the most substantive points of the contract, there were many areas worth clarifying. And all the while I had to fight my intense impulse to just sign anything so Sarah wouldn't change her mind. I felt like a negotiator without leverage.

But I have been on the other side of negotiations too. Everybody has *some* leverage, even if it's only an appeal to fairness. Like any business, United Media depends on the goodwill of the people they work with. My brain said I was safe. Besides, after a first reading of the original contract draft, we had "agreed to agree," and I

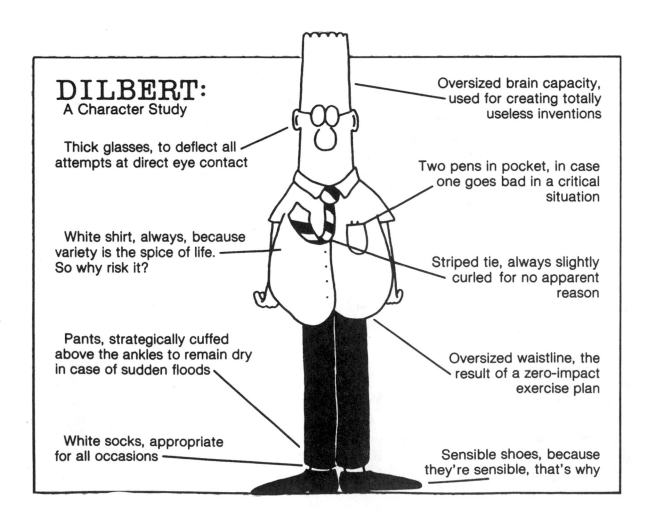

DILBERT:
A Character Study

Oversized brain capacity, used for creating totally useless inventions

Thick glasses, to deflect all attempts at direct eye contact

Two pens in pocket, in case one goes bad in a critical situation

White shirt, always, because variety is the spice of life. So why risk it?

Striped tie, always slightly curled for no apparent reason

Pants, strategically cuffed above the ankles to remain dry in case of sudden floods

Oversized waistline, the result of a zero-impact exercise plan

White socks, appropriate for all occasions

Sensible shoes, because they're sensible, that's why

was already working with Sarah informally with the expectation that the contract would fall into place.

More important than the contract was my feeling about the general trustworthiness of United Media. Ideally, neither of us should have to rely on the contract after it was completed. I asked for a reference from one of their newer artists. Sarah put me in touch with Pat Brady *(Rose Is Rose),* and Pat's unqualified recommendation supported the good impressions I was developing already by working with Sarah and her staff.

Eventually the contract was signed, and I think all parties were pleased with the result. I was glad I made the effort to negotiate the contract and become comfortable with it. And hiring a lawyer was a good move.

The Routine

I'm often asked how I find time to keep up with cartooning and still do my day job. My morning starts at four-thirty A.M., when I roll out of bed, hit the button on Mr. Coffee, and amble over to my drawing table. By five-thirty I've completed one penciled cartoon and two cups of coffee. Then it's shower, work all day, come home, buy dinner at the salad bar at Lucky's, eat, work out at the health club, and back to the drawing table for inking and other mechanical tasks. I leave the television on so I won't think I'm really working.

Then I go to bed and start over. On weekends I put in another ten to fifteen hours, much of that on the

DOGBERT:

Dogbert is a furry, egg-shaped sidekick who guides Dilbert and adds meaning to his life—the meaning of sarcasm, cynicism and snide humor. Any resemblance between Dogbert and any other creature, living or dead, is purely coincidental (and purely impossible).

dreaded Sunday strip. The rest of my life gets taken care of by skimping at one or more of the evening activities. (If I could just stop eating I should have enough time to squeeze in a social life.)

My real secret is the first hour of the morning. That's when I'm most creative. I wake up instantly but I stay relaxed. Everything seems clear and simple, yet off balance at the same time.

Humor is nothing more than ordinary situations slightly twisted. At four-thirty A.M., everything seems slightly twisted. That's when Dilbert and Dogbert talk to me. We split the writing responsibilities. I come up with the situations and they come up with the jokes. I usually don't know what the punch line will be until the last panel. Sometimes I think I know when I start, but I end up surprised.

About 90 percent of my strips are unplanned these days. The rest are crafted backward from punch lines that occur spontaneously in nature. For example, a coworker was reminiscing about the good old days and ended, "But I'm dating myself now." It occurred to me

that it was just as well, since nobody else would want to date him.

I do other things to nudge the creative process along. I never leave the house without a pen and some note cards to scribble down thoughts as they occur. The hardest things to capture are the thoughts I most often think. The little insecurities, emotions, and idiosyncrasies that make good cartoon fodder are so much a part of me they are often invisible. It's too easy to think in terms of objects and events, where humor is harder to find. I try hard to think about what I'm thinking about.

I also wrote a program for my computer to generate random silly sentences and combine unlikely objects and events. I stare at it for a while, which helps shake me out of the logical mode that I lock myself into during the day.

I think a lot about what makes a joke funny. I know a joke when I hear one, but I don't know why one joke is funnier than another. My theory is that there are only a hundred joke patterns in the universe and all of us jokesters are just filling out the patterns with differ-

ent characters in different situations. Beyond that, it's just instinct and trial and error.

Working with the Syndicate

Some people are surprised to hear that Dilbert was not invented by United Media to satisfy the vital "engineers-with-talking-dogs" demographic group. The syndicate does influence the direction of the strip but in ways that are quite compatible with my own creative needs.

The title of the strip, the basic characters, the concept, and all the jokes are mine. I draw rough art and send copies to Sarah at United Media for editing. Those that make the cuts, typically 70 to 90 percent of the submissions, are later inked and finished. I determine the order in which they will appear.

We have a good artist–editor relationship. Sarah doesn't tell me what jokes to write and I don't whine when she says they don't work. The editorial direction is mostly in a yes-or-no format, as opposed to suggesting specific creative changes to individual strips. Sarah has turned editing into its own art, constantly gener-

ating innovative ways to say "this one isn't funny" without actually causing me to burst into tears and stick my head in the oven.

Editing does have an important macro influence on the creative direction of the strip. For example, the frequency of appearance of some characters and the degree of risk I take with the humor is definitely influenced by which jokes made the cuts last time or, more importantly, which ones didn't. I haven't felt restricted by the editing process yet.

Fragile Fate

So that's the story of Dilbert. No matter how it turns out, it's been the highlight of my life so far. I often wonder what would have happened if my car hadn't broken down that winter night. Would I have moved to California and seen Jack Cassady's cartoon special on television? What if Jack had just thrown my letter away instead of writing back? And then writing again?

Thanks, Jud.

BILL AMEND AND *FOXTROT*

Story from Issue No. 84, December 1989

During the National Cartoonists Society convention in San Francisco in the spring of 1988, we had a chance to sit down with Bill Amend to talk about his strip *Fox Trot*, which he does for the Universal Press Syndicate, and about his career to date. Bill lives in Burlingame, California. Our conversation follows.

HURD: I know you've said that as a child you spent a lot of time reading *Iron Man* comic books and watching countless episodes of *The Wild, Wild West*. Then, when comic book prices soared to 40 cents an issue,

Bill Amend

you began drawing your own, featuring the invincible Super Monster and his archenemy, the dreaded Six-Gun Toad. Also in high school you did artwork for various school publications and made a number of short films, including the epic *Trek Wars*, a *Star Trek* meets *Star Wars* spoof. All these activities earned you Most Creative status in your senior class poll. Tell us more, Bill.

AMEND: My first big passion was a desire to be a filmmaker. I used a little Super-8 movie camera that Dad had gotten to shoot Christmas movies. After our family went to Disneyland when I was in seventh grade, I read everything I could lay my hands on about Disney and about cartooning, with the result that later on in high school I took a filmmaking class in which the final project was making your own movie. A couple of classmates and I made an animated film, using clay, toy rubber monsters, various G.I. Joe figures, and so on.

HURD: You went in several different directions in college at Amherst, didn't you?

AMEND: Yes. With filmmaking in mind I thought I'd major in English or drama, and I did take a number of drama courses my first year. But I didn't feel I was learning anything good and solid. Then, that spring, I took a physics course, and since I'd always been mathematically inclined, I loved that.

HURD: Did you have any formal art training either in high school or college?

AMEND: I took an art course my freshman year in high school, and at back-to-school night my teacher told my parents she thought I was going to be a cartoonist someday. Then—to jump ahead a bit—I took a basic drawing class during my senior year at Amherst, and about this time I began to think seriously about pursuing cartooning as a career. The professor hated me because I would make a very careful sketch of the human body in the life class and then top it off with a funny caricatured head.

HURD: What started you on the road to becoming a syndicated cartoonist?

AMEND: All four years at Amherst I did an editorial panel for the college newspaper, which came out twice a week. And over those four years I began to get better at cartooning, to the point where I thought maybe I'd have a chance to make it a career. So in 1983, during the summer between my junior and senior year, I decided to try a comic strip. I drew up about a week's

worth of strips, sent them off to syndicates, and got some rejections, but one note said, *This is pretty good but send more.* As a result, after college I decided to postpone a serious job search in favor of spending three or four months trying to develop this strip I'd started, *Bango Ridge.* It was about an animal psychologist who goes off to Bango Ridge in the jungle to study animals, and it turns out that most of them are more human than he is. They're running around with Michael Jackson records, and you can imagine what else was involved in that kind of a scene. Again, I got a bunch of rejections but a couple of these were encouraging rejections, if there is such a thing. At this point I decided to try a second comic strip. Meanwhile I got a job doing animation here in San Francisco for a couple of months, working on some commercials and a music video as an in-betweener. Following that I went with a new movie production facility in San Francisco, which involved a lot of administrative work and not much hands-on opportunity. So I developed my sec-

ond strip, *Fox Trot,* and sent it off in January of 1986. It was rejected by various syndicates, but David Seidman of the Los Angeles Times Syndicate called me, said the strip was good, and wanted to see additional samples. He liked the writing but felt my art needed work. After a while Lee Salem of Universal Press Syndicate also became interested, and a year later, in the fall of 1987, Universal brought me to Kansas City and offered me a contract.

HURD: Would you clarify this sequence of events a bit?

AMEND: My first submission of *FoxTrot* went to a number of syndicates simultaneously. They all sent rejection slips except David Seidman, who wanted more samples. So I did another batch for him but also sent this second bunch of samples to all the other syndicates. In other words, every time I did more samples, they went to all the syndicates. This procedure, as I mentioned a moment ago, eventually led Lee Salem and Universal to decide to take the strip on. After I'd sent out about three batches to everyone, I had a note

Cartoon Success Secrets

from Lee Salem's secretary, saying that he'd like to see still more, maybe a couple of dozen strips. Following this Lee wrote me a long letter, going over some of the concerns the syndicate had, what they thought the strong points and the weak points of the strip were. Later he had to be out in San Francisco, so I had a chance to talk with him here about what needed to be done.

HURD: What were some of the syndicates' concerns?

AMEND: The strip had sort of an ensemble cast of five family members, and the syndicate was afraid that readers would get lost trying to follow each one and would be confused as to who was who. I hadn't really wanted to focus on just one of them—to make that character a star character. But they wanted me to try it and see if it would work. Later I did narrow things down to two characters, but they felt it lost something in the process so we went back to the original arrangement. I had taken the drastic step of just going with the daughter, Paige, and the little boy, Jason, and it was purely a sibling-relationship strip at that point.

HURD: What was it that most interested Universal in *FoxTrot*?

AMEND: I think the strong part of the strip from their perspective was that it has a very contemporary setting—it contains a lot of the trappings of our times. You'll see a lot of Coke cans around, *Wheel of Fortune* will be on the TV, and there'll be evidence of 1989 paraphernalia everywhere. That probably separates it from other family strips. Universal had some criticism pertaining to the early strips because they didn't show much movement of the camera or the viewpoint. They were very static, so we've been trying to intersperse some different camera angles as we go along. I was reluctant to do this early on because I felt it might detract from the writing. But I've been getting better at camera angles and have discovered that there are ways you can help the humor with these variations.

HURD: How do you go about producing ideas?

AMEND: I drink a lot of coffee and hope my brain will vibrate enough so ideas will pop out. Seriously, I just try to be observant—the world's full of humor—little nuggets of funny situations wherever you go, and this is particularly true when you're doing a family strip. I suppose that for about 50 percent of the strips I depend on some sort of blurred memory of my family: things that happened, recollections of how I felt at different times, and so on.

HURD: Do you have a set routine in producing your week's output?

AMEND: I write much better in the morning. I try to set aside an entire week each month as just a writing week. Then I do the month's art in the remaining three weeks. I have difficulty drawing while I'm trying to think of ideas. I'd rather concentrate on one of these tasks at a time.

HURD: What's your writing routine like?

AMEND: I start out with a clean yellow legal pad and begin scribbling down a two- or three-word description of some idea that may work, such as the birthday of one of the characters, back to school, or a family vacation. I may do a dozen of these in ten minutes, and they get the brain wheels going along the line of an isolated strip or of a whole week of strips on the same subject. I then write my dialogue, without any pictures; the results look almost like a movie script. Previously I have Xeroxed sheets with the outlines of the four panels indicated. I write the dialogue in each panel and make rough sketches of the characters involved. Finally I send a batch of these to Lee Salem and Jack Morrissey at the syndicate. Then maybe a week later I'll get back a *yes*, or a *no*, or a *maybe* from them. Occasionally they'll have a brief comment on several of the ideas, maybe suggest a word change or something like that.

HURD: Some cartoonists like to hear what kind of pens their colleagues use. How about it?

AMEND: Early on it was suggested that my lines were too thin and weak and I ought to vary them in weight. I started out drawing the strip with pen and ink, but that requires a very steady hand and it meant drinking no coffee, so I've switched to an Osmiroid fountain pen. I use what they call a sketch tip. It seems to be flexible enough to get some heavier lines in my strips, and it's firm enough so that it doesn't splatter.

HURD: I think you said, when you were at Amherst drawing for the college newspaper and were the star cartoonist, that drawing a strip would be easy. Have you found that to be true?

AMEND: No. I'm working nine to nine, practically seven days a week. My girlfriend hates me because she never sees me. I hope sometime to be able to manage everything in six days.

Let's go back for a moment to your question about my method of getting ideas. Every Sunday night I'm with our church's high school group, which includes twenty-five or thirty young people, and although obviously I don't do it in order to get strip ideas, it's a wonderful source of material for me. I get a chance to talk with teenagers in a general social sense, can see what they're wearing, hear what's going on at school, what their interests are, et cetera. Of the hour-and-a-half meeting, only about half is structured time, the other half is for games and chitchat. The kids are very interested in how the whole comic strip process works, and often one of the group will say, "Do a strip with me in it!" The subjects of the meetings deal with some of the problems in the lives of young people: how to deal with stress, with peer pressure, with drugs. The youth pastor at our church will ordinarily give a short talk and then we break up into small groups for discussion.

HURD: Good luck with *FoxTrot*, Bill!

Bob Weber and *Moose & Molly*

Story from Issue No. 96, December 1992

A description of Bob Weber's workweek is a whirl-wind example of what has made him a successful cartoonist. For almost forty years, he's been writing and drawing the comic strip *Moose & Molly* daily and Sunday for King Features. And his wasn't the usual case of a cartoonist anxiously trying to sell a feature to a syndicate. Instead, legendary King Comics Editor Sylvan Byck had seen his gag cartoons in the *Saturday Evening Post* and other magazines and tried to sell *Bob* on the idea of doing a strip for King.

Nowadays, he also works with his son, Bob Jr., on the very popular King strip *Comics for Kids,* featuring Slylock Fox.

And, if that's not enough, he does frequent chalk talks for kids at schools and libraries.

HURD: First of all, Bob, would you describe the characters in *Moose* for the benefit of those readers who may not see your strip regularly?

WEBER: Sure. Moose Miller, the head of the family, is the main character. He has a wife, Molly, and they have three children—two small ones and a teenage boy. There are also a lot of animals involved in the strip. What makes it easy for me to do a strip like *Moose* is the fact that he's very lazy. My own mother had nine children, and if you'd stopped her on the street and asked her, "Who's your laziest child?" she would say, "Robert!" So the personality of Moose is a lot like mine.

HURD: It's hard to picture you as lazy, considering the energy you display in running around to all those book sales, seminars, and lectures, but I'll take your word for it that you're like Moose when you're around the house.

WEBER: Molly is the kind of wife that every husband would like to have. She doesn't find any fault with Moose, although he has lots of them. Even though he

doesn't have a job, she doesn't urge him to go out and find one—that's left to his mother-in-law. Molly waits on Moose hand and foot, so I suppose I'd like to be in his position myself. Naturally, she acts as the straight woman on whom Moose can bounce a gag. Neither of them tries to destroy the other with any comments—I save these for the mother-in-law! Moose has a thick skin, so he's not destroyed by these cracks by Granny.

Moose has a very messy yard, lots of animals, tall grass, and a garage full of junk, and his yard is the only one in the neighborhood like it. He lives next door to a man who's just the opposite. That's Chester Crabtree, who has a very neat yard and hates Moose and all he stands for. Moose will end up in Chester's swimming pool when his neighbor isn't looking, and all the animals will be found in it too. Moose can also sometimes be seen in Chester's house, raiding the refrigerator.

The Moose world consists of his occasionally looking (not too hard) for a job, finding one, and losing it by messing up within a few days. Being out of work a lot, at home, he spends much time involved with Chester.

HURD: Speaking of the book sales I mentioned a moment ago, I run into you at every one that's held anywhere in the Westport area. And I know you make more effort than the average cartoonist does to attend every lecture, seminar, or public appearance of anyone having any relationship to our business. So I'm wondering whether you do this in order to help you come up with as many cartoon ideas as possible.

WEBER: I do this not so much to keep the ideas flowing as to keep excited. I like to know as much about every phase of cartooning as I can. I also scan the newspapers; as a case in point, here's what developed from an item I saw recently in the *Hartford Courant.* The paper tells you who's coming to town and where, and last Saturday I read that a cartoonist, Ellis Pyle, whom I'd never heard of, was going to appear at the Cel Market in New Haven, next to the Shubert Theater. The announcement said he'd been an animator for Disney, worked on *Pinocchio,* and was going to appear from eleven to four. Normally, I have lunch on Saturday with a bunch of cartoonists, and when we were about to break up at five-fifteen, I could have given up, figuring that Pyle would no longer be at the Cel Market, since it was past four. But I decided to try, picked up the phone, dialed New Haven, said I was in Westport (about forty-five minutes from New Haven), and wondered if the animator would be there for another hour or so. They said, "Come on up!" Jerry Marcus was with me, so we jumped in the car, headed for New Haven, and soon discovered what a fascinating story the animator had to tell. He had gone to Disney in 1937, had worked with Sam Cobean, Virgil Partch, Hank Ketcham, Ed Nofziger, and others. We learned that after the war Cobean had gone to New York, begun to work for *The New Yorker,* and suggested that maybe Pyle would like to do the same. Well, Pyle didn't become a *New Yorker* artist, but he opened an animation studio that has been in operation for the past thirty-some years. During the time we spent with him that day, we heard lots of fascinating stories.

From time to time when I mention an event like this to fellow cartoonists, I often find they'll shrug off various happenings that I usually go to on a whim.

HURD: I admire your enthusiasm. It goes far beyond what one expects from people.

WEBER: As I get older, I still get excited, and I like to think I'm a better cartoonist now than I was ten years ago *because* of experiences such as I've just mentioned. All of a sudden, animation really fascinates me. I study more cels, more drawings from the various animation studios, and observe carefully how different characters and backgrounds are drawn. I really think my own drawing is being uplifted because of this enthusiasm. Also—since, as you know, I teach so many groups in so many places—I get a certain pleasure in telling the kids to do the same things I do. If they're interested in cartooning or children's book illustration, I'll tell them, "Watch the paper and have your mom or dad arrange for you to sit in the audience if an illustrator comes to town and talks in your local library." I remember that the sports cartoonist for a Baltimore newspaper told me, when I was seventeen, "You can learn from everybody. Whether better than you are, not as good, or whatever, he or she is going to know something you don't know, and you can constantly learn from these people."

HURD: What kinds of books are you usually picking up at all these book sales I mentioned at the beginning of our conversation?

WEBER: Generally, I'm looking for books about cartoonists and cartooning. Naturally, when I look through

them, I might get some ideas, but that's incidental to my main purpose.

HURD: Would you say something about the methods you use to come up with the constant need for new *Moose* ideas?

WEBER: Sometimes flipping through a magazine will produce something. *Moose* likes to spend a lot of time at the refrigerator, as you know. Recently I noticed a drawing showing somebody partially *in* a refrigerator, and I built a whole gag around this. In my strip, the mother is saying to the mother-in-law, "I'm looking for Moose. He's not in the cellar, he's not in the attic,

he's not in the backyard, not in the garage!" Mother-in-law replies, *"He's in the refrigerator!"* When I was a kid my mother would say, "Get out of the refrigerator!" Well, none of us were really *in* it, but you know what I mean.

I use many different methods—I like working alone, and I also really get a kick out of working *with* someone, as you've told me that Johnny Hart does. That other person may suggest something, and I'll say, "Yeah, that's it!" Then, when the colleague sees what I've done, he may come up with a slightly different version on top of mine, and it will make my idea even better. My ideas always seem to be better if I work *with* someone. Although occasionally one of the cartoonists at our lunches will jot down some remark that has been made, in order to convert it later into a usable idea, I seldom get ideas at these times. I usually have to be in a working mode to produce anything.

I've worked with a number of cartoonists, and really started doing this with magazine cartoonist Orlando Busino about thirty years ago in New York City. At

that time we might have begun with a theme, or one of us might randomly have said something like "man overboard in a diving suit." He had a pad and pencil in front of him, I had the same, and each of us began sketching his own version. I knew he was trying to come up with something, which was a challenge for me, and the competition brought results for both of us. We compared ideas. I might think of something that would make his idea better, and he might come up with something to improve mine. Obviously, each of us would hope to end up with different gags, which each of us could sell independently. Working by myself, as I frequently do, I may look at another gag and try to think of either a switch or a variation. This is pretty stimulating. I have lots of cartoon collections that have been published over the years, so there are plenty of examples with which to try the switching I've just mentioned.

HURD: Please tell our readers how you came to be doing the *Moose Miller* comic strip for King Features.

WEBER: It's a long story. I came to New York in 1959, and my style really hadn't taken shape. I was very fortunate in eventually living across the street from Orlando Busino, who was a selling cartoonist at that time. This was in Hollis, Long Island. I had met him when I'd come up occasionally from Baltimore, where I'd grown up. He was nice enough to invite my wife and me out to his house to meet his wife, and while we were there, he suggested, "Why don't you move up to New York and be a cartoonist?" Shortly after that Orlando called us at our home back in Baltimore, during which he mentioned that there was an apartment available right across the street in Hollis. We took the apartment. I can't say enough about how beneficial this meeting was for me professionally. It was like going to college. Here I was just getting started, and right across the street from me was a terrific established professional! He didn't have a car, nor did I, so if we needed anything we'd walk to the store, talking shop both ways.

HURD: How far had you gotten with your cartooning before your arrival at the Businos in 1959?

WEBER: Back in 1953, when I was eighteen years old, I had attended the school that later became the present School of Visual Arts in New York City. A bout with pneumonia took me back to Baltimore, where I began selling to the trade journals. But I had only developed to a certain point and my work didn't have a really professional look. But in 1959, when my association with Busino began, I commenced to make the Wednesday rounds to the various magazines that bought cartoons and was lucky enough to make a sale to the *Saturday Evening Post* on my first trip. This was a fluke, but the

cartoon editor thought the gag was funny. A lot of cartoonists who were much more talented than I'll ever be would give up, after they had come to New York expecting to sell very well and discovered that they weren't living up to their expectations. My philosophy was different. I kinda thought I might succeed, but I also knew I might not, so I was prepared *not* to sell all that well. I was prepared to wait it out. I didn't sell the *Post* for another year, but in the meantime I was selling a bunch of trade journals and smaller magazines.

HURD: The late magazine cartoonist Stan Stamaty once told me he actually got to the point where he wasn't crestfallen when he didn't sell a market, because the

editor would sometimes tell him what was wrong with a cartoon, and Stan would later enter this criticism in a little notebook and remember not to make that same mistake again.

WEBER: I like that thinking, because I also apply it to other things. I will get turned down and learn from the experience. I'm not easily destroyed by turndowns. I tell my classes, "It's nice to be talented, but those of you who aren't should know that what will *really* help you to succeed is *drive!* This is even more important than the talent.

HURD: I realize I've led you astray from my original question about how you came to be doing *Moose Miller* for King Features.

WEBER: For the first year and a half, beginning in 1959, I didn't sell that much to the majors, but for some reason I started selling regularly to King Features' *Laff-a-Day* panel. At one point, several weeks had gone by, I was owed for three panels, and I needed the money. When I phoned King to ask the reason for the delay, the young lady put me through to Sylvan Byck, who was the most prominent syndicate comics editor in the business. He said he'd expedite my payment and asked my name. When I gave it to him, he said, "You notice that we've been buying your cartoons quite regularly." When I told him I'd been pleased about that, he continued, "You have a very funny style, and if you ever think about drawing a comic strip, we'd certainly like to see it." You can imagine how that comment from somebody like Sylvan Byck completely knocked me out! But I didn't feel I was quite ready.

Two or three years later a writer at King asked me to do the drawing for a strip he'd written. The strip was rejected by Sylvan, but the writer told me that Byck was really enthusiastic about my cartoons. So I waited about a year and a half and submitted a strip of my own called *Bunky,* which was also rejected. Another year went by and I thought to myself, Maybe Sylvan will be interested in *Bunky* this time. I was afraid to show it to him in person so I left it with his secretary. When I went back the following week, I was told by the secretary that my strip had been rejected but that Byck wanted to see me. As I sat down in his office he said, "You know, I saw this a year ago, and I haven't changed my mind about *Bunky.* I like your work, but I suggest you go home and do another comic strip and bring it in and show it to me." If he hadn't encouraged me, I might have waited still another year before I tried again. But with this impetus, I went home, and within a couple of weeks I had formulated the idea for *Moose.* To show you how anxious I was to have Byck see what I'd done as soon as possible, I drove to the post office in deep snow to send him my idea. I had just done an outline for a strip, naming the characters and what was expected of each one, along with a sketch of him or her.

I hadn't actually done any strips with this submission, so naturally Sylvan asked to see some. I did nine strips, and a week later he called and said, "Bob, we're going to buy this idea. We like it." This was in 1964, but King had just bought Bud Blake's *Tiger* strip, so they decided to wait a year before introducing *Moose.*

HURD: Did Sylvan make any suggestions for changes in the strip?

WEBER: Yes, he didn't like the name *Benny Buttons* that I had given it. He asked me to come up with a hundred names, at which time he and I would sit down and pick out the best one. After looking at all our selections, we circled *Jake, Gus,* and *Moose.* I said, "Let's go with *Gus.*" The syndicate took publicity pictures of me sitting at the board with a huge drawing I'd made of the character with the name *Gus* prominently displayed. After a couple of weeks I decided I preferred *Moose* and suggested the change to Byck. I think he was a little afraid that readers would connect the strip with all the Loyal Order of Moose lodges around the country, but after consulting with the president of King, he gave his OK to the switch.

I had thought that, since *Moose* was lazy, he might be the type of guy to go to a bar and have a drink. I did one gag on this theme but Sylvan told me, "We're not going to use this gag. I'd rather that he *not* be in a bar." Maybe he thought the strip might become too closely associated with *Andy Capp,* since Andy was always at the bar. In the beginning, Sylvan was very much against the character Chester Crabtree. Probably he was right, because *Moose* was a very happy-type strip, and all of a sudden I brought in this very violent man. When he first came into the strip, he was very mean, very violent, and Sylvan was upset when he saw this fellow screaming all the time. He didn't insist that I eliminate the character, so I didn't. Chester has softened some over the years, but he's still upset with Moose.

HURD: I know you wanted to say a word or two about readers who write letters when you've disturbed them one way or another.

WEBER: Yes. One has to be careful. I remember doing a strip in which a dog on a leash, tied to a tree, had wrapped himself around the trunk so far he couldn't reach his food. That brought a letter from a reader who thought I was being cruel. On another occasion, I had some kittens in the strip and showed one of them being slipped into the mailman's pouch without his being aware of it. A follower of the strip pointed out that I should have shown the animal being given to someone who would love it, not sent off to who knows what fate.

HURD: I can't resist kidding you, as many cartoonists have done, about your tendency to work too close to the deadline. I recall friends telling me they'd seen you walking up a ramp in Grand Central Station, on your

way to King Features, and stopping at one point to finish up the inking on one of your strips.

WEBER: I can tell you of one instance worse than that. One time I was driving to New York to deliver strips, and every time I stopped for a red light I'd grab my board and continue inking till the light changed. Pulling up in front of King, I still wasn't finished inking, so my brother, sitting beside me, would dry the ink with matches. I wouldn't believe it if you told me something like this about another cartoonist.

On the occasion you mentioned in Grand Central, I was spread out on a marble slab, inking and putting in the blacks, so I had sheets all over the place. People coming up from the subways would bunch up behind me, because I looked as though I was getting something ready to sell. I had a growth of beard, because I'd been up all night trying to make headway on my strips. Nowadays I'm in better shape deadline-wise, simply because, as I've gotten older, I can't physically go through the routine I often followed in years gone by.

HURD: Readers of *CARTOONIST PROfiles* know of your son Bob Jr.'s *Comics for Kids* Sunday page, which is scheduled also to become a daily. You've been helping him occasionally with his feature, haven't you?

WEBER: Yes. He does all the writing—he created the comic strip—and asked me if I'd work with him. I agreed and have found it a joy to do. He'll call me in from time to time to illustrate one part of the feature. On other occasions I may illustrate a different section. The feature draws quite a bit of mail, I'm happy to say. To tell you the truth, I think this experience is making me a better cartoonist because he'll give me an assignment that may well be more difficult than one I'd give myself, so it's a challenge.

HURD: I know you teach a number of cartoon classes for young people. Let's hear something about that project.

WEBER: I really started teaching some years ago at the Smithsonian in Washington, when I lived in Baltimore. A few years ago, Orlando Busino told me that

Cartoon Success Secrets

the Ridgefield, Connecticut, YMCA was looking for a cartoonist to teach a class for kids. That started me off. Next, the Westport YMCA asked me if I'd add an afternoon class here in town. Darien and New Canaan followed, as did Wilton. I'm now doing this five days a week, but each class lasts just an hour. It pleases me that the kids are interested in cartooning, and I like showing them shortcuts which, if I'd had them when I was a boy, would have saved me several years of work in learning them.

HURD: What advice do you give young people who want to get into cartooning?

WEBER: I'm really torn when I'm asked this question. I don't have an art education background—I don't know anything about anatomy. I realize that if you're interested in animation, it's necessary to know anatomy.

For my style of cartooning, my background has been OK. When I was coming up in our profession, I admired a lot of cartoonists and did a little bit of copying, but if I were starting over, I'd do a whole lot more copying. If, let's say, you copy the way Mort Walker draws a chair, a certain amount of that sticks with you. Or you may copy the way in which another cartoonist handles a walking character. But be sure and copy a great variety of cartoonists. To this day, when a new cartoonist comes along, I'm still interested and love to study the way in which he or she gets different effects. Incidentally, if you want to become a sports cartoonist, it's *essential* to know anatomy.

HURD: Thanks, Bob, for talking about so many different aspects of your career.

RAY BILLINGSLEY AND *CURTIS*

Story from Issue No. 101, March 1994

In December 1993 we had a long and interesting talk with Ray Billingsley, the cartoonist who sparked the public's interest in black strips, first with his *Lookin' Fine* for United Feature Syndicate and currently with the popular *Curtis* strip for King Features. Our first surprise, on the day we talked, was to discover that Ray had become a professional cartoonist at age twelve!

HURD: I know there have been several ways by which you've been able to get your creative corpuscles going during your cartoon career, Ray. What's the current one?

BILLINGSLEY: Right now it seems to be music. I sit quietly, play some music, preferably jazz as performed by all the greats, and just let my mind wander. For relaxing I've got a wonderful chair. It looks as though it's right out of the old TV show *Dynasty,* it's so huge.

Curtis

by Ray Billingsley

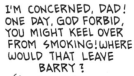

All my friends love it. I just sit there for a while and let the ideas stream over me. Before I know it, there's something I can pick up. A situation will pop up that maybe I can use. During this relaxing process, I may think of something that actually happened the other day, or something I saw on the news that interested me, or I may recall an interesting conversation I had. As far as the news is concerned, I have to be sure that readers' interest is likely to last for at least six weeks, because that's how far ahead of the *Curtis* publication date that I have to work. Some potential strip ideas that stream over me date from my own childhood, my past. Eventually the flowing of these images seems to produce ideas that will work.

HURD: Do you make an effort to read a considerable variety of publications?

BILLINGSLEY: Oh, yes, that's really the only way a cartoonist can stay current. I get a few out-of-town papers, and for a little while I even bought a London paper just to keep up with what's happening over there. I read a Vancouver paper too, and in all these journals I pay particular attention to the Letters to the Editor columns. People write in about their concerns and express their feelings on all kinds of matters. Many times I can salvage ideas from reading these letters. You find out what's on the minds of people, what's bothering them. But I have to make sure that *everyone* can relate to whatever strip ideas I come up with. Naturally, the problems here in New York aren't exactly the same ones that concern people in Vancouver. I read a lot of magazines, some science fiction, and the *New York Times,* and I try to stay abreast of everything.

HURD: Many cartoonists have reported that various members of their families were natural gagmen, ready with a quip for any situation. Has that been true in your family?

BILLINGSLEY: Oh, yes. Both of my parents were stand-up comedians—not in the sense that they went out and performed at clubs but rather in the family. If my brother, my sister, or I complained about the way a certain meal turned out or asked, "What is this you're putting in front of us, Mom?" she'd come back with "It's Maggot Stew. Eat up." She'd say this with a straight face, very calmly. So obviously humor began with my parents. They came up during very hard times—we were all in the South, in Wake Forest, North Carolina. My father was originally from Alabama. He came along during a time when there was still separatism, racism, and it was a rough time for him. So I think he developed his humor (and the same was true for my mother) to help cope with the times.

My older brother, Richard, was the number-one push in my life. He gave me the competitive edge at a very young age. I was about eight years old when it all started. He was a fine artist; he could draw portraits and still lifes perfectly. I used to see all the praise he was getting. He's eight years my senior, so when I was eight, he was sixteen already. But I didn't realize I was competing with a much older person, I was just competing. I started doing fine art, but I noticed that most of the response I got was laughter. People were laughing at my work, which wasn't exactly what I was looking for. So at that early age I switched to cartooning. I started to draw characters with big bulbous noses, fat squishy feet. All these things seemed to click together, and at age twelve I turned professional. I had read quite a bit about other cartoonists. I want to say that Mort Walker is one of the men I've really admired, because I discovered that he also started when he was about eleven.

It was always a battle to get people who bought artwork to look at my stuff, but at the time I didn't think of it that way. I was contending with grown-up artists for the same space, and many times I did win out. I used little tricks to get to an art director's office. I'd put my portfolio in a large manila envelope and tell the studio receptionist that the art director had to sign for it. In those days everything was a little more lax, and the secretary would often let me through. When I got into the inner sanctum, I'd take my portfolio out and show it to the art director. They seemed to think I had a lot of heart by succeeding with my little ruse, and I got a lot of jobs that way. I guess it's a mixture of a certain amount of talent, luck and perseverance, and just plain buttin-skyness!

Here's a little story for you: I was twelve years old and my art class was into recycling even in those days. My art teacher was quite creative, and we were constructing a fifteen-foot aluminum-can Christmas tree outside a hospital. There was a small amount of media coverage of this project, so while the other kids were busy with the tree, I sat on the side, took out a pad, and started drawing. A woman approached me and asked

to look at my efforts. She asked if she could keep the drawing and wanted my name and phone number, so I gave it to her. Back in that time I figured that since I was only twelve years old she wasn't hitting on me. A couple of days later the woman called my home, and it turned out she was the editor of *Kids* magazine! She asked if I would come down to her office and do some sketches. Believe it or not, they liked my drawing and hired me as a staff artist. From that day on, there would be a car waiting for me as I was about to leave school, and I'd be taken to the *Kids* office. This was from about three-thirty to five-thirty P.M., Monday through Friday, and I took work home on weekends.

HURD: I'm sure your parents were extra pleased about this development.

BILLINGSLEY: Oh, yes, the job kept me out of trouble, and they knew where I was. My mind was concentrated on my job, while my buddies out on the street were interested only in playing basketball or baseball. I can still see this difference in direction. At so many of the schools and universities I visit, the kids come up to me and say they want to be a basketball or rap star. They aren't aware of the type of future they could have in cartooning. They may not want to do the hard work, because I always tell them that cartooning is not a job for the squeamish. If you don't have the stomach for it, do not try it, because you will just wind up with a lot of heartache. When I was growing up, a lot of my friends thought I was some sort of nerd because I didn't do anything they did. I told them I was thinking of the future, but they just couldn't get the idea. Kids should work their minds more. They're looking for easy ways to make a living, but that easy money is not out there in journalism. I've met kids who've said they'd only do a comic strip if they could do one just as they wanted to with no outside interference. I've told them they'd better stay out of our business, because we all have editors.

Cartoon Success Secrets

HURD: You went to the well-known High School of Music and Art in New York City, didn't you, Ray?

BILLINGSLEY: Yes, but as time went on I didn't spend full time there. Two friends, Richard Klein, who was the principal, and Eugene Wexler, my college counselor, gave me a big push. I got special permission to be absent from school during the times I was working on professional assignments in connection with my cartoon work. I was doing a lot of independent study also, because the school gave me homework assignments for when I was at work on advertising projects or storyboards for art studios. I was very fortunate to have a lot of adults on my side. During the time I was at Music and Art, cartooning was not considered serious work. I was told by many people, "Ray, when are you going to grow up?" Little did they realize that I was already being published. Probably I had been published more than my art teachers had.

HURD: After high school you got a full four-year scholarship to the School of Visual Arts in New York City, didn't you?

BILLINGSLEY: Yes. This is a very competitive school—very hard—but I loved that drive. I was there from 1975 to 1979.

HURD: I guess I should ask you to describe the characters in your *Curtis* comic strip, which is distributed by King Features.

BILLINGSLEY: The title character, Curtis, is an eleven-year-old mischievous city youth. He's a kid who's open to a lot of ideas, and he loves music a little too much—to his parents' dismay. He's into his family and into his friends, and he's got a love affair going with a girl named Michelle, who doesn't like him. She's really the little spoiled girl of the strip. Her father is half owner of a record company, and I guess you could say she's stuck on herself. She's a singer for the church choir but she's sort of a deep character with a few problems. Her parents are divorced. Her mother is somewhere in France; Michelle doesn't even know where. Her father often leaves her for days at a time, traveling to promote his new groups. She appears rather hard-crusted, but there are lot of reasons for her attitude.

Then there's Chutney, the other girl in the strip, who loves Curtis. She's a spicy type of girl—just like the relish. She's very outgoing and has no trouble telling Curtis how she feels. She's independent and sweet as an angel, until Curtis tries to use her. When that happens, she can become a holy hellion.

One of the thorns in Curtis's side is his little brother, Barry. Barry is eight years old and a nosybody. He's the type that will sneak over to the extension, when Curtis is on the phone, listen in, and then try to blackmail Curtis later. I get a lot of mail on Barry—people really like this character. I guess he's a little more complex than I thought he was. I just wanted him to be a little nuisance with an angel face. He gets away with things with adults because he's so cute. But Curtis knows how bad the real Barry can be!

I get mail from people who identify with all these characters. It's so weird. I even had a Gunk fan club for a while—I don't know whether it's still out there or not. There was a group of students who liked the character Gunk, who comes from Flyspeck Island, which is at the northeastern tip of the Bermuda Triangle. We don't see the island because it's usually clouded over and has escaped detection. It's almost a paradise. Gunk is visiting the United States. I guess you'd call him sort of a foreign exchange student, since he came here to go to school. He's always talking about things that happened on Flyspeck Island. Basically I use him as a storyteller, especially if I'm trying to get a moral across. Gunk is one of the easygoing characters in the strip. Nothing seems to faze him, he has a charming and engaging personality, and he's become Curtis's best friend.

HURD: Tell me a little more about how you use this character and this island from time to time to get your point across.

BILLINGSLEY: There are certain unique things about Flyspeck Island, such as its soil, which is the most fertile in the world. Anything organic that you plant in it will grow. Gunk has brought a packet of Flyspeck Island soil to the States with him, and it doesn't mix well with American soil. I did a sequence where just a pinch was added to an ivy plant: the clinging ivy started growing like wildfire, and Curtis was in danger of being suffocated. So Gunk had to battle the plant to save Curtis. With this sequence I was trying to get over the following point: If we Americans latch on to something, especially if it's a natural resource, we tend to overdo it. We keep taking and taking until it's almost destroyed. It only takes a pinch of Flyspeck Island soil to make things grow. The trouble started when Curtis added more than he needed out of greed. This symbolizes the American tendency to take more than we should. And the results are often catastrophic.

HURD: You're quite a storyteller, Ray. Where did this ability come from?

BILLINGSLEY: I haven't thought much about it, but some of it may come from my dad, who worked for the Metropolitan Transit Authority in New York City at one point. He came in contact with lots of strange characters every day, and he'd come home and tell us about these occurrences. He spun these tales in such a fascinating way that we kids loved to sit there and be entertained. And of course my mother urged us to read. She'd hand us a book and say, "Read that and let me hear what you think of it afterward." Since we were from the South and a tightly knit family, we depended on one another for our warmth, our closeness, and our solace. We could talk about any problem, and it would always become a family matter. It sounds sort of dull, but it worked. Also, because I'd become a professional artist at such an early age, both family and school authorities cooperated in seeing that I got to and from my responsibilities safely.

HURD: Here's an interesting question. Why is it that the *Daily News* in New York City runs the Sunday *Curtis* but not the dailies?

BILLINGSLEY: The *News* has been subscribing to the *Curtis* dailies since the strip started, but hasn't actually run a single one. They've told me they have to wait for space and that a strip has to be dropped to make room for *Curtis*. At one point there *was* a strip dropped, and of course, all of us went tumbling for that spot. Rick Detorie's *One Big Happy* got the nod on that occasion. I was almost promised that space, but that's the way the business goes. (Author's Note: In 2003, *Curtis* appears in the *News* daily and Sunday.)

HURD: I guess we got sidetracked from your descriptions of the characters in *Curtis*. Who else is there?

BILLINGSLEY: There's Gunther, the barber. He started out as a one-note character; he seemed to be just a perennial liar. That's the way my own barber was. Once he told me he had discovered some diamond mine in Harlem and nobody would believe him! Gunther has become one of the main characters—he's a lot meatier now and not just a liar. He comments on social hap-

penings, just as real-life barbers do. He's become something like a second father to Curtis, who comes to him with problems.

Greg and Diana, whom I just named recently, are Curtis's parents. These two were examples of how public interest can motivate a cartoonist to do something. When *Curtis* first started there were no parents in the strip. But Paul Hendrix, one of the editors at King Features, told me I had to introduce parents because people would be asking about them. Up to this point I was just developing kid characters. Curtis's father made his appearance, but I didn't know what his face looked like, so I did what many other cartoonists have done: I either had his face off-screen or I had words covering it. When the strip first started, I hadn't even thought about Curtis's mother—her personality hadn't hit me yet. But as time went along, people started asking for these characters. "What do they look like? I want to see them." So, a year into the strip, I finally introduced the parents. They took off right away, I got a lot of mail on them and people said they loved them. They've gone from being secondary characters to becoming major characters. Curtis's father is a heavy smoker, and Curtis is always trying to discourage this habit. He'll use any means necessary—he'll walk up and take the cigarette out of his father's mouth; he'll squirt his dad with a water gun—you name it. But of course even these methods aren't enough to discourage the hard-core smoker, so it's a continuing battle.

HURD: I know *Curtis* gets quite a lot of fan mail. Do you answer a lot of it?

BILLINGSLEY: I try to answer all the letters, but it may take me a couple of weeks. Of course, one has to be careful about people asking for originals, because there are some slickers out there. I remember getting a request via a letter scrawled with a thick child's crayon, but it contained words only an adult would use. Cartoonists who have given originals have sometimes discovered them later on sale at cartoon shows.

HURD: I've heard that you have students you help through the mails. How does that work?

BILLINGSLEY: I do this with about twenty-five of them. The kids write in and ask me for advice, which I give them, which prompts another letter, and so on. In this way we build up a correspondence, and I now have about twenty-five steady kids. Some of them are starting to get published in their hometowns—one kid ecstatically sent me a tearsheet of his comic strip from his local newspaper. He credited some of the pointers I had given him, and that makes me feel really good.

HURD: I know you always have a number of projects in mind. What's the latest?

BILLINGSLEY: Well, I'm the coauthor of a play called *Precious Memories,* which is scheduled to open in Lincoln Center on December 28, 1994. As for other projects, I'm working on two books larger in format than two previous ones I've done for Ballantine. And I'm also storyboarding an animated special involving Curtis. I want it to have real substance and not be something people will dismiss quickly. I've already come up with a few highlights, but I don't have the real meat of the story yet.

HURD: What's your schedule like, Ray?

BILLINGSLEY: My day starts at about eight A.M. I have a good stiff breakfast because that may be my only meal till late at night. Then, once I get into my work, all my bodily functions stop. I'm not hungry anymore, I'm not tired, I'm just doing my work. When I'm finished, then I'm back to normal. I usually work on the strip from about ten A.M. till about six or seven o'clock at night. After that, these days, I go to the rehearsals of the play I mentioned a moment ago. Back home at eleven, I may do some writing. Usually I'm up till two A.M., just making sure I'm prepared for the next day.

HURD: Wow, a whirlwind routine allowing for only about six hours' sleep!

BILLINGSLEY: Luckily, I can deal with it so far. One reason I can handle all the stresses and pressures I've been under is because I started professional cartooning so early in life. So I was used to all those deadlines.

CABLE ADDRESS KINGSYN NEW YORK
(800) 526-KING • (212) 455-4143

King Features
216 EAST 45TH STREET, NEW YORK, NY 10017

JAY KENNEDY
Comics Editor

July 7, 1994

Mr. Jud Hurd
Cartoonists Profiles
P.O. Box 325
Fairfield, CT   06430

Dear Jud:

Greg Evans showed me a rough draft of the article he is writing for
<u>Cartoonist Profiles</u> about "getting syndicated". It's well written,
but beyond that it's an article that I think people will be
referring others to for years to come because what he says in it
needs to be said.   It's an important article for aspiring
cartoonists.

With great precision, Greg Evans zeroes in on the real issues
aspiring cartoonists should concern themselves with.   Too often
discussions of getting syndicated veer towards discussions of
premises, art styles, pens and paper.   Those things are secondary
to the points Greg Evans articulates. Every cartoonist aspiring to
become syndicated should read the article.   It focuses on the
basics that are easy to lose sight of.

I'm glad you're publishing his piece and hope that you can get it
the attention it deserves.   I know my job as a syndicate editor
would be made much easier if every aspiring cartoonist took Greg
Evans' words to heart before sending me their submission.

Sincerely,

Jay Kennedy

JK:km

GREG EVANS AND *LUANN*

Story from Issue No. 103, September 1994

In a few months, *Luann* will turn ten: the strip, not the character. Luann the character possesses that incredible cartoon ability to stay the same age forever. I wish *I* could do that. Unfortunately, I'm not ink so I'm ten years older—and maybe two years wiser.

To mark *Luann*'s decennial, I'd like to share what little wisdom I've gained in this business. For if there's one thing I've learned in ten years of producing a syndicated comic strip it's this: Most everything I thought I knew, I didn't.

A lot is written about how to get started, how to become syndicated. But I've seen little, if anything, on how to *stay* syndicated. Regardless of what you may read in books or magazine articles, getting syndicated requires nothing but talent. Staying syndicated requires talent, luck, timing, competitiveness, flexibility, and a willingness to promote. Knowing how to *stay* on the comic page will help *get* you on the comic page. With that in mind, here are my pearls of wisdom:

1. Don't create a hit comic strip. If you're trying to come up with the "great concept," you're doing it wrong. Whenever someone tells me they have a great concept for a comic strip, I flinch. Great concepts are for movies and TV shows. Twenty years ago you might have been able to sell a strip about "the wacky people on a cruise ship," and a few years ago you might have gotten attention with a strip about "a single mom coping with modern life." But concepts are not what give a strip life. Readers don't come back day after day to read a concept. A concept is only a starting place; it's not the strip.

2. Be original. *The Far Side* has been done. So has *Luann* for that matter. Ask any syndicate comic editor and they'll tell you they get more copycat material than anything else. In rare cases, a syndicate will buy a worthwhile copycat strip, but the copycat never does as well as the original. And anyway, do you *really* want to be the creator of a strip that's "like *The Far Side* but not as popular?" Be yourself. Do something original.

3. But don't be too weird. Newspapers are very conservative. They want their comics to be conservative too. Editors don't like to think too much about comics or worry about their content. As a result, comics are very mainstream, populated by average families and comical animals. This doesn't mean that some cartoonists aren't pushing the boundaries and trying to move comics from being twenty years behind the times to only ten years behind. And, yes, there are strips (*Outland, Zippy the Pinhead, Sylvia, Ernie, Dilbert, Ballard Street, Fusco Brothers*) that are not exactly mainstream. But they're more offbeat than downright weird. If you tend toward weirdness, you may want to consider the underground press or else self-syndication to alternative and college newspapers. If you're only offbeat, try the syndicates; they like to see different things. But realize that most of the strips just listed don't have huge client lists and they often have small—though *very* devoted—readership. If you can't deal with a love/hate relationship with your readers or you just really want to have a mega-blockbuster strip, don't do weird.

4. Don't do plain vanilla either. You probably look at your paper's comic page and say, "I could do as good as this!" Depending on what paper you're looking at, three-fourths of the strips are decades old. They've developed a strong following through years of careful character development, and if the gag isn't tops, it doesn't matter, because readers simply enjoy the characters. But if you created a similar strip today, no one would buy it. Why? Because most newspapers are happy with the comics they have. They don't especially want to change anything and deal with reader wrath. So offering them something that's as good as what they already have is futile. Syndicates don't want strips that are just like what's already out there. What they want are strips that are *kind of like* what's out there but

better. And what does *better* mean? Well, it could mean more humorous, a little more current, a bit off-center, a tad wild. Somewhere between *weird* and *vanilla* is the tone that most appeals to editors and, therefore, syndicates. "But," you say, "I see new strips in my paper all the time that don't seem better at all." True. Which is a measure of the syndicate's skillful salesmanship and the newspaper editor's uncertainty about what readers may like. However, look for those "as good as" strips a year or two from now. Chances are, they won't survive.

5. Getting in and staying in are two different things. As difficult as it is to break into newspaper syndication, it's much harder to stay in. The mortality rate for new strips is about 65 percent. If ten new strips come out in any given year, only four will survive. And of those, maybe one will get lucky and flourish (150 or more clients) while the others will do OK. And it's getting worse. Not that long ago, nearly every major city had a least two competing newspapers. Not anymore. In 1984, there were 1,701 daily papers in the United States. In 1994, 1,556. The number continues to go down. Less competition, fewer papers; it's extremely difficult for a new strip to get a toehold. Only the very best strips have a chance to get in and survive. So how do you create a great strip? You don't.

6. It's not the strip, it's you. You don't read *Peanuts,* you read Charles Schulz. You don't read *The Far Side,* you read Gary Larson. Syndicates aren't looking for another *Calvin and Hobbes,* they're looking for another Bill Watterson. Let's be honest: If you or I or anyone else did *Calvin and Hobbes,* it wouldn't be the same. I hear aspiring cartoonists say, "Man, if only I'd thought of *Calvin and Hobbes!*" But that's just the point—they didn't. It's not as if there are incredible, fail-proof ideas floating around in cartoon space, waiting for anyone to come along and claim them. There's only one person

Greg Evans and *Luann*

on earth who could bring forth *Calvin:* Bill Watterson. Only Schulz could produce *Peanuts*. The greatest strips are the product of one person's vision and talent. It's not the strip that's great, it's the person. Or, more exactly, it's a creative person combined with a perfect vehicle to express that talent.

7. A hard pill to swallow: Be honest. You won't read this in many instructional cartoon books, but the most important element in a successful comic strip isn't the drawing or the lettering or the ages or genders or races or occupations of the characters or whether they're a fat cat, a bumbling husband, or a teenage girl. It's you. And you either have the ability or you don't. How do you know if you do or you don't? Look at the comic page and ask yourself honestly if you could produce a strip, every day, that's *better* (see No. 4) than the strips you enjoy reading. Would your strip have the depth and richness in twelve years to be as good as (preferably better than) it is now? Can you create characters that are fresh and endearing and have interesting personalities that generate emotions? Can you conceive of a cast of characters who interact in ways that produce gags unique to your strip and are not interchangeable with five other strips? In other words, do you have an ability to produce a strip that will make editors say, "*This* strip is like nothing else and deserves to be on my comic page!"

8. Analyze yourself. When I started submitting strips, I followed the usual thinking process: "Let's see, what hasn't been done? How about two bumbling clowns in a traveling circus . . . two bumbling detectives in Los Angeles . . . two bumbling astronauts on the moon?" These were actual strips I developed and submitted, recycling the same two bumbling characters with each rejection. The trouble is, I knew nothing about any of these occupations. And the strips revealed that. They were shallow gag-driven efforts that might have had a chance in 1950, but were just not relevant thirty years later. Plus, I was creating artificial people doing formula-funny things in contrived settings. After enough rejections, I realized I was doing something wrong. For guidance, I read some biographies of famous cartoonists and learned that the secret was in that age-old adage: Write about what you know. Examine yourself. What are your interests, talents, life circumstances, experiences, attitudes, philosophies, convictions? What in your life is interesting or unusual that would provide fodder for a comic strip? What's your sense of humor like? It is ironic, satiric, pessimistic, uplifting, corny, literary, clever, insulting, nostalgic? Write a strip that comes from inside you instead of some external, artificial concept. If it doesn't come naturally, it's either the wrong strip or . . .

9. Maybe you're not mature enough. How come all the stuff I did before age thirty-five was awful, and then it all came together with *Luann*? I think it has to do with maturity or life experience or whatever you want to call it. I hate to admit that it took me thirty-five years to mature, but before that, regardless of how hard I tried, I simply couldn't produce anything worthwhile. Do *you* have to wait until you're thirty-five? I certainly hope not. Kevin Fagan (*Drabble*) was only twenty-two when he was syndicated. I was a late bloomer—you may not be.

10. Develop good characters. The second most important element of a successful comic strip, right after you, are your characters. Ask any cartoonist whom they pattern their characters after, and they'll say "me." And it's true. All my characters contain at least some small aspect of myself or someone in my family. This is how it should be. It's the only way to put real depth into your characters. What kinds of characters should you create? Interesting ones with flawed personalities and unique traits. "A husband who works for an irritable boss" describes millions of men. "A husband who naps, eats huge sandwiches, and is always running to catch the bus" describes only Dagwood Bumstead. "A kid who likes to play baseball" could be any kid. "An insecure kid who never wins and always has the football pulled away" describes only Charlie Brown. Also keep in mind that success isn't funny, failure is. Who would you rather read about, a sweet loving feline who purrs contentedly in his master's lap or a fat sassy cat who eats his owner's dinner and kicks the dog off the table? That illustrates another rule: Conflict creates humor. When strips fail, it's usually because the characters just aren't interesting; they lack conflict. You should develop your characters in such a way that when you place them in certain situations or in combination with other characters, sparks fly. The humor that comes from the dynamics of unstable and opposing personalities is far more satisfying than generic "joke" humor. Look at the most successful strips and you'll find this demonstrated again and again: Sarge vs. Beetle, Cathy vs. Irving, Dennis vs. Mr. Wilson, the King vs. everyone in Id. OK. So after you've developed good characters, you have to face it. . . .

11. Writing. You can't teach it, you can't explain it. The world's greatest artist can't produce a comic strip without the ability to write. And in the beginning stages of a comic strip's life, nothing is more important than writing. Don't write fourteen gags and think you've created a strip. If you spend more time drawing than writing, you're doing it backward. It's your writing that will sell your strip, not your artwork. It takes a lot of writing to get into your characters and flesh them out. The more you write, the better your work will be. Write a hundred gags, then write a hundred more. Then pick the best twenty-four to submit. If the syndicate likes your strip, they'll want to see more. Your second batch should be even better than your first. When your strip hits the papers, you want to grab the readers with excellent material, because newspapers don't give new strips a whole lot of time to prove their worth. Neither do readers. You've got to come out of the chute at top speed and keep it up for at least the first year. That's when readers are test-driving your strip to decide if they'll add it to their daily routine. Editors talk to other editors, and you want your strip to be a hot topic. You get only one chance to make a splash—make it a big one. Be prepared. Write.

12. After you've made your splash, keep splashing. Wouldn't it be great if we could all be like Bill Watterson and produce a strip that's exalted far and wide and is snapped up by thousands of papers in record time and all we had to do was sit in our studio and occasionally go to the bank? Well, face it, that's not likely to happen. Instead, you have to be willing to promote yourself. If you think your syndicate isn't working hard enough for you, be the squeaky wheel. Give them a new character to promote or a new situation to tell editors about. Be willing to part with originals to help grease a sale or thank a new client. Do you *have* to do this? No. Some cartoonists do it a lot, some not at all. Ultimately, the success of a strip always boils down to how good it is. Still, nearly every strip goes through periods of sales stagnation, and a little promotion never hurts.

13. On the other hand, don't harass your syndicate. Your relationship with your syndicate can be a honeymoon, a nightmare, or a big nothing. Every cartoonist complains about his syndicate; it's part of the deal. Ideally, each side should gain equally with neither party feeling shorted. No cartoonist appreciates an indifferent syndicate just as no syndicate enjoys a whiny cartoonist. Try to make friends with your editors. Hold them to high expectations but respect their limitations and other obligations. A good relationship will pay off in the long haul.

14. Ignore all these pearls. In the comic strip business, nothing is more true than the fact that there are no truths. For every rule, there is a strip that defies it.

Jay Kennedy, comics editor at King Features Syndicate, tells me he gets six thousand strip and panel submissions each year. One of them may be yours. It may flaunt every rule I've outlined here and end up in two thousand newspapers in twelve months.

Then I'll realize that in the past ten years I've gained absolutely no wisdom at all.

But, hey, I've had a hell of a lot of fun. Best of luck to you.

BRIAN WALKER, GREG WALKER, AND CHANCE BROWNE ON *HI AND LOIS*

Story from Issue No. 103, September 1994

At the invitation of the three cartoonists who produce *Hi and Lois,* your editor sat in on a gag conference for this popular strip, just before it celebrated its fortieth anniversary. The strip was created by Mort Walker and Dik Browne in 1954. The three we talked with are Brian and Greg Walker, Mort's sons, and Dik's son, Robert (Chance) Browne. As you will see, they talked about how they work together in considerable detail. On another occasion, I asked Brian Walker to say a little bit more about his process of creating gag ideas. His response follows the story of the gag conference.

BRIAN: What you're sitting in on today, Jud, is the gag conference that we have every two weeks. Greg and I do the writing for the strip, and I bring in thirty gags for each of these sessions. It's very important to include in each of these gag sketches an indication of what the characters' expressions are, whether they're inside or outside, in the kitchen or the backyard, whether it's a cold day or a hot day, and so on. All these little elements determine whether the gag comes across or not. If I simply typed up a few words such as *Hi says to Lois* and *Lois replies to Hi,* we'd be losing about 90 percent of the visual material that reinforces the gags. Greg adds an additional fifteen gags to my pile. Chance doesn't do any writing on the strip, but it's a great advantage to have him here at the gag conferences because he's the one who ultimately has to *draw Hi and Lois.*

We grade these idea sketches on the Mort Walker system. A gag is either a *1* or a *2*—either you like it or you don't. Of course, there are shades of liking—*1-plus* and *1-minus.*

GREG: *1* is a usable gag; *1-plus* means use it right away. These gag sketches are done on sheets of typewriter or bond paper.

BRIAN: Greg and I have a tendency not to draw the characters exactly as you see them in the paper. Each of us has his own style and we don't fuss over a lot of little details that have to go into the finished artwork.

GREG: Unless one of those little details is visually important.

BRIAN: Going on to the next stage in this process, Chance will call me periodically and say he needs

Mort Walker and Dik Browne's

Hi and Lois ®

by Brian and Greg Walker
and Chance Browne

Hi and Lois was created by Mort Walker and Dik Browne, two of the most celebrated cartoonists in comic art history. This loving portrait of an ordinary family provoked a strong emotional response from readers right from the beginning. With each new generation, readers have seen themselves reflected in *Hi and Lois*.

another batch of gags. At this point, I'll get together four Sundays and twenty-four dailies that we've previously OK'd. Sometimes I'll add editorial suggestions such as "Make sure they have their coats on because it's cold outside," or I may note briefly some things that maybe aren't really clear in our rough sketches.

GREG: We've been writing *Hi and Lois* all our lives in a sense; it's only now that we're getting paid for it. When we were kids and did something funny, that would be written into the strip by our dad. I've been doing gags for over twenty years now. Here's a comparison for your readers, Jud: When I used to work in comic books, I would sometimes get a script to draw up from someone who wasn't an artist. It would be typed up almost like a movie script, with elaborate stage directions in detail. In our case, we can set the scene with our *sketches,* and we don't have to write out suggestions such as "Hi goes out the door," "Hi looks mad," or whatever.

BRIAN: One of the things I learned from my dad was not to beat a dead horse in a gag meeting. Mort has very little patience with too-lengthy discussions pro and con a gag we're considering. Either it works or it doesn't! We do have discussions sometimes about changing a word here or there. You can actually fix a gag, and turn a *1-minus* into a *1,* but you can waste a lot of time with haggling and you'd be better off starting all over again.

JUD: Chance, are there basic things you've changed about the strip since you've been doing it?

CHANCE: Well, Hi doesn't drive a Studebaker anymore—it's a Volvo—and the kids wear seat belts. Lois is working now. She's in real estate and Hi is pretty much a house husband. He still goes to work, but you don't see Lois in the apron too much—Hi's got the apron on now! Her real estate adventures do provide a lot of the gags.

BRIAN: In the late seventies or early eighties Mort and his staff made this change for Lois. But I will say that we are very respectful of the traditions in the feature and we're following the old saying, "Don't fix it if it isn't broken." Whatever changes the three of us have made in the strip have been very subtle, over a long period of time.

GREG: What we've done more than anything else is just update the strip to modern situations and conventions—things that are important nowadays. Naturally, there's a lot more emphasis on recycling, the seat-belt issue, and so on.

BRIAN: We try to avoid the old clichés, such as making fun of the wife's cooking, or showing her burning the roast and appearing to be a horrible cook. That doesn't really seem fair nowadays when you show the mother holding a job. She works all day, she comes home and cooks for the kids, and it doesn't seem funny to show the kids giving her a hard time about her cooking. As a result, in the 1994 *Hi and Lois,* we turned this situation around a bit and are still able to take advantage of the fact that there's a lot of humor in burnt roasts, spillage, and so on. We show Hi trying

Left to right:
Brian Walker,
Chance Browne,
Greg Walker

to cook periodically, which is positive, because he's trying to do his part. But he's not very good at it, so it's OK for the kids to make fun of *his* cooking, whereas in the case of Lois, gags about her cooking wouldn't seem fair. When we first started writing the strip regularly in the early eighties, I often noticed that even though she had a newborn baby, Trixie, at home, she didn't seem to do the kinds of things a mother with a newborn would usually do. We all had young children at the time, so in our writing we started dealing with diapers, day care, babysitters, and other logical activities. We realized that a lot of what young mothers do is talk about their babies with other young mothers. It didn't seem to us that Lois had enough friends in the strip for this to happen, so we tried to correct that situation.

GREG: One of the reasons that Mort turned the writing of *Hi and Lois* over to us was the fact that we *did* have young kids, and our families were a lot more like the *Hi and Lois* family than *his* family was.

BRIAN: This is a reality-based strip. Readers perceive our comic strip family as being composed of *real* people.

JUD: Do you have time to answer the letters you receive?

CHANCE: We answer all of them. I feel these characters are real. I grew up with them and have been aware of their distinct personalities for the past forty years. People complain about Ditto's always getting the short end of the stick, for instance.

BRIAN: And readers are concerned about anything in the strip that might put Trixie in danger.

JUD: At this point maybe it would be a good idea for you to describe the various members of the family.

CHANCE: Hi and Lois are a modern nineties couple—he's pretty much a house husband, even though he has a job, and she's in real estate. They share parenting duties, of course. (Incidentally, I don't know how many of your readers are aware that Lois is a sister of Beetle Bailey.) Chip is a young teenager who's just on the brink of getting his driver's license but probably never will. He's somewhat grumpy and moody, as members of that age group often tend to be. Dot is Little Miss Perfect, who can't do wrong and is always looking askance at her twin brother, Ditto, who almost can't do anything

right. The poor guy always has his shoes untied, and his perfect sister is forever horrified by his behavior. These twins are about six or seven years old, perhaps in second grade.

BRIAN: Dot is something of a little feminist. She's always telling Mommie to stick up for her rights, demand equal pay in her job, and so on. This is our way to get into a slightly more strident point of view on the subject of feminism. We don't want to make Lois like that because she's a soft, gentle soul, whereas Dot can be made a little pushier and more demanding.

CHANCE: I certainly can relate to Trixie, the baby. Our own baby is now twenty-one months old, starting to say actual full words and walking—she's probably just a little older than Trixie. Trixie crawls around making wonderful, sometimes incorrect, often on-the-money observations about everything that's going on around her. She has this special relationship with her sunbeam, which comes through the window. She also has a huge English sheepdog, Dawg. Her classic pose is to be resting back on Dawg, in the sunbeam, musing about what's going on around her.

BRIAN: Hi is the nineties father-husband type. He's a very sympathetic character in that he tries to do his part around the house, babysitting, taking the kids for outings on weekends, and so on. He feels, as we nineties dads often do, that he's doing much more than previous generations did, changing diapers and all the rest of the current father-husband routine, and he gets a little frantic and frazzled at times.

GREG: We have an extended family in the strip also—their neighbor, Thurston. Thirsty is a slob who doesn't take proper care of his yard. Then we have Mr. Foofram,

Hi's boss, who owns Foofram Industries. And of course, there are the garbagemen, Abercrombie and Fitch. A newer character, Mr. Strivemore, is the antithesis of Thirsty, in that *his* yard is always perfect, in contrast to the sloppy mess on Thirsty's property.

BRIAN: Jud, you brought up the subject of the changes we've gradually made in the strip. Take the case of Thirsty: He's a key character in the strip, in that he's everything that Hi is not, so he ends up making Hi look good, a dutiful father, husband, and sympathetic character. Thirsty is lazy, lets his wife mow the lawn, and goofs off at work. Traditionally, he always was shown with a cigarette hanging out of his mouth and a beer can in his hand. There were a few shading lines on his nose, making him look a bit like a drunk. We have downplayed and phased out the overdrinking side of the character. But recently we had some comments from the *Los Angeles Times,* indicating that they were still concerned about the red nose, so we played around with the character, with the result that he's presented as someone who's pretty much reformed—maybe back from the Betty Ford clinic or something like that.

JUD: I know you both do gags for *Beetle Bailey,* and I've heard that there's a possibility that Beetle will be visiting Hi and Lois. Is that true?

BRIAN: The fortieth anniversary of the strip is October 1994. Actually, Amanda Haas of King Features thought of this idea. After doing a little research, she was intrigued to discover for the first time that Lois was Beetle's sister. This relationship was disclosed after the Korean War, when Mort was attempting to decide whether to have Beetle return to civilian life for his fur-

Cartoon Success Secrets

ther comic strip activities. We wanted to do something special for this anniversary, so we worked up a story line in which Beetle actually leaves his own strip to go visit his sister for a short period—maybe a little less than a week.

GREG: Brian wrote some gags to run in *Beetle Bailey* pertaining to this brother/sister visit. It's worth noting that this relationship between the two comic strip families is paralleled by the close relationship that has existed for many years in real life between the Walker and the Browne families.

JUD: Chance, you do the daily and Sunday drawing. Do you have any help with that?

CHANCE: Yes. I do the dailies and the Sundays with the help of Frank Johnson, who inks, and who, if necessary, can also draw the feature, since he's been working on *Hi and Lois* for thirty-five years. I come from what I'd consider a straight fine art background. I went to college as an art major for two years in the Midwest and then spent two more years in New York City at the School of Visual Arts. Later I worked as an art director for several record units, since I'd been playing blues and had been involved in the music scene for many years. I do freelance graphic design, such as the logo I did for the newly established Connecticut chapter of the National Cartoonists Society. I paint and also have been a longtime student of my late dad's work. I started to work regularly for him when I turned thirty in 1978, but I'd worked part-time for him years before that. I'm still trying to master that wonderful style he developed, so I guess you could say that basically I'm following the methods of the Dik Browne school of cartooning.

BRIAN: I can say that I think that *Hi and Lois* is one of the best-drawn strips in the papers. In that connection I sometimes notice the lack of backgrounds, the static design, and the talking-head format of many other strips in the field.

GREG: That reminds me of the difficulties Brian and I had when we were working on the *Betty Boop & Felix* strip. We had a problem with her because she's never really been shown in profile, rarely ever from the rear, or from any angle other than a three-quarter or straight-front view. Sometimes we'd have to show her body twisted around with the head still facing forward.

BRIAN: Sunday pages are really special for us. Greg and I try to write episodes that are challenging to Chance and will put the Flagston family in a different environment—maybe at the July Fourth fireworks or at the beach.

CHANCE: Madeline Brogan, down in Florida, helps part-time with the color work and has written the lead-in panels for the Sunday strip.

GREG: Ever since *Hi and Lois* started, the Browne and Walker families have been relatively close. It's almost as though we've been like cousins—part of an extended family. Dik was my godfather, by the way.

JUD: Chance, do you chip in with suggestions that might punch up further the gags they've brought in, as far as the drawing is concerned?

CHANCE: As I look at them the first time, I'm thinking about how I'm going to draw the gags, and occasionally I may say, "Maybe this would work a little better if it was drawn this way." And of course I have my own ideas as to which drawings look funny and which don't.

GREG: I think readers *like* the Flagston family. In this age when so many families are dysfunctional, I believe people look at *Hi and Lois* as a good role model. *The Simpsons* and *Married...with Children* and *Roseanne* TV families may be funny in their struggles and difficulties, but you don't want to live your life that way.

BRIAN: I find writing *Hi and Lois* gags is much easier and more natural for me than writing *Beetle Bailey* gags. Some *Hi and Lois* gags literally come out of the mouths of my children and out of the things my wife does.

GREG: I find it somewhat constraining not to be able to do the fantasy type of thing I do in occasional *Beetle* gags. Beetle can be beat up and crushed and still pop up fine the next day. Obviously we can't do that in *Hi and Lois*, which is much more reality-based than a lot of other strips.

CHANCE: I think we should also mention Fred Schwartz, who works at King Features and who has been lettering the feature since the beginning. He's doing a wonderful job. Frank Johnson is heavily involved—he does all the inking, handles special projects, lays out stuff—he's very big in the mix. His touch has been apparent in the consistent appearance of the strip. *Hi and Lois* is a team effort.

Now to Brian Walker's comments about his method of creating gag ideas.

JUD: A classic question asked of cartoonists by members of the general public has always been, "Where do you get your ideas?" I know this is a favorite subject of yours, Brian, and that you taught a class at Fairfield University in which you tried to provide some answers.

The Hi and Lois Family Tree

Hi Flagston | Lois Bailey | Beetle Bailey

Chip | Dot | Ditto | Trixie

Dawg

BRIAN: You'll be glad to hear, Jud, that in preparation for the course, I looked through a lot of interviews that had appeared in *CARTOONIST PROfiles,* and found quotes from various cartoonists, in which they told how *they* had answered this eternal question.

In my own case, I almost have to put myself in sort of a trancelike state in my studio all by myself. That's the reason I work in a studio away from my home. I'll sit down with a yellow legal pad, just staring into space for half an hour, writing down anything that comes to

"THIRSTY"

"THURSTON"

mind, to get my gears turning, and maybe I'll write two or three pages of stuff. Quite possibly, when I look over what I've written, nothing will be usable till I come to something I've jotted down on the third page.

Unlike my father, I don't carry around a little book in which to write down things I hear people saying. However, when I'm sitting there in my reflective state, I *will* recall things that people have said to me, or observations I've made, because I think I have a pretty good memory. And many of my scribblings result from various reading I do constantly. I look through collections of other people's cartoons. This isn't with the thought of switching gags, but I'll study their styles of writing, their mechanics, and so on. I'll read columnists like Dave Barry, Anna Quinlan, or Calvin Trillin, in order to absorb something of their sense of humor and point of view.

I feel like sort of a sponge, everywhere I go. I watch television, I go to movies, I read books, and I talk to people; I guess I'm a pop-culture addict. I watch stand-up comedians too, and somehow all that material soaks in, so when I sit down in that quiet state I mentioned, ideas come.

Since we're writing a strip that does have established characters and established traditions, I will often look through books or proofs of old *Hi & Lois* strips. This keeps me focused on the characters and on the kinds of situations that readers are used to seeing in the strip and seems to put necessary reins on my imagination. For instance, I might come up with a scuba-diving gag involving Hi in my dreamlike state. This would really be out in left field for *Hi and Lois*. People would say, "What's he doing scuba diving?" So in order to use a gag like this, I'd have to establish that he's on vacation. I think you find in any strip a certain number of set situations that occur regularly. In *Blondie*, for instance, Dagwood may often be seen sitting in the living room, in bed, sleeping on the couch, at work, and so on. The same thing applies in our strip. We've traditionally shown Hi and Thirsty playing golf together, Lois at the grocery store, the kids in school, and the family in other often-repeated locales. But I don't go beyond certain parameters by putting them in situations that wouldn't be characteristic for the Flagstons. Of course, we have to be careful not to repeat old gags. In fact, looking over previous material helps prevent repetition.

JEFF MACNELLY AND *SHOE*

HURD: Twenty years ago, Jeff, when you were an editorial cartoonist in Richmond, you said you were too new at the game to give any cartooning advice. But now you've won three Pulitzer Prizes, two NCS Reubens, and other honors, both for your editorial cartoons and your comic strip *Shoe*. First of all, how did you arrive at the name *Shoe,* and would you describe the strip's characters for the benefit of any new readers?

MACNELLY: It would be nice to think that I have new readers. I named the strip after a guy named Jim Shumaker, who was my first editor in the newspaper business at the *Chapel Hill Weekly*. He was a beloved journalism professor at the University of North Carolina, known to all his friends as Shoe. (I think I always addressed him as Mr. Shumaker.) It seemed a natural to borrow his name for the title character of my proposed strip. He was the type of person I was leaning toward for the cigar-smoking character. At this point it was really just a working title for my own focus. Back then he always wore high-top black sneakers to work and smoked cigars. He had a great sense of humor and was one of these guys who is very gruff on the outside but totally the opposite on the inside. He tried hard not to let the inside get through to the outside. He was a real straight-shooter, a very honest guy. My basing this comic strip character on him doesn't do him justice at all as a human being.

HURD: What was his reaction when you first came out with the strip?

MACNELLY: I'm sure he was pissed—people would constantly ask him about the connection. I think it took him about fifteen years to get used to the idea, when he probably decided the continual comments wouldn't go away. But to get back to your second question. The guy who's turned out to be the main character is Professor Cosmo Fishhawk, who's famous for the messy desk and for falling asleep at the wheel all the time. He is basically autobiographical and seems to have become the star. I read something years ago by Al Capp, way before I started the strip, which I still remember. Talking about Li'l Abner, he said, "A comic strip is *all* autobiographical; *all* the characters are based on me."

At first this sounded like a lot of baloney, since his comment couldn't possibly apply to Daisy Mae. But then you realize, sitting there at two o'clock in the morning, trying to think of an idea—it all has to come from your own head. So the professor has wholly evolved into me and vice versa.

Skyler is the little kid type. He is perpetually in sixth grade (or seventh grade, I can't remember which), but he's really me. He's the little guy with glasses, he's *me* at the age of twelve or thirteen. Definitely not as tall, of course. Through Skyler I can deal with these wake-up nightmares I had about that term paper that was due in the morning and with other psychoses of mine.

Another character is Irving Seagull. He runs the junkyard. He's *exactly* like me: He can take anything apart and so can I.

HURD: Are these various characters just one species of bird?

MACNELLY: When I started drawing them, I was going to try and make Shoe a purple martin, the professor a fishhawk, and Irv a seagull. But they turned human pretty quick.

HURD: And they can operate both up in the trees and on the ground, can't they?

MACNELLY: Oh, yes . . . and I try to do them flying every once in a while, but this seems a little too energetic for these characters.

HURD: Any other characters you want to mention?

MACNELLY: There's Roz. I don't know what her whole name is. She runs a kind of hangout, the diner deal. She's the bartender, the confidante, and everything else.

HURD: Shoe is editing the local paper, right?

MACNELLY: Yes. He's always been the editor of the *Treetops Tattler-Tribune*. Every once in a while he goes to the track, but basically he's every-boss. And once in a while I like to have anonymous crazy characters wander in, just to do something new and interesting. These occasional geeks that wander into Roz's place

Shoe

by Jeff MacNelly

are fun to draw. Also, there's sort of a bimbo character who really doesn't have a name, but the professor is usually going out on a date with her. She's sort of anonymous—every-bimbo, I guess.

HURD: Before you came up with *Shoe,* had you found yourself creating gags that weren't usable in the editorial cartoon? I remember that Henry Martin, a cartoonist for the *New Yorker* and other publications, was very often coming up with magazine gags in which the scene was at some business office—so frequently, in fact, that he developed a syndicated panel consisting exclusively of this type of idea, in addition to his magazine work.

MACNELLY: I think in the back of my mind I *always* wanted to try a strip. It was something I just wanted to see if I could do. Also, I had the energy at the time!

HURD: Cartoonists everywhere have always enthused over the mechanical details that have been pictured so authentically in your editorial cartoons. Did you have a lot of formal art education?

MACNELLY: As a kid I always wanted to be a painter or an illustrator, and I used to draw a lot. I guess I'm self-taught, however.

HURD: Do you do a lot of sketching?

MACNELLY: I try to—I do painting and sculpture stuff when I have some time or get a burst of energy. And I try to set aside a period during the day to do something other than cartooning.

HURD: Do you have any set schedule in order to juggle the editorial cartoon, the strip, and now your panel *Pluggers*?

MACNELLY: The only thing that has settled in pretty much is the political cartoons, which I do on Tuesday, Thursday, and Friday. I do three a week and send them over the computer so they show up the same day in Chicago at Tribune Media Services. They then run the next morning in the first edition. I usually devote the entire first half of the day on these three mornings to the editorial cartoon. I'm always watching something on C-Span and keeping up on the news, which I would be doing anyway even if I weren't working for a newspaper. But these days really are the only *rigid* part of my schedule, and of course I set aside a lot of time to get those three cartoons ready for the syndicate. I change my style around—I'm always changing something—paper, pens, or ink. My latest change involves me drawing a hell of a lot longer than I used to. I'm now doing the work with a *ballpoint pen,* which sounds really terrible, except that's how I learned to draw. I got back to this way of working about a year or so ago.

HURD: What tools had you been using before you went back to the old way?

MACNELLY: Oh, brush and ink, for instance. Nowadays I just look for a ballpoint that's black—whatever they're selling at the local art supply store. Doing a lot of traveling, I found myself carrying ink everywhere. Going up and down on an airplane tended to squirt the ink out of whatever I carried the ink in. It made quite a mess. I dealt with this problem for a long time because I enjoyed doing the brushwork. But now I really like the *control* that's possible with the ballpoint pen. And what's really been fun lately is that drawing is an adventure again. Now I can spend three or four hours working on a piece, whereas formerly I'd better be through with it after an hour and a half.

HURD: What brought on this newfound excitement with the drawing?

MACNELLY: The best way to explain it is that, as I mentioned a moment ago, I have a lot more *control* over what I put down on paper. The final result is much closer to what I had in mind than it was during my brush-and-ink period. With a brush, a lot of times you get some real happy accidents, and that's wonderful, but often I used to get halfway through a cartoon and wish I'd handled the brush and ink some other way. With a ballpoint I can be a lot more sketchy. I can go back over certain areas—it's kind of like doing a painting. I think that's why I like this method so much. I can work over a cartoon for three or four hours and have *fun* with it.

HURD: I believe I've had a similar experience. For years I did all my *Health Capsules* and *Ticker Toons* entirely with brush and ink. With these materials I tended to draw sweeping curved lines, which look pretty slick, in an attempt to demonstrate what I'm able to do with a brush that is difficult to handle. Although I haven't shifted over to a ballpoint for my syndicated work, I've been aware, when sketching for my own pleasure, that

I can add interesting and subtle little details with a ballpoint that can't be duplicated with the brush.

Do you have any help in your juggling of the editorial cartoon, *Shoe,* and *Pluggers?*

MACNELLY: I didn't have any for a long time, but nowadays I've got Chris Cassatt helping me. He is my electronic inker. Chris has been a cartoonist for years for the *Aspen* (Colorado) *Times Daily.* Mike Peters introduced me to him a few years back, and I learned that Chris was big with computers. At one point I told him my dream was to be able to use the computer to help out with *Shoe,* as long as it didn't detract from my being able to draw it, and with the understanding that its use would improve the final product. Of course I was interested in reducing the drudgery in doing a strip too. I was amazed, when I visited his studio, by the various programs he used to do *his* panel.

So here is how we work together these days: I draw the images for *Shoe* a lot bigger than I used to, really

Jeff MacNelly

Pluggers are dial-tone people
in a touch-tone world.

freehand on a big sheet of paper. These are scanned into the computer. For an average daily strip I'll do three big drawings and then Chris compiles them on his computer. We do all this, by the way, over the phone. Then he sends me the strip about 90 percent completed, and I do some finished work on the final version. He's got all the various-size boxes and balloons in his computer, as well as my style of lettering. Incidentally, this larger size in which I draw the images is more comfortable for me. I'm now able to do a lot more aspects of the characters and put more life in them. You know, a cartoonist gets a little frustrated these days drawing little talking heads. The computer has made it fun to draw the strip once again. I fax Chris a week's worth of stuff, including the dialogue, and I kind of art-direct things, telling him what I had in mind. He then adds the necessary balloons and lettering to my three big character drawings, reduced to the proper strip size. He can move everything around to make things fit.

HURD: Is there any general advice you give to young people who come to you for advice about our profession?

MACNELLY: Both my sons have really good instincts along that line. My older son just graduated from college, and he enjoys doing part-time cartooning. The kind of advice I give him (which seems strange coming from me) is this: "If I were you, I would learn all I could about computers, graphics, and Internet stuff." If I had an idea for a comic strip right now, I'd try to do one every day, making sure I had enough material so that the finished product was good on a daily basis. And I'd copyright the material. Then I'd get it an Internet site and just stick it out there for the world to see. The Internet is such an exciting place. You're not going to be making any money, but if you are a dedicated lunatic cartoonist just starting out, with a real job on the side, it would be great at night to be able to self-publish in the way I've indicated. You would immediately have such a vast audience out there that you would establish a following after several months, if your stuff is good, and you could do something with that following. That might lead to your being published in many places!

Reagan-era cartoon, done with brush and ink on Graphix paper.

Balance

Recent ballpoint cartoon

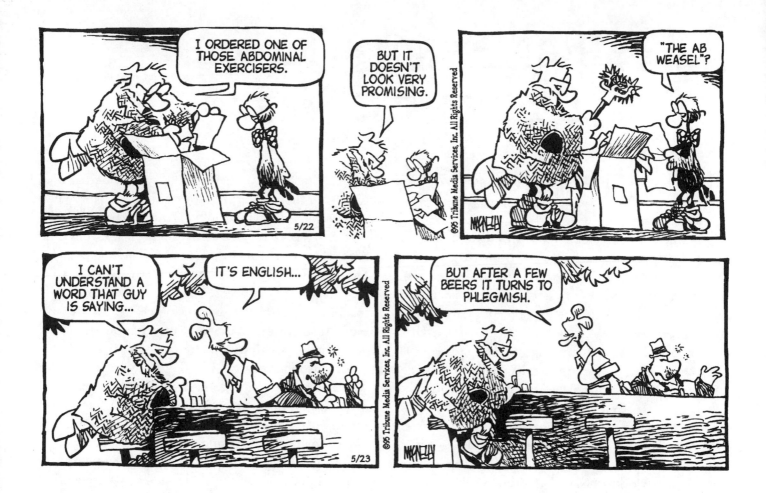

HURD: Would you just add a few words about your own particular method of stirring up *Shoe* ideas?

MACNELLY: I spend a lot of time listening to the radio, watching C-Span, or looking at some old movie. Usually I write stuff down on little pieces of paper, which I used to lose all the time, but now I put a star in front of a word or phrase that has occurred to me, and these accumulate in my pocket. When my wife, Susie, runs across this starred junk around the house, she saves it, and after a few weeks I have a little batch to work from.

HURD: By the way, I'm delighted that we've been able to reproduce here cartoon samples showing the difference between one of your brush-and-ink cartoons and one done in your ballpoint style. One last item: Would you say something about your latest venture, the syndicated panel *Pluggers*?

MACNELLY: It's a daily and Sunday feature (I've enclosed one of the first ones we did). It's based on the concept that we are all pluggers, in that we plug along through work, play, and family, encountering and conquering obstacles along the way. It's a way to recognize all the quirks and foibles we all share as humans (even though I draw them all as animals).

Several months into this, I started getting suggestions and letters from the readers. I let them take over the writing, since they were coming up with much better stuff than we could. (I have four partners. They're the guys who came up with the original concept and I'm the factory.) It's not in many papers so far, but Tribune Media Services is enthusiastic, and Disney has entered into a development deal with us. (A book will come out this fall.)

RON FERDINAND AND DENNIS THE MENACE

Story from Issue No. 112, December 1996

Some years ago Hank Ketcham, creator of *Dennis the Menace,* decided that the time had come for him to delegate some of the production of his legendary feature to others to make time for the painting he had often dreamed of doing someday. Here is the story of one of those artists who helped make that dream possible. We are particularly appreciative of the fact that in the following interview with Ron Ferdinand, who does the Sunday *Dennis the Menace* page for King Features, he credits *CARTOONIST PROfiles* with starting him off on a successful fifteen-year career with Dennis and his creator, Hank Ketcham. Most of that time was spent with Hank in California, but nowadays he works in New York State.

HURD: One of the most frequent questions we are asked by our readers is, "How can I become an assistant to an established comic strip artist?" I can't think of a better answer than to tell them about your progress, Ron, from your first interest in cartooning to the time when you sat down as an assistant in Hank Ketcham's studio.

FERDINAND: I had graduated from the School of Visual Arts in New York City in 1972 and I wanted to work for Disney. With this in mind, I took all the usual courses that are available in art school and, in addition, a class in animation history, taught by John Culhane. My term paper required me to do some research on *Terrytoons,* and I did a one-minute film to complete the class.

Following art school, I worked six years for a firm where I was involved with printed circuit boards—a far cry, I might add, from my Disney dreams. My employer was pretty sympathetic with my plans, though, and agreed to let me take Mondays off to work at home on enlarging my portfolio. I did a lot of Marvel-type pages just to hone my abilities in comic-book-style work. I wasn't selling to Marvel, but later I *did* show some pencils to *Archie Comics* and worked for them for a while. Following this I spent some time working in a real estate office.

Ron Ferdinand and Hank Ketcham

I had been reading *CARTOONIST PROfiles* about comic strip artists, but it never entered my mind to try to become an apprentice to one of them. At this point, I'll have to jump back a bit to say that Milt Kahl, one of the famous nine old men at the Disney Studio, had come to the school as part of their training program, accompanied by the noted Richard Williams. There was a lavish demonstration of Kahl's animation. He suggested that I send life drawings to the studio for consideration. That was all they wanted to see. No comics.

HURD: It's been widely known that the Disney Studio isn't interested in cartoonists who already have been working in a distinctive style of their own. They're looking primarily for artists with very good basic drawing ability, who can then learn the Disney way of drawing.

FERDINAND: Of course every year I had taken life drawing class at Visual Arts, but a lot of my time had been spent on the film I made, work in illustration, and so on. After they saw the drawings I sent, they said, in effect, "You have certain talents, but we want Michelangelo." Obviously, life drawing hadn't been my main thrust in

art school. After that I did spend about a half year at the Art Students League studying with John Groth.

Anyway, I was married at the time I was at the real estate office and had new responsibilities, when my eye caught your story about Hank Ketcham in the March 1981 of issue of *CARTOONIST PROfiles* where he said he'd like to train people to help draw *Dennis* and gave an address for sending samples.

With this exciting invitation, I got some Dennis books, made some pencil drawings, and mailed them out to Hank within a week. I never expected anything to come from my efforts, but three or four weeks later, I got a letter saying that he liked my pencils and would like me to send him a résumé and a photograph. Although he said I could take my time, since there was no rush, naturally I fired these items back to him the

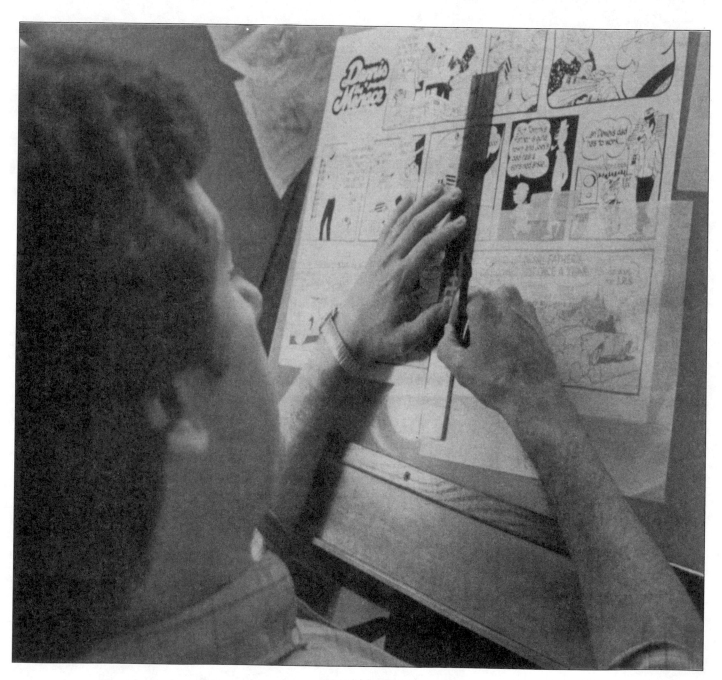

Ron at work

next day! Several weeks later he sent me a few gag slips and asked me to rough them out. I didn't hear from him for about a month, and then a phone call came one day, asking if I'd be interested in coming out to Pebble Beach for two weeks. Hank had hired a couple of assistants who were working on the Marvel comic books featuring *Dennis*. He was working with them furiously to get them to learn the style, and they were having a hard time meeting the monthly deadline. Luckily for me, he needed still another artist to get the comic book done. I went out for two weeks, he set me up in the studio he was renting in the Carmel Valley, and I went to work the first day on the comic book. At the end of two weeks, Hank asked if I'd be interested in moving out to California and working in a beautiful area. My wife and I flew out within the month, and we were there for fifteen years.

As a result of your *CARTOONIST PROfiles* story, Hank was flooded with submissions from fine illustrators around the country, but I guess it was my foresight in sending drawings I had done after carefully studying *Dennis* pages that got me the job. Hank's staff had done about seven issues of the monthly comic book when I

arrived, so I was involved in the balance of the issues for the year. The contract had been for one year, and Marvel wanted to renew it, but Ketcham was dissatisfied with the distribution in airports, liquor stores, et cetera. As it happened, a year passed after my arrival in California before I started work on the Sunday page.

HURD: Can you give us some examples of the type of critiquing that Hank did when looking over an assistant's work?

The model sheets and sketches accompanying this story, as well as the text itself, are copyrighted 1990 by Hank Ketchum.

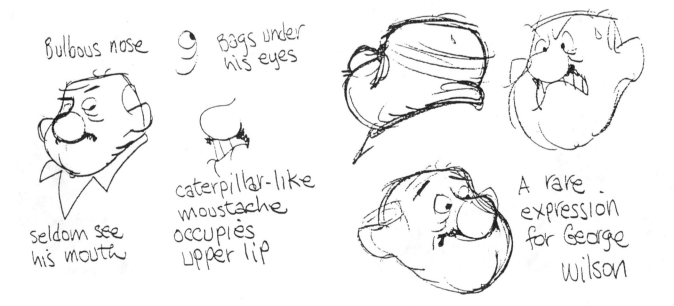

Bulbous nose

Bags under his eyes

seldom see his mouth

caterpillar-like moustache occupies upper lip

A rare expression for George Wilson

Marcus Hamilton, Hank, and Ron

FERDINAND: Mr. Wilson's nose might be too big, and the fingers might look like bananas. Finger criticism was big with him. And research was everything. If you did a toaster, Hank might ask, "Did you go to a Sears catalog and look at a toaster to see what it actually looks like?" Anything that detracted from the actual gag, such as an inaccurate background item, had to be taken care of. If, in looking at *Dennis*, a reader felt that a toaster didn't look just right, he'd concentrate on it and forget about everything else. Badly drawn chairs—all kinds of poorly rendered background details—detracted from the reader's appreciation of the gag.

HURD: What were some of the other details that required a lot of effort to master?

FERDINAND: Size relationships were particularly important. Dennis was three heads high, Wilson five

heads, and everything had to be just right. Maybe I was making Dennis too small or too large, his head too big, and so on. Of course, Hank's own work was evolving too. The 1950s Dennis was very different from the 1970s character.

HURD: I suppose Hank had a pretty sizable morgue, didn't he?

FERDINAND: Of course. He had practically everything he needed in a collection of Sears catalogs, plus the *World Book* and *Childcraft Encyclopedia*. If he couldn't find what he was looking for, he'd send one of us out to research it. If he needed to draw a butcher shop, we'd find one and make sketches. The same thing would happen if he needed a sailboat or whatever. Especially in the beginning, just so we'd practice our sketching, whenever we had a little extra time, he'd say, "Go out

Wilson Living room

High forehead.
Nose like her
husband's...Tho
a bit smaller

Hair
rolls tightly
around head

Ample/plump
wears
corset

Heavy legs

Martha
Wilson

soft hair on
top of head

Granny
glasses

3-HEADS
TALL

SHORT
EYEBROWS
HIGH ON
HEAD

SMALL "M" INSIDE
PUG NOSE

NO TEETH!

EAR & COWLICK
HELP ILLUSION
OF HEAD TURN

and sketch houses or people." So of course, anything we sketched was going into our mental computers. This practice was very valuable.

HURD: I think I first met you about five years ago when I visited the studio in Monterey and met everyone who was working with Hank at the time.

FERDINAND: That was about our third location. First there was the office in Carmel Valley where I began. Then he built a house in Pebble Beach where he spent thousands converting it into a studio. At that point, there were six of us: three artists; a secretary; Fred Toole, who was writing the comic books; and Hank. Six cars

coming in each morning, six cars leaving for lunch, six cars departing at night. The nearby neighbors were getting very nervous so we had to leave that location.

HURD: During the fifteen years that you spent at Ketcham's studio in California, you could look directly over Hank's shoulder whenever any correction of your handling of *Dennis* was necessary. But now that you're back East, I know our readers would be very interested in the seemingly complicated exchange of faxes that you are engaged in.

FERDINAND: There are five or six freelance writers involved with *Dennis*. Half of them supply ideas for the daily panel, which is done by Marcus Hamilton in North Carolina, and the other half concentrate on doing gags for my Sunday page. The writers I deal with live in various parts of the country, and each sends ideas independently. The first step is for me to screen this material and fax the best of it out to Hank in California. He will return the approved scripts to me here, in Pine Bush, New York, with suggestions or alterations. Next, I do my first rough of the page, and since I work in fairly large size, I will reduce what I've done so I can fax the entire rough Sunday page to him on one 8½-by-11-inch sheet. (Obviously, because the use of a fax requires it, everything we send back and forth has to be on this standard-size sheet.) Hank may say, after viewing what I've sent, "I want a close-up here (or a silhouette there)." As soon as he faxes these suggestions back to me, I start work on the final pencil drawing for the page on a tracing vellum. When this is finished, I fax half the page on one sheet and the other half on a second sheet for final approval. (Formerly, I reduced my drawing and sent the entire page on one sheet. Hank later asked me to use the two sheets so it would be easier for him to indicate corrections.)

After getting Hank's approval on my final pencil drawing and adding his corrections, if any, I lay the drawing I've done on the tracing vellum on my light table, place a sheet of two-ply plate-finish Strathmore on top of it, and proceed with my inking, "skating across the surface" as Hank likes to describe the process. I use Gillott 170 pens and regret that the present-day aluminum black ones aren't the equal of the old-time copper ones. I use Pelikan black ink, in case your readers are interested. The finished drawing goes to Hank for final approval. I do the color guides for the page. Hank, as a rule, doesn't see these unless he happens to drop in on Dottie Roberson, the office manager in California, to whom I regularly send them. Dottie, of course, sees to it that the inked pages and the color guides go to King Features Syndicate.

HURD: Ketcham's continuing dedication to *Dennis* and the fine way you've responded to his guidance certainly have maintained *Dennis* as a beautiful Sunday page. Congratulations, Ron!

DENIS LEBRUN AND *BLONDIE*

Story from Issue No. 119, September 1998

Denis Lebrun

Over the years we have published several stories about our friend Dean Young, who took over the supervision and writing of the *Blondie* strip after the death of his father, Chic. We now have asked Denis Lebrun, who draws the famous feature so expertly, to talk about his part in the saga of the Bumsteads.

by Denis Lebrun

In 1981, I got the call to move up to the majors. At the time, I was working as art director for the *Burlington* (Vermont) *Free Press*. As I recall, I was in the bathroom when the managing editor burst through the door and said, "Lebrun, some guy who claims to be Dean Young is on the phone for you." Hmmm. Not the most ideal locale for a memorable moment, but that's how it happened that I started assisting Dean with *Blondie*.

I had met Dean Young when I was only eighteen years old (far out!). It was quite a thrill to meet a big-time cartoonist, but as much as I was in awe of him, I had no idea what the real consequences of our meeting would be in just a few short years.

In the early years on the strip, I was primarily doing backgrounds and lettering. Years before I started working on *Blondie,* I had done a comic strip of my own that I sold to a few newspapers. Because of that strip, I was aware of daily deadlines. Of course, the work on *Blondie* was much more intense than a strip with only a few newspapers.

Although *Blondie* is drawn in a style that has become very familiar and comfortable to readers, there have been changes. Over the years we've updated peripheral parts of the strip, and as far back as I can remember, Dean has continued to evolve *Blondie* to fit the times.

We went to three panels a couple of years ago. I think this was a great move. Dean felt we could get the graph-

me live in their house, and Dean refers to our household as a Teen Lab. In fact, it has turned out to be a great source of reference material. All I have to do is remember back when I was a teen. Hip huggers, bell bottoms, and tight tops have made a second appearance; *far out* is out but *coo* (cool) is in (you don't pronounce the *l*, it's not coo). We've also kept in step with fashions for Blondie and Dagwood. Dean sends me clothing catalogs he receives in the mail and circles the apparel he'd like to see Blondie in. I have a "Blondie fashion album" that is broken down into seasons.

Since Stan Drake's death in 1997, the responsibilities of drawing *Blondie* have been mine, but for many years Stan and I shared the workload. During those years, we also shared many observations about this American fixture called *Blondie,* and both of us came to understand that we were hired to continue a legacy. While the work was now drawn by different hands, the essence of the strip had to stay intact. I recall several conversations with Stan when he would wonder how Jim Raymond would have drawn a certain situation Dagwood was in. Still, as much as you try to keep the style and nuance of *Blondie* true, there will always be a little of yourself mixed in. This was true for Stan Drake and is now true for me. Fortunately, I grew up working on *Blondie.* More than three-quarters of my adult life has been with the strip. So the whole *Blondie* way of drawing has become instinctive. That's not to say it has been easy. I'd even bet that from time to time Dean doubted whether I would be able to handle it.

Back when I first started, Dean sent me ten years of *Blondie* proofs to study. They have been indispensable. *Blondie* is not an easy strip to draw. You have Dagwood, with his hair and all, verging on bigfoot style. Then you have Blondie; she's about as close to being anatomically correct (with a few enhancements) as you can get and still be a cartoon. One of the enduring traits of *Blondie* is that it's still drawn pretty much head to toe. Some of the most fun I have is drawing the incidental characters. Some pretty wacky characters show up at the Bumsteads' front door and as employees at Dagwood's office.

A typical workday never seems to happen. The direction of my day can sometimes change several times. I need at least fifty to sixty hours a week for six dailies and a Sunday page. This can vary, depending on how

ics a bit larger. Also, the three-panel layout gives me more room to work with and a little more white space, making it less busy. Blondie and Dagwood's offspring, Alexander and Cookie, have acquired love lives. Some great stuff is written for the kids, including jobs, driving, and all your run-of-the-mill teen problems. I myself have two teens who are graciously letting my wife and

Here's a Sunday pencil that I typically fax to Dean. We then discuss any changes in dialogue, expressions, or scenes over the phone. Sometimes there's nothing to change at all, and other times there may be major changes. Fortunately, the latter is rare.

part of my routine. Merchandising is unpredictable at best; we can get a bunch of work all due at once while still having to maintain the deadlines on the comic strip.

There are no shortcuts to drawing *Blondie*. Each line has to be deliberate, while still making it look spontaneous and simple. I use Pelikan Drawing Ink A with either a Hunt 103 or Gillott 1290 pen. I've been disappointed for the past several years with the Gillott 1290. It seems to wear out faster and the point is not as fine. I age my ink like a fine wine; I leave the cap off a lot to get the consistency I like to work with. If I'm not careful, though, it turns to sludge. For lettering, we use a Speedball A-5 filed down to the size and shape I feel comfortable with. My assistant, Jeff Parker, does most of the lettering now. I've passed down this filing and shaping thing I do to the lettering pen to him. I think it took him longer to figure out how I shaped the penpoint than to learn the lettering style. Jeff is also learning how to draw the *Blondie* way, and at the same time he's drawing editorial cartoons for the *Florida Today* paper. He's doing a fantastic job!

As for paper, I use a Strathmore two-ply plate finish. What a great paper! It holds ink on the surface, doesn't bleed, and is very smooth. I use an electric eraser with an eraser strip for pencil on those ink lines that go astray. The Faber Castell white pencil eraser strip is great for taking out the ink line and smoothing the paper, so I can re-ink over the very same area. For penciling, I use an HB but, more importantly, it's a .05mm technical drawing pencil. When you're drawing half-inch tall Blondie heads, you need a thin pencil lead. (Chic Young and Jim Raymond used to whittle and shape a normal pencil using a knife and sandpaper to get a nice fine point.) There's just one other tool I use to do the strip: coffee. I drink a lot of it. It's my stimulant of choice, and it's legal. When I die, I could be dry-roasted.

Since we are on the subject of tools, I have to mention that we've been using computers for various tasks since 1989. While the strip and merchandising work is still done by hand, we use the computer for coloring and post-production work. Since December 1995, we've been e-mailing the strip to King Features. We scan the strip in at 600 dpi and reduced to the size it appears on the proof sheet, about 6⅜ inches. After it's scanned and compressed, we attach it to e-mail and send it on its way. I've got a cable modem, so it's about two hundred

many characters are in each panel. When I read a script Dean has sent, I can usually tell how long it will take to pencil and ink. I know if Dean has written a gag that takes place in the post office and Dagwood is standing in line with lots of other people, I'll be camping out at my board for a couple of days. Merchandising is another

part of the future of our industry. We'll be able to broaden how we deliver a gag to the reader, utilizing animation and some interactive features. I still have to say, though, that many of my friends, myself included, still like a good old ink-on-the-fingertips newspaper. There is nothing that quite replaces its mobility and convenience. Besides, I'd miss digging around in the bushes for my morning paper.

Well, that's it for me. In closing, I'd like to thank you, Jud, for allowing me to stop all the work I have piling up to share some things with your readers. Actually, I'm honored. What a wonderful job you've done over the years. *CARTOONIST PROfiles* has been an inspiration from the very beginning of my career, and I'm proud to be a part of your ongoing look at our profession. Thanks again.

times faster than a 28.8 modem, plus I can watch reruns of *Gilligan's Island* while uploading to King.

This way of sending the strip now gives us the advantage of sending any corrections or changes instantaneously. Merchandising work can be like noontime at a popular restaurant. We'll get a sudden rush of work and deadlines are tight. Many times the client needs the work yesterday, and with the Internet we can almost do that. Overnight delivery is great, but sometimes we need an industrial-strength delivery system, and the Internet gives it to us. We do the color work on the computer, which makes changes and revisions a whole lot easier. The programs that we use are PhotoShop for the coloring and, occasionally, Illustrator.

Dean and I are wired now. Typically, I'll send pencils for him to review using a fax, but more often we're using the Internet to transfer art. I think the computer, and now the Internet, has opened the door to another dimension for comic strips. I'm not sure if anyone knows exactly how comics on the Internet will fit in, but I do know this: It's going to be a noticeable

AARON MCGRUDER
AND *THE BOONDOCKS*

Story from Issue No. 123, September 1999

Aaron McGruder was born in Chicago but grew up in Columbia, Maryland. Being one of two or three black faces in a predominately white neighborhood is familiar ground for the cartoonist. He attended the University of Maryland, although he had no formal art training. He was voted one of *People* magazine's twenty-five most intriguing people of 1999. When *The Boondocks* launched he was working out of his bedroom at his parents' house. He now lives in Los Angeles.

Aaron McGruder with Huey R. Freeman, the central character in *The Boondocks*

HURD: How did you go about being syndicated?

MCGRUDER: I took the standard route, I guess. I collected all my strips that had run in college papers (about thirty) and sent them off to the big syndicates. The return results were mixed: some flat rejections, some promising phone calls that eventually led to rejection, and some wait-and-see. During the summer of 1997, I attended the National Association of Black Journalists' annual convention with the hope of making some newspaper contacts who would support the strip, and I actually met a Universal Press Syndicate executive. I was offered a contract at the end of that summer.

HURD: Your strip is quite different from anything in newspapers today. Do you feel that you are pioneering a new voice for minorities?

MCGRUDER: That's how people seem to be taking the strip. I'm coming from a hip-hop foundation, which is about honest creative expression that isn't watered down or scared. I'm coming from the perspective that

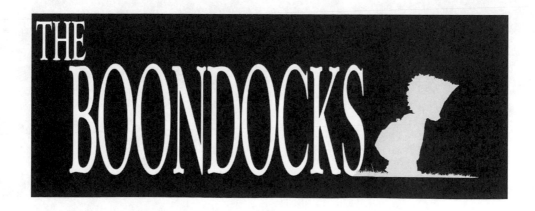

Cartoon Success Secrets

if you have something to say, you should do so without fear or hesitation but with great thought and preparation. People are amazed I say the things I say to mainstream America, but really it shouldn't be that big of a deal. The problem is that, because information is so controlled and limited in this country, different perspectives are quickly seen as offensive or subversive.

I have a responsibility to the black community to represent us accurately, depicting us both in writing and in art in a way that black people will be proud to allow their children to read. Also, it has been really important to me to try to expose the beauty of black children artistically in a way that exhibits the intelligence and sophistication of young black kids today. Then I build upon that in the writing of the strip. Black people are going to be watching very closely to see if something is misrepresented, and for good reason. They've been horribly misrepresented in the past.

HURD: Your characters speak frankly—as if you're trying to get away from the standard gag production. Talk about this.

MCGRUDER: Why on earth would I want to do anything standard? And why wouldn't the characters speak frankly? I don't think what I'm doing is so different from other strips that have come before. My favorite was probably *Bloom County*. There's some frank talk in that strip.

I'm a generation younger than most cartoonists so, admittedly, things may come off a little strong sometimes. That's good, though. It helps the strip get attention and helps me get my points across quicker.

HURD: What does the success of the strip represent to you?

MCGRUDER: I'm very grateful to the newspaper editors who signed on to *The Boondocks* early and made the launch so successful. To me, judging not only from

the launch but the overwhelming response, I would say it's an indicator that, while America has a long way to go before it tackles its racial issues, people from all walks of life are ready to start talking about things openly and addressing these taboo issues with candor and honesty. That's a good first step to solving problems.

HURD: How do you get your ideas? Are many of them patterned after things you have heard in conversations with friends?

MCGRUDER: Ideas come from everywhere. Sometimes they seem to manifest out of thin air like magic; sometimes I'll say something or a friend will say something that's just enough of a spark to ignite a strip or a week of strips. I think coming up with ideas is just about being conscious of what's around you, of what you're laughing at and why. I make sure to keep my eyes and ears open and then see what I can do with what I observe and absorb.

HURD: Talk about your love of cartooning. How did you first become interested? What need in you did it fill?

MCGRUDER: Honestly, I'm not sure if I have a love of cartooning. I love hip-hop, and I love drawing (sometimes). I love telling stories and developing characters. I love arguing and debating and getting a point across. I have a strong interest in the global racial dynamic and how it shapes politics, sociology, culture, and so on. So to me, cartooning seemed to be one of the few ways to express all these things simultaneously. Some people cartoon just for the love of the medium. I don't think that's me, yet. I'm still struggling to make the medium work for me. The spaces are too small, the deadlines are too unforgiving, and the industry is still too nervous and sanitized for my taste. But I'm working on that.

HURD: Talk about where your work was first seen and published.

Huey, radical scholar and central character of the strip, is the eternally scornful champion of the dispossessed.

Caesar, Huey's best friend, is the rambunctious and fun-loving Brooklyn native who dreams of microphones and lyrical dominance.

Jazmine, a young biracial girl, struggles to find her identity at the border of the color line.

Riley, Huey's younger brother, is the brash product of a popular black culture obsessed with gangsters.

Aaron McGruder and *The Boondocks*

MCGRUDER: *The Boondocks* started out online. It appeared on a small urban-oriented Web site in February 1996. At the end of the year, it started in my campus newspaper, the University of Maryland's *The Diamondback*. I did a three-month stint at *The Source* (where the strip will probably be returning in a few months) in the summer of 1998, and the newspaper launch was April 19, 1999.

HURD: How would you characterize hip-hop?

MCGRUDER: You don't have space for that here. Hip-hop is a culture that, to me, represents the latest manifestation of the always-evolving artistic expression of the black collective experience. The standard definition of hip-hop is an urban culture with four primary elements: graffiti, break dancing, Ding, and Ming. But its foundation is soul, which is a point of contention in contemporary hip-hop as it moves further and further away from the people who created it: black people. Many believe that what the mainstream media currently accepts and celebrates as hip-hop isn't really hip-hop at all, it's just commercially driven rap music with little artistic or cultural value.

HURD: How do you feel about the reader comments received by newspapers running your strip, both pro and con?

MCGRUDER: The strip is slowly accumulating a growing number of rabid fans, which is good. The strip also seems to have a lot of curious onlookers. That's good too. To the extent that pro and con comments lead to debates and discussion of sensitive racial topics, I think it's all wonderful. Then again, some of the people who attack this strip are just not getting the joke and do not understand the nature of satire.

HURD: What do you say to people who say the strip has racist overtones?

MCGRUDER: People throw words like *racist* and *stereotypes* around without much understanding of what they really mean in a society and culture as complex as

Cartoon Success Secrets

this one. I've found that often the accusation of racism comes from whites who simply cannot stand the thought of dealing with black people on our own terms. When we demonstrate true independence of thought and action, we are accused of widening the racial gap. It's as if "acceptance" of black equality is conditional on our behaving and speaking as much like white people as possible.

HURD: What are your passions? Movies, books, favorite music.

MCGRUDER: As I said, I love hip-hop music. I don't like the way it's going now, but it's like I'm married to it, and for good or ill I have to stick with it. I don't read as much as I should except for other comic strip collections (I'm constantly trying to figure out exactly what the hell I'm doing). Movies—well, they've been pretty bad recently, as well. I'm pretty open to all genres of movies, but everything has been more "miss" than "hit" recently. My biggest passion has always been *Star Wars*.

HURD: Talk about the opening of *Star Wars*.

MCGRUDER: I saw an early screening with a bunch of people, and we were all really excited when we left. Part of it was the sheer relief of having lived long enough to see this thing, and part of it was because the best part of the movie was at the very end. Even then the flaws were readily apparent. I've seen it four times since then, and it's just not a good movie. It is racist. I know lots of folks are skeptical on that whole issue, but you're just going to have to trust us on this one. It was boring, it was effects driven, and quite frankly there is no excuse for the movie to have any flaws after sixteen years of preparation. As if that wasn't bad enough, I

see where George Lucas is being called out for ripping off the creator of *Dinotopia*. What was he thinking?

Lucas needs to remember what was in his head when he made the first two movies. He needs to find Gary Kurtz and Irvin Kirshner (or another director), dump David McCallum, grab the reins on ILM, and stop using children as an excuse for bad screenwriting. The *only* part of *The Phantom Menace* that lived up to my expectations was the final duel—which was undoubtedly the cheapest part of the whole film.

HURD: Where do you go from here?

MCGRUDER: I hope *The Boondocks* will continue to grow and remain funny. I've become interested in other mediums as a vehicle for the strip in addition to print, like animation and possibly some merchandising. But that's a bit into the future. My goal for right now is to become the best cartoonist I can be. It's a great medium because there is so little standing between myself and the readers. Sure, the editors at the syndicate and the newspapers have some say, but Universal Press Syndicate doesn't alter my voice—there aren't a lot of hands in the strip trying to alter its direction—which is good. It's not like TV or movies, where you have to contend with so many different forces because someone else is paying the bills.

HURD: What advice can you give young aspiring cartoonists?

MCGRUDER: **1. Work from your heart.** This is a job that requires a lot of creative output. Ignore market forces or what people may tell you is the right way to go to sell a strip.

2. Believe in yourself but be flexible. Remember that only so much of this is in your hands. Tenacity, perseverance, and all that stuff are a necessity, but they still won't guarantee you success. More than 99 percent of the people who aspire to be syndicated cartoonists will not make it. For those who do make it, the struggle takes decades. Be open with your creativity. Know all the options for your talents. Don't be so focused on one medium that other opportunities go to waste or slip by unnoticed. I was interested in illustration, screen-writing, doing fine art, and comic books while I was pursuing syndication. I knew if I didn't succeed in one medium, I would in another. That's the mentality to keep. Know that you will succeed, and keep your mind open as to how it will happen.

3. Master your craft. No amount of flash, quick talking, or fine color reproductions from Kinko's can make up for good writing and good artwork.

4. Get your work noticed. Once you've mastered your craft, you have to sell it. Here's where a tasteful amount of flash, quick talking, and fine color reproductions from Kinko's *can* come in handy. All of the above helped me when the time came. The best art does you no financial good if it's never seen. Be totally unafraid of rejection. If it's at all possible, make them like you as a person. Know the difference between being persistent and being a pest.

5. No, the syndicates don't know everything. Yes, they might all be wrong about your strip.

MARCUS HAMILTON AND *DENNIS THE MENACE*

Story from Issue No. 124, December 1999

by Marcus Hamilton

Mr. Hurd—Jud—you had requested a follow-up article to your interview with my good friend and fellow *Dennis* artist, Ron Ferdinand. I am honored to have the opportunity to share with your readers this account of how my career and my life were dramatically changed when Hank Ketcham and *Dennis the Menace* crossed my path at a very opportune time.

As you acknowledged, it would have been more fun to have conducted this interview face-to-face, as you did with Ron at the Pen and Pencil in New York City, but the logistics of a Connecticut–Carolina rendezvous make it difficult. I do hope the opportunity will present itself at some point, as I would love to meet the legendary Jud Hurd in person.

The irony of my new career is that I didn't start out with the ambition to become a cartoonist. The opportunity to work with Hank Ketcham on *Dennis* just seemed to drop in my lap.

I read your profile of cartoonist Marshall Ramsey, and his earliest memory of drawing—when his mother gave him a note pad and pencil to keep him quiet in church—is exactly the same as mine. My childhood heroes were Walt Disney and Norman Rockwell. I thought it would be great to make a living drawing, and Disney's *Peter Pan* kindled a desire in me to pursue animation. However, after receiving the standard Mickey Mouse rejection slips, I turned my sights toward a career in magazine and book illustration.

I submitted printed samples to every publishing company whose address I could find in our local library. Countless negative responses from art directors did not stifle my determination to land that first national project. In 1971, that opportunity came when the art

After a visit to the New York offices of 'King' Features, Marcus gave his 'KONG' impression of the DENNIS crew's descent upon the BIG APPLE.

  By *Hank Ketcham*

Marcus Hamilton visiting the comics wall
at King Features in New York City

On March 14, 1996, DENNIS celebrated his 45th birthday!

"I MAY BE SIX YEARS OLD, BUT I FEEL LIKE I'M STILL FIVE!"

director for *True* magazine called to offer an illustration assignment.

I don't think you ever forget the feelings you experience when you get that first job! Those milestones in your career make all the struggling and perseverance worthwhile.

With my freelance toe in the publishing door, other assignments began coming along, so in 1972 I abandoned the security of a steady income (from my job at a design studio) and plunged into a full-time freelance career as an illustrator.

It was satisfying work that gave me many rewarding opportunities. My regular clients included *Golf Digest, Changing Times,* and *Saturday Evening Post.* I would have to say that one of the real highlights of my career as an illustrator was when I was asked to do a portrait of Bob Hope in a Santa outfit for the Christmas cover of the 1978 *Saturday Evening Post.* Quite a thrill!

But at some point during the eighties, the market for my style of illustration began to decline. Dependable clients stopped calling, and for a freelancer, a silent phone is deadly to your income. As my assignments dwindled, the creative challenges gave way to the financial problems of being self-employed . . . and I lost my enthusiasm for drawing. As I approached the half-century mark, I really felt I had peaked, and now it was all downhill.

My faith became my foundation for persevering and not giving up. My wife, Kaye, had always been supportive during the dry spells of my career, but now our situation was getting desperate. The few assignments I received could not sustain us and meet our financial obligations, so we decided that my illustration career had reached an end; I needed to find a *real* job. It was a scary proposition to start over at age fifty, but I did manage to get a minimum-wage job at WalMart, transferring photos to video.

The same day, Hank celebrated his birthday. This 'mock' panel was faxed to him as a Birthday greeting.

"I MAY BE 76, BUT I DON'T FEEL A DAY OVER 75!"

Art Director: Kwonk Wong
Client: Doubleday

MARCUS   HAMILTON
12225 RANBURNE ROAD
CHARLOTTE,   NC   28212
704·545·3121

On June 22, 1993, I was channel-surfing and caught the opening teaser to *The 700 Club*. They were previewing the new *Dennis the Menace* movie, premiering that week, and promised an interview with *Dennis*'s creator, and real dad, Hank Ketcham. I was hooked!

In the interview, Mr. Ketcham was asked what he wanted to do with the rest of his life, now that he had spent over forty years drawing *Dennis*. I'll never forget his response, because it changed the course of my life. It went like this: "I'd love to travel, and paint, and play golf, but I'd have to find someone to draw *Dennis* so I could retire."

I didn't have to hear any more. I went to the phone, called my friend Jim Scancarelli (cartoonist on *Gasoline Alley* and fellow Charlottean), and asked if he might have Hank Ketcham's phone number in California. He did, and I dialed.

Mr. Ketcham answered, and I told him that I had just seen his interview. I asked if he was serious about finding someone to draw *Dennis;* if so, I was an illustrator and would love to have the opportunity. He asked me to send him some examples of my work, which I did, and within a couple of weeks, I received his response. It was encouraging. He said he liked my work, and that if I was interested in pursuing *Dennis,* he would like to see some sketches of the DTM characters.

I can't tell you how excited I was at that point. Another one of those milestones.

I sent sketches to Hank, and he responded with his tutorial comments. Although his blue-line critique was extensive, his comments were always encouraging. He asked me to get some two-ply Bristol board and India ink and try my hand at inking with the Gillott 170 pen points that he had sent.

After years of using an Artograph overhead projector and working in acrylics and watercolors on canvas and illustration board, this new process of inking on thin Bristol over a pencil sketch on a light box was an exhilarating challenge! Hank's instructions were to have *fun* with it. Make it sing! Simplify!

As I studied every piece of *Dennis* reference I could get my hands on, I practiced sketching the Ketcham characters over and over. I kept a sketch pad in the car, and at each stoplight I would see how many *Dennis* heads I could draw before the light changed. That self-discipline paid off, since I now need speed to stay up with our weekly deadlines.

Hank agreed to train me to take over the responsibilities of producing the daily *Dennis* panel, so that after forty-five years, he could get out from under the unrelenting demands of doing a daily comic feature. I can

Cartoon Success Secrets

Preliminary sketches...

Finished pencil sketches; ready for final inking.

Z6129

"CAN THE MONKEYS COME OUT AND PLAY?"

"CAN YOUR MONKEYS COME OUT AND PLAY?"

First, Second... third... and FINAL, approved panel.

"CAN THE MONKEYS COME OUT AND PL..."

"CAN YOUR MONKEYS COME OUT ANT..."

"CAN THE MONKEYS COME OUT AND PLAY?"

"CAN THE MONKEYS COME OUT AND PLAY?"

understand why. Also, he wanted time to channel his creative energy into fine arts painting.

Thanks to the fax machine, I have had the opportunity of staying here in Charlotte and being taught by one of the true masters of cartoon illustration. One of my fears about doing a daily feature was that I would run out of compositional ideas and the panels would become mundane reruns. But through his guidance and encouragement, Hank has been able to stretch my thinking beyond that old limited view to see the many poses and situations and unlimited possibilities for the characters.

I think that next to his classy penmanship, what I admire most about Hank's work is his ability to take the same characters, and similar situations, and always make them look distinctively different and fresh. *That* has inspired me to strive to see everyday situations as a creative challenge.

Your interview with Ron was also encouraging. I had admired Ron's work on the *Dennis* Sunday page before I ever knew he was the one doing it. His creative use of color, silhouettes, and composition present a standard of quality that I hold in high regard.

One of the great by-products of this whole situation has been the opportunity to get to know Hank, of course, but also Ron and Dottie Roberson. Dottie is Hank's executive secretary and right-hand person, totally involved in the whole enterprise. So her willingness to keep me in the loop has certainly made me feel like part of the Ketcham Funny Factory.

In Ron's interview, he mentioned that we work with several experienced gag writers. Hank has allowed Ron and me to have more creative input in the gag selection process, so it is definitely a team effort.

I'm always asked how long it takes to do one daily *Dennis,* and there's no pat answer. Most of my time is spent on research and penciling roughs. The process goes basically like this: As I read the gag, which is just a quote by one of the cast, I take the who-what-where-how approach: *Who* is saying this? *What* has caused this situation? *Where* are they? *How* am I going to show this in an eye-catching way?

I do my thinking in sketch form, placing the figures inside the roughly drawn box shape of the daily panel. Hank explains that it's like a window on the scene. He says the artist is the director and the cameraman. The

SHADOWS can provide a dramatic impact!

"BOY, LOOK AT ALL OF THE STARS! I WONDER WHICH ONE IS TOM HANKS?"

"JOEY ISN'T SCARED OF THE DARK. HE'S SCARED OF THE *STUFF* HIDING IN IT!"

I've always appreciated Hank's great sense of DESIGN through his placement of solids, patterns, etc. I try to maintain quality in the panels.

"I DON'T SEE WHAT'S SO *GREAT* ABOUT PARADES!"

A <u>simple</u> approach

"AW, COME ON, MOM. I'M NOT A **KID** ANYMORE!"

a more <u>complex</u> approach.

"I'VE GOT ENOUGH CANDY. THIS YEAR I'M GOIN' FOR THE **HARD CASH!**"

actors and props can go anywhere in the frame, but you must move your eye, your camera, to the best vantage point to emphasize the focal point of the gag. And you have ten seconds to capture and hold the reader's attention.

This philosophy has encouraged me not to be afraid to draw the same scene over and over from different angles. Hank has worked diligently to instill in me his perspective on *Dennis*. And after three years, I have conditioned myself to try different approaches to everyday scenes to capture the humor in each gag. It's not always easy, but it is always a challenge. I told Hank that drawing *Dennis* is the most strenuous fun I've ever had at the drawing board!

Once I've completed sketches for a week's worth of dailies, I fax them to Hank for his input. And he always has comments, not always flattering to my efforts but always his honest opinion (for which I'm grateful).

Occasionally I hit a brick wall and can't seem to get a particular scene to work. It's then that I really appreciate Hank's little thumbnail roughs. They quickly shake me out of my tunnel vision and give me a broader perspective. I don't know how he does it . . . it's like he never runs out of new ideas. I envy that!

When my pencil roughs are approved, I enlarge them on the copier to the actual art size, 6¼ by 7⅜ inches, and do a final loose pencil tracing on vellum. That tracing is placed on the light table, and a piece of two-ply plate-finish Bristol is taped over it (so the sketch shows through). Then I begin the inking process. The border is drawn free-hand with a Speedball B-4 nib. The lettering at the bottom of the panel is also hand-drawn, with a Speedball C-5. The panel is drawn with the Gillott 170 pen point, with heavy black areas added with a No. 3 brush.

Once I have six panels completed, they are reduced on the copier to fit on one sheet to fax to Hank for final (I hope) approval. Even at this finished stage, the panels are not guaranteed an OK. Usually some fine-tuning is required, minor revisions to noses, fingers, or chairs. Another couple of hours are required to make the necessary cut/glue/whiteout changes.

Then, into a Priority package, and another week of *Dennis* dailies is on its way to North America Syndicate in New York, to be copied, put into a one-page format with publication dates, and sent out to newspaper

Research, for accuracy, requires occasional visits to the Mall, or a bowling alley.

"I'LL BETCHA THE SMELL KEEPS ALL THE MEN AWAY, HUH?"

"YOU'RE SUPPOSED TO *KNOW* IF I'VE BEEN NAUGHTY OR NICE, SO HOW COME YOU ALWAYS ASK ME IF I'VE BEEN A GOOD *BOY*?"

"LET'S ROLL THEM BOTH AT THE SAME TIME, JOEY, THEN MAYBE WE'LL GET A STRIKE."

DENNIS' annual visit to his Uncle Charlie's farm calls for some extensive research, and allows me the opportunity to escape the studio long enough to carry my sketchpad to a local farm for on-sight sketching.

"NO WONDER THOSE COWS LOOK SO COOL. THEY HAVE THEIR OWN *FAN*."

"ANOTHER GREAT THING ABOUT A FARM, JOEY... DIRTY HANDS ARE *PERFECTLY NORMAL*!"

"WHERE DO YOU PUT THE *MONEY* TO MAKE IT GO, UNCLE CHARLIE?"

Although the background technique implies complexity, the simplicity of the foreground figures carries this panel.

"FIREFLIES BLINK LIKE THAT, JOEY, WHEN THEY'RE GOING TO MAKE A *TURN*."

Snowy, winter scenes are fun! With just a few lines you can create a 'chilling' atmosphere.

"LOOK, MOM. AN ICICLE BUILT FOR TWO."

My favorite in the cast is JOEY... he's trusting and gullible. I guess I relate to him because my family accuses _ME_ of being gullible.

"...BUT LOOK AT IT THIS WAY... *NOW* YOU HAVE THE ONLY BUGGY WITH A *SUN-ROOF!*"

I get a chuckle from some of Wilson's facial reactions to DENNIS' innocently-pointed statements.

"THAT GUY SAID IF YOU USED TO BUY THESE FOR A DIME, YOU MUST BE A *HUNDRED YEARS OLD!*"

As Dennis leans on Marcus' shoulder... creator and Mentor, Hank Ketcham keeps a watchful eye OVER his shoulder.

Wow! Talk about a spittin image!

Thanks heaps, Marcus! I've never looked better! You are a mountain of talent!

Hank

After my first trip to Hank's Monterey studio, I sent him a color portrait in appreciation. This drawing was his response.

offices worldwide. The next time I see those panels is six weeks later in our local *Charlotte Observer*. What a process!

I am truly grateful for the opportunity to work with Hank, Ron, and Dottie; to get to know the good folks at King Features; and to be part of the team that is committed to continuing the legacy of *Dennis the Menace*. I hope the popularity of Hank Ketcham's little mischief-maker continues for another forty-five years and beyond, and that I will have the privilege of being on the Ketcham team.

Two well-known American personalities who have provided highlights in Marcus Hamilton's career: *Dennis the Menace* and Bob Hope in a painting for the cover of the *Saturday Evening Post*.

FAMILY CIRCUS:
THE NEXT GENERATION

Story from Issue No. 127, September 2000

by Christopher Keane

Author's Note: Before you read the following article, you should know that I am more than a reader of the *Family Circus,* I am also a member. As Bil Keane's son, my every childish blooper was recorded and exposed in a daily panel. Gee, Dad, thanks—maybe I can do the same for you someday. Anyway, Dad asked me to write this article for him; in exchange, I won't have to clean my room for a week. Thought you all should know.

Life's a circle. And so is the *Family Circus.*

For more than forty years, that simple circle in the morning funnies has held a lens on American family life. Its humor has been described as nerve-touching,

Bil and Jeff painting a mural at McCormick-Stillman Railroad Park in Scottsdale, Arizona. It is in a hundred-year-old relocated railway station, now an ice cream parlor. Bil says he was asked to do it because they wanted the mural done by someone older than the building.

tear-in-the-eye, lump-in-the-throat, warm, fuzzy—actually, that sounds more like the flu—let's just call it gentle humor. Or take two aspirin, and get plenty of rest.

In addition, *Family Circus* is a chronicle of middle-class parents and children: a daily look at their foibles and fancies through the years, from color TV to Web sites, from Captain Kangaroo to Pokémon.

However, the continuity of the feature has recently come into question. Since the loss of Charles Schulz from our lives and the disappearance of new *Peanuts* strips from the comics pages, there is a greater focus on the longevity of these older comic strips. Editors and fans alike have asked Dad about the future of *Family Circus*. Will Bil Keane retire? Will the *Family Circus* continue afterward?

As to the first question, Dad is absolutely adamant. He says he has no plans of retiring in the near future. You can believe it; he barely retires each evening. This is a guy who still sits behind the drawing board in his Arizona studio seven days a week, often starting at sunrise and working till Leno. We would have to pry the pen from his grip before he'd take afternoons off.

As to the long-term future of the strip, Dad says, "I can see Sparky's point of view. He didn't want anyone else to ever touch *Peanuts*. "But I'm on the other side. What I spent my lifetime building, I'd hate to see fold

and go under. The feature is a reflection of family life, and since family life goes on and on, so should the *Family Circus*."

Toward that end, Dad handpicked his eventual successor. Actually, he created one years ago—his youngest son.

No, not Billy. That kid never could draw. After four decades, seven-year-old Billy still scrawls only crude stick-figure cartoons. Oddly enough, many long-time *Family Circus* readers still think those cartoons are penciled by a first-grader.

"Those are some of the hardest cartoons for me to draw," said Bil. "I have to keep thinking, How would a seven-year-old draw that? How would he draw a computer, for instance? It's not easy."

What was easy was choosing his successor.

My brother Jeff has assisted Dad with the *Family Circus* for the past twenty years. As Jeffy in the cartoon, he grew up with an intimate knowledge of the feature's inner workings. As a family man, he lives in southern California suburbia with his wife, Melinda, and their three kids: Spencer, age eight; Matilda, six; and Olivia, three. Jeff has a front-row seat at his own family circus. And like his father, Jeff works at home.

"That's one of the things I've really enjoyed—always being at home with the kids. Of course, come to think of it, that's also one of the things I sometimes hate."

"If you help me with history, I'll help you with the computer."

"What's the magic word to get what you want?"

"Grandma!"

The Keane Family in 1960, the year *Family Circus* was created. Front row: Glen, now directing animator with Walt Disney Feature Animation; Jeff, Bil's assistant; Christopher. a writer in Tucson; Neal, a musician and computer design engineer in LA. Back row: Gayle, only daughter, lives in Napa, handles Bil's mail and book orders, and is operations assistant for Bil and Thel; Thel, the heart of *Family Circus,* model for Mommy, inspiration for Bil, and business manager; and Bil.

Jeff's first collaboration with Dad was a cartoon strip called *Eggheads.* Jeff had recently graduated from the University of Southern California with a degree in fine arts when Dad asked for his help on a new feature.

"I've always loved puns, but I found they didn't lend themselves to *Family Circus,*" said Bil. "So I started *Eggheads.* It was simply drawn and had a kind of vaudeville-type humor."

(First guy: "Did you take a bath?" Second guy: "No, is one missing?" Rim shot, groan.)

Bil wrote the gags, and Jeff drew the strip. It only appeared in about thirty newspapers, and after two years they stopped it altogether. "The sameness of the material caused it to falter," said Bil.

But by then, Jeff was helping on *Family Circus.*

"He was the obvious choice whenever I needed help," said Bil. "He's a very thorough guy and makes sure what he does is letter perfect. He gradually took over all the inking and coloring for the Sunday pages."

Jeff said, "I didn't consciously go into this with the idea of doing the *Family Circus.* It just gave me a firm schedule and an income. I understood the main ideas, the humor. The main thing I had to learn was drawing in Dad's style. But the more I did it, the more I had a sense of what was going on.

"I remember as a little kid going into Dad's studio and trying to draw his cartoons. Trying to trace them. There was one in particular of all these kids at a birth-day party that I spent hours tracing. Of course, I'm still only half done with it. . . . Maybe I can finally finish it now."

In their current working relationship, Dad remains the idea man and Jeff finishes the art. "I rough out the

THE FAMILY CIRCUS,   **By Bil Keane**

2-15
©2000 Bil Keane, Inc.
Dist. by King Features Syrd.

"Harry Potter IS a wizard. He's taken Billy's mind off Pokémon."

Cartoon Success Secrets

ideas for the daily and Sunday pages and FedEx them to Jeff," said Bil. "Jeff takes a kneaded eraser and erases all my lines. Then he redraws it in pencil. Finally he uses a No. 2 sable brush and imitates the visual line in ink.

"Many times a cartoonist can't control the brush smoothly. I always used a croquill pen and leaned heavily on it. But in 1965 I started with an assistant, Bud Warner. Bud was able to imitate my style with the brush, and it looked much smoother. He developed the smooth finished look of the *Family Circus* cartoon. Jeff has also mastered the brush.

"Jeff has been a godsend," Bil added. "He not only can do the physical labor, he can discern what's funny and what isn't. I lean on him for how a gag works with modern-day kids, which TV show they watch, which toys they play with."

"And Dad never hesitates to tell me when I'm wrong," Jeff said.

Of course, there were no grandiose schemes when Bil Keane first started drawing *Family Circus*. What became an icon in cartoon history began for the same reason most cartoons do. It brought in a few bucks.

The next generation of inspiration for their dad and granddad, Jeff's idea people: Spencer, Olivia, and Matilda

"With five little kids to feed and a mortgage, all I wanted was a little more income," said Bil. "Back then I had *Channel Chuckles* in a few newspapers." (*Channel Chuckles* was a panel gag about television that appeared in the TV sections of about two hundred newspapers from 1954 to 1976.) "I was picking up about two hundred dollars a week doing freelance magazine stuff, but the income was up and down. I figured if I could get another daily syndicated and pick up another hundred and fifty a week, I could quit the freelance gags and have some good predictable income."

For the new daily cartoon, Dad went with his strength.

"When I'd send off a bunch of freelance cartoons, the editors at *Collier's* and *Saturday Evening Post* and the other magazines always seemed to pick the stuff that had to do with kids. I figured I was good at that, so I picked that direction. I think that determined the success of *Family Circus*.

"I also put it in a circle because I wanted it to stand out on the comics page. I think editors liked that because it was a little different.

"When I first started *Family Circus*, it was more exaggerated family humor. Everything would go toward the big laugh, the kind of stuff that Jerry Scott and Rick Kirkman are doing so well now in *Baby Blues*. But I think

To answer many inquiries, here is the secret of how the dotted line behind Billy is produced.

THE FAMILY CIRCUS. By Bil Keane

5-29
©2000 Bil Keane, Inc.
Dist. by King Features Synd.

"At least you won't hafta worry anymore about that vase gettin' broken."

the injection of warm tear-in-the-eye humor is what built a particularly strong following for me.

"Consequently, since I didn't always have to be funny I could change the pace of the cartoon, going day to day from funny, to a warm loving look, to a commen-

tary; I even went so far as to inject religion. It all made it more interesting to the reader."

Jeff agrees that formula is necessary for the continued success of the feature.

"I don't feel there's a great difference between Dad's and my approach," Jeff said. "If I've had any influence over the years, it may be keeping the cartoon a bit more current. But the cartoon is still more about Dad's ability to observe. Kids are still just kids. Only now it's Pokémon instead of G.I. Joe.

"I wouldn't ever seek to change things for the sake of changing them. That's just ego. I guess it might be fun to make it really funny, but then you'd kill the quiet quality that *Family Circus* has. I like to see cartoons remain the same type of cartoon."

Both Jeff and Bil cite Dik Browne's *Hagar the Horrible* as a great example of a cartoon that successfully passed between generations.

"Chris Browne does a beautiful job, just like his father did," said Jeff. Bil added, "Chris has carried on very well; the cartoon looks pretty much the same. In fact, Chris looks pretty much the same as Dik, too."

But Bil Keane's grooming of a successor would be almost moot if he didn't own his cartoon. And like most cartoonists, he didn't.

In 1960, when the Register & Tribune Syndicate agreed to distribute his new feature, they required Dad to sign over all rights to them. Dad understood that as just common practice, the industry standard for cartoonists and syndicates. So it wasn't an issue for him—until 1978.

During new contract negotiations that year, Dad felt justified in asking for a higher percentage of the revenues and a five-year contract. *Family Circus* had become hugely popular. As an anchor of the comics page, it practically sold itself. In fact, the syndicate could use it as a package headliner to sell less popular features.

But R&T refused Dad's request for more money and demanded a ten-year deal. When Dad balked at signing, R&T threatened to take the panel away from him.

"I felt like they put a gun to my head," Bil said. "I was afraid I would lose my life's work. They even got a guy in Des Moines to start practicing on *Family Circus,* trying to imitate my artwork. So I knew they were serious."

Faced with the possible loss of his creative heart, Dad caved in. He signed "under protest." Control stayed with

This 1965 cartoon is the one Jeff recalls trying to trace as a little kid. *Sideshow* was the part of the Sunday page that pulled in volumes of reader mail. Street addresses of contributors were eventually eliminated as a precaution against unwanted mail, sent to kids even back then.

Jeff Keane, right, along with older brother Christopher, in 1967, opening reader mail solicited in Bil's *Sideshow* feature

A special drawing done by Bil for a magazine cover on the occasion of his Reuben Award in 1983

the syndicate. But from then on, Dad wanted to regain the rights.

In 1986, King Features bought the Register & Tribune (which by then had become Cowles Syndicate). Another round of contract talks began. Dad had one overriding demand—copyright to the feature. King was just as adamantly opposed to the idea.

A long and often bitter contract battle ensued. Fortunately, Dad's efforts were led by the *Family Circus* mommy, Thel Keane. As the business mind behind the success of Dad's career, Mom led the negotiations, along with their lawyer, and took a hard-line stance. When King talked about taking the feature away from Dad, she urged him to stand his ground. Finally, in 1988, King gave Dad what he wanted: the copyright to his own creation.

On January 30, 1989, © *Bill Keane, Inc.* appeared beneath *Family Circus* for the first time. It ensured that the panel would never again be out of Keane control. And it allowed Dad to plan for the future.

Every true cartoonist bleeds India ink—at least the best ones do, or those prone to paper cuts. Their work reflects their heart and soul. That has never been truer than for Dad and his *Family Circus*. And now for Jeff Keane too.

Family Circus is a reflection of family life. More specifically, it's a reflection of the Keane family. With the assistance of Jeff, life in that circle will roll into the next generation.

Editor's Note: Christopher Keane is a journalist and author. He lives in Tucson, Arizona, with his wife, Mette, and their son, Oliver.)

CATHY GUISEWITE AND *CATHY*

Story from Issue No. 133, March 2002

by Cathy Guisewite

To my left are four hundred newspaper articles I've ripped out, thinking they'd be good material someday. On the floor are sixty newspapers and magazines I haven't even looked through yet. Next to them, a foot-high stack of "miscellaneous joke fragments." On the file cabinet, heaps of mail I haven't answered, piles of bills I haven't paid, bank statements I haven't balanced, offers I haven't opened, receipts I haven't filed, two broken Barbie dolls, a bag of clothes to return, a fat-gram guide, Federal Express form for the dailies I sent this week (really late), Federal Express form for

the Sunday I'm sending today (really, *really* late), five belated birthday cards, four belated wedding cards, a "to do" list that's virtually unchanged since the mid-eighties, and, in front of me, this: a really, really, really overdue story about the twenty-fifth anniversary of *Cathy*.

This story is late because I decided to create four books to celebrate the strip's anniversary, and the books were all late. The books were all late because I found the most complicated way possible to take apart and reassemble twenty-five years of work. The books are titled, *Food, Mom, Love,* and *Work*—what I've always referred to as the four basic guilt groups. For each book, I went through every strip I'd ever done on the subject, made a copy, spread them all over my office, and then completely rearranged the strips, divided them into chapters, and wrote a sort of narrative to connect it all. It's the exact same psychotic approach to life that prevents me from ever getting caught up on anything—and provides most of my subject matter.

I quit drawing when I was eight years old because my big sister, Mary Anne, was the artist of the family, and I didn't want to compete with her in an area where she was so brilliant. I also felt it was pointless to learn to draw since it would be of no use in my chosen career, which was to be a cowboy like my hero, Roy Rogers.

My first real drawing was a self-portrait—twenty-five years old, forty-five pounds overweight, miserable love life, eating everything in my suburban Detroit apart-

Cathy Guisewite

CATHY   **by Cathy Guisewite**

This is the first *Cathy* strip that ever ran, November 22, 1976.

Cathy Guisewite

I sent my drawings to Universal Press Syndicate just to get Mom to quit nagging me, and they sent me back a contract within a week. I immediately bought a drawing board and a box of donuts and frantically tried to learn how to draw. My how-to bible was a book Dad found for me called *Backstage at the Strips* by Mort Walker. I told no one I was working on a comic strip. The day the first *Cathy* ran in the paper, I was so embarrassed and insecure I hid in the ladies' room at the office for most of the day. I kept my advertising job for a year, partly because I loved it, mostly because I was sure the syndicate was going to call and tell me they were just joking about me being a cartoonist.

Universal Press Syndicate told me they bought *Cathy* because the writing was so genuine. It was 1976, and they had been hoping to find a strip that dealt with how radically the world was changing for women. All the submissions they'd seen before mine had been created by men and didn't exactly have the same emotional honesty about the massively conflicted feelings women my age were experiencing in the late seventies. Lee Salem, then an editor, worked with me to help me define main characters (all the men problems became "Irving," all the feminist lectures were condensed into "Andrea," all the other girlfriends became "Charlene.")

ment kitchen while waiting for Mr. Wrong to call. It wasn't even a drawing so much as an explosion of frustration that wound up on paper instead of in my mouth. It made me so happy to see a picture of me at my worst that I started coming home from my job as an advertising writer and summing up my disaster of the day in picture form pretty regularly.

My mother, an extremely private person, had always taught me to write about feelings instead of sharing personal things with others. I sent the drawings home with letters to let Mom know I was keeping my feelings private and that I hadn't completely lost my sense of humor.

Mom, the champion of privacy, immediately went to the library, researched comic strip syndicates, and typed a list of the ones she thought I should submit my drawings to, in the order I should submit them, so that millions of people could share my humiliating personal moments. Universal Press Syndicate was at the top of Mom's list, mostly because they represented *Ziggy*. Mom and Dad had had a long correspondence with *Ziggy*'s creator, Tom Wilson, when I was in college. I had written a little book for Mom for Mother's Day one year, and Mom and Dad (lifelong proud, pushy parents) had sent it to Tom, who was at American Greetings, about possibly publishing it.

Cathy Guisewite

These are the covers of my four anniversary books.

For a few years, I sent pencil roughs of all strips to Lee, who would work with me to figure out what worked and what didn't. When I quit sending pencil roughs, I used to read him everything over the phone before I drew it. Somewhere around year four, he told me to start sending the finished strip in without going over roughs, and I remember being virtually paralyzed with fear.

Universal Press has been an incredible support system for *Cathy* from the fragile first years on. Between my different art style, writing style, and subject matter, the strip wasn't exactly an easy sell, especially in the late seventies when almost all the potential buyers were men. The people at Universal Press have been unwavering in their willingness to stand by me; they're known not only for supporting but for encouraging creative risks, and because of this they have really helped create a comic strip page with more unique points of view. Even if another syndicate had been willing to take me on in 1976, which I doubt, I know I wouldn't have lasted more than a year.

In the first years of the strip, it used to take me eight full hours to draw one daily strip (after it was written), and two full days to draw a Sunday. I worked seven days a week, from the second I got up until two or three in the morning. Because drawing anything new (like an arm raised, a leg crossed, a person walking) took so

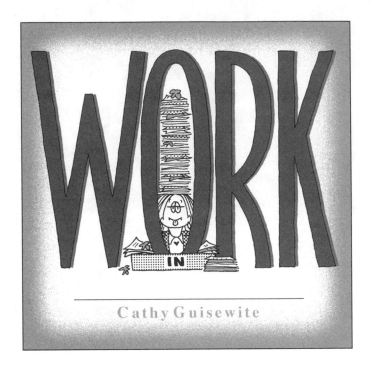

many tries, I developed a system of drawing each frame over and over on tracing paper until I had it sort of right and then tracing the best versions of each frame onto Bristol board with a light box. This is still the system I use. I draw everything—even the first roughs—with a rapidograph pen. I don't use pencil at all except to draw some straight guidelines for backgrounds.

The single most amazing moment of my career was in 1977 when the late great Ed Mitchell invited me to the Northern California Cartoon and Humor Association meeting in San Francisco to talk about being a new cartoonist. I had never known a cartoonist before and couldn't believe I was getting to fly across the country to meet a whole roomful of them. I remember standing in the room before the event started and hearing a little commotion at the door. I looked across the room where—it seemed like in slow motion—the crowd was parting and this tall astoundingly handsome man was walking toward me. "Hello," he said, "I'm Sparky Schulz."

I felt as though I had just met God. I was new to cartooning, but a lifelong worshiper of *Peanuts*. It had helped define my sense of humor. The characters were like my best friends; they had already given me a lifetime of comfort and perspective and made me feel I was never alone. I'm sure I never would have thought

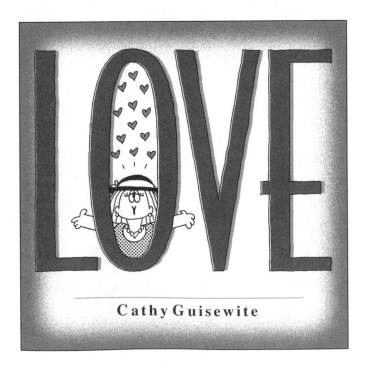

FOOD - '70s

FOOD - '80s

FOOD - '90s

FOOD - '00s

MOM - '70S

MOM - '80S

MOM - '90S

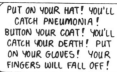

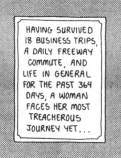

MOM - '00S

Cartoon Success Secrets

LOVE - '70S

Panel 1: WELL, WELL. HOW'S MS. HOTSHOT TODAY?
IRVING, I DON'T KNOW WHY YOU RESENT MY CAREER SO MUCH.

Panel 2: MY CAREER IS SUPPOSED TO BE MAKING ME MORE VIBRANT AND INTERESTING TO YOU. SEE?

Panel 3: MY CAREER IS ADDING A FRESH NEW DIMENSION TO OUR LIVES! IT'S MAKING US A DYNAMIC YOUNG COUPLE OF THE 70'S!

Panel 4: YOUR CAREER IS MAKING ME SICK!
THESE ARTICLES ALWAYS LEAVE SOMETHING OUT.

LOVE - '80S

Panel 1: OKAY, I'LL SEE YOU LATER, CATHY.
"LATER" AS IN "TONIGHT," OR "LATER" AS IN, "SOMETIME IN THIS LIFETIME"?

Panel 2: OH, HA, HA. GIVE ME A CALL SOMETIME.
"GIVE YOU A CALL" AS IN "YOU RESPECT MY RIGHT TO TAKE THE INITIATIVE" OR, "GIVE YOU A CALL" AS IN "CALL ONLY WHEN YOU SPECIFICALLY ASK"?

Panel 3: YOU'RE A RIOT, CATHY. WELL, I'VE GOT TO GO.
"I'M A RIOT" AS IN, "YOU LOVE ME" OR "I'M A RIOT" AS IN, "WE JUST BROKE UP"?

Panel 4: MEN SHOULD COME WITH INSTRUCTION BOOKLETS.

LOVE - '90S

WHAT A WOMAN SAYS:
I KNOW YOU THINK I'M TOO JEALOUS, BUT WHY SHOULD CHARLENE GET GIFTS ALL VALENTINE'S WEEK WHEN YOU AND I GO BACK SO MUCH FURTHER? CAN'T YOU PLAY ALONG WITH ROMANCE A LITTLE?? IS YOUR WHOLE HEART USED UP BY YOUR STUPID GOLF GAME??

WHAT A MAN HEARS:
I KNOW YOU THINK I'M TOO JEALOUS, BUT WHY SHOULD CHARLENE GET GIFTS ALL VALENTINE'S WEEK WHEN YOU AND I GO BACK SO MUCH FARTHER? CAN'T YOU PLAY ALONG WITH ROMANCE A LITTLE?? IS YOUR WHOLE HEART USED UP BY YOUR STUPID GOLF GAME??
OK.

LOVE - '00S

Panel 1: HAPPY VALENTINE'S DAY FROM MY LAPTOP TO HIS PALM PILOT...

Panel 2: HAPPY VALENTINE'S DAY FROM MY AUTO-DIAL CELL PHONE TO HIS DIGITIZED VOICE MAIL / PAGER SYSTEM.

Panel 3: HAPPY VALENTINE'S DAY FROM MY HIGH-RES, FLATBED SCANNER TO HIS WIRELESS WEB MESSAGE RETRIEVAL DEVICE.

Panel 4: WHAT HAPPENED TO "HAPPY VALENTINE'S DAY FROM ONE HUMAN TO ANOTHER"??
TOO COMPLICATED.

WORK - '70s

WORK - '80s

WORK - '90s

WORK - '00s

Cartoon Success Secrets

Examples of what I submitted to the Universal Press Syndicate. They liked the "energy" of my art and were confident I would learn to draw if I had to do it 365 days a year.

to sum up my insecurities in picture form if Sparky hadn't done it first. A strip like mine would never have had a place in the paper if *Peanuts* hadn't paved the way. That Sparky, who hated to leave his home, drove more than an hour to come that night to meet me and offer his encouragement, changed my life and is a perfect example of why he was so beloved in our world.

Sparky became a wonderful friend and mentor. Because of him, I moved from Detroit to California, even-

tually winding up in Los Angeles. I asked him once how long I'd have to do the strip before I wouldn't wake up fearing all the papers were going to drop me on that day. He said, "Ten years." On the tenth anniversary of *Cathy* I called him up and told him he'd underestimated. He laughed and said he hadn't wanted to discourage me with the truth, which was that we'd all signed up for a lifetime of insecurity.

My "work routine" is the same today as it has always been: flinging myself at whatever is most overdue and letting everything else stack up. I have a fantasy work routine—write on Monday, draw Tuesday, Wednesday, and Thursday, spend Friday on mail and special projects—which I have never yet once achieved in twenty-five

years. I spend a really, really long time writing the strip. I've heard of cartoonists writing a couple of weeks of strips in a day. It sometimes takes me a full day to write (and not even start to draw) one strip.

I worked solely out of my house until I started doing so much licensing that my whole house was taken over, so I got an outside office. I don't do the licensing anymore, but now I have children and have kept the office because I have to be in a different zip code to form a coherent thought.

The biggest change in my life is that I now have to apologize for being thin. After years of trying to hide my fat, I now have to carry *before* pictures to prove I actually have a fat person inside still screaming to get out. The other specifics of Cathy's and my life are different, but the basic life challenges are exactly the same. We share the "bathroom cupboard problem," the "ten years of miscellaneous photos not in albums problem," the "weeping on the floor of the swimsuit department dressing room problem." We share the same dreams: finish last year's Christmas thank-you notes before this Christmas gets here, stay on a budget and/or workout program for more than twelve hours in a row, begin and finish a phone call with Mom without turning into a five-year-old.

I live in Los Angeles with my husband, Chris Wilkinson (screenwriter of *Nixon* and *Ali*), my daughter Ivy (age nine), stepson Cooper (age five), and the constant undying belief that sometime next week I'm going to be ahead of my deadline and have everything under control.

A DAY IN THE LIFE OF ZITS

Story from Issue No. 136, December 2002

by Jerry Scott and Jim Borgman

JIM: Every day in recent years I have awakened thinking of new ways to cartoon the antics of the most famous adolescents in America. I am speaking, of course, of Bill Clinton and George W. Bush. But when my editorial cartoon is done and the republic is safe for another day, I turn my attention to *Zits,* the comic strip Jerry Scott and I launched in the summer of 1997 about the world of fifteen-year-old Jeremy Duncan, his parents, and his friends.

JERRY: We're often asked how we can create a comic strip while living almost 2,500 miles apart (I live in Malibu, California, and Jim lives in Cincinnati, Ohio), and the best answer we've come up with is *electricity.* We keep in touch daily by telephone, fax, and e-mail in a constant dialogue about story lines, ideas, and themes. Collaborating on a comic strip the way we do from this distance would have been impossible even ten years ago.

Jim and I met several years ago while reluctantly serving as members of the board of directors of the National Cartoonists Society. One day on the way to one of those fascinating meetings, we ended up on a plane together for a short flight from Atlanta to Sarasota, Florida. Fortunately (in retrospect), the plane blew a tire on the runway and we ended up with three or four hours to kill, so we talked. About everything. Jim is a

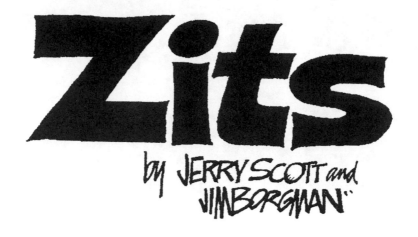

Jerry's first concept scribbles (step 1)

SOMETHING
STUPID
JUMPS OUT

JEREMY!

LOOK!

I GOT THE JACKET!

I GOT THIS COLOR BECAUSE IT LOOKS GOOD WITH MY HAIR

DON'T YOU TOTALLY LOVE IT?

YEAH. AND IT REALLY MINIMIZES YOUR COMPLEXION, TOO

I - BEG - YOUR - PARDON?

EVERY TIME I OPEN MY MOUTH, SOMETHING STUPID COMES OUT

Jerry's daily sketch (step 1)

great conversationalist, and it was refreshing to talk with another cartoonist about things that don't necessarily involve ink or punch lines. This is where our friendship started and the foundation for this collaboration was formed.

JIM: Fast forward. In 1996, I agreed to give a talk in Phoenix and, with a free plane ticket to a sunny place in hand, hoped to parlay the trip into a mini-vacation. I called Jerry, who lived outside of Phoenix at the time, and picked his brain about Sedona, two hours to the north in red rock country. He sold me—and himself—on a couple of days of hiking, so we rented cabins and spent a weekend avoiding all cartooning shop talk—almost.

Before we left Sedona, Jerry showed me the first scribblings of a comic strip idea he had about a teenage boy. It didn't have the look he hoped for, he said, and did I have any thoughts? I have always enjoyed drawing teenagers in my editorial cartoons. Their clothes, posture, language, and actions are so expressive and colorful that they make for fun drawings. Also, my son was entering those years and so my thoughts were rich with texture. I drew what turned out to be the first sketch of Jeremy, and we sat up much of the night talking about what the strip could be.

We went home to our respective lives, decided they were much too busy already, and swore off the joint project altogether. After a month or two, though, Jerry's roughs began slipping through the fax machine again, and my inability to resist tinkering with them meant we were on a journey into the belly of the teenage beast.

JERRY: I'm an unconscious observer of people and things. My wife thinks I'm just plain unconscious, but the fact is that I'm working all the time. I often carry around a sketchbook, but it seems like most of my ideas come from things I didn't pay much attention to when I saw them. My brain is like a big empty soup pot of a space somewhere, into which interesting sights, words, phrases, and behaviors that pass through my field of vision are deposited. Sometimes ideas just present themselves, but more often things have to simmer in my brain for a good while before they become material for the strip. Most of what I daydream into material for *Zits* comes from remembering parts of my adolescence and then adding some excitement, emotion, personality, and humor in order to make it interesting.

Like Jim, I think teenagers are fascinating beings. The fact that most of us experience those years totally unaware that we are on the most incredible journey of our lives makes this subject all the more appealing to me.

Jerry

Jim

Jim's pencil sketch (step 2)

I like to start early in the morning in my study, where I read the newspaper first thing. On lucky days, I might find some pages on my fax machine from Jim with ideas, scribbles, news items, or just funny sketches of our characters in odd situations. These are great idea starters and often become complete strips with very little adjustment. Then I sit, pace, draw, read, answer mail, bang my head against the wall, talk on the phone, or whatever else it takes until a batch of promising ideas have made it onto the pages of my sketchbook; this can take a few hours or a few days. Although we work about ten weeks ahead of publication, there is no grand plan or master script that we follow. With few exceptions, Jeremy's experiences occur as unexpectedly to us as they do to him.

Then I grab a pencil and make rough sketches of the strips, working out the dialogue and visual timing as I go. When I'm satisfied with them, they're faxed to Jim, and I start all over again.

JIM: When the fax machine yields up Jerry's roughs, I feel like the work is at least halfway done. Jerry has a gift for storytelling and pacing, and his storyboarding saves me hours of wrestling with a concept. It frees me up to tweak the fine points and challenges me to see what I can add to improve the strip another level.

JERRY: Meanwhile, Jim redraws my roughs, improving vastly on the art and making adjustments in the dialogue and timing to his tastes. He then faxes those roughs to me, and we spend a considerable amount of time on the phone discussing each strip. This is my favorite part

Jim's finished strip (step 3)

Cartoon Success Secrets

Jerry's Sunday pencil sketch (step 2)

Jim's Sunday pencil sketch (step 3)

Jim's finished Sunday strip (step 4)

of the process, because it's where our partnership really shines. When you're working within a panel roughly two inches square, the tiniest of details can make a huge difference in getting your message across to the reader. From slightly tilting an eyebrow to poring over a thesaurus for a punchier word, we fine-tune each strip until it's right . . . or at least as right as it can be. With attention to detail, mediocre ideas turn into good strips, and good ideas become great strips. It's collaboration at its best.

JIM: Finally it's time to ink over my pencil lines, which I do with a fine-tipped red sable brush, permanent markers, and gobs of white-out. Inking takes an hour or two per strip, and Sunday strips take most of a day, including scanning the drawing into my Macintosh and coloring in on the monitor. The various stages of

Cartoon Success Secrets

the strip you'll find in today's comics section are shown on pages 303 to 308.

The biggest challenge in doing the strip for me has been learning to draw our characters consistently over and over again. It's counter to my instinct in my editorial cartoons to present an entirely different pageant every day. In comic strips, familiarity is part of the bond readers come to feel with the characters. The trick is to present a familiar world day after day while surprising the reader with new stories and ever-revealing aspects of character.

I'm pleased to find that my editorial cartoons and *Zits* coexist peacefully on my drawing board. When the news is a little too much with us, it's refreshing to retreat to the strip, where Jeremy lives at ground level and grapples with the basics of life. Then, when I need an escape from my own head, the editorial cartoons provide a chance to comment on the outside world and talk about another layer of concerns.

JERRY: Producing a syndicated comic strip is a process. There's no manual on how to do it right, no school at which to learn the proper techniques. The only way to tell how you're doing from an artistic perspective is to look at the comics each day in the paper, see if that day's strip works, and make adjustments accordingly. It's sort of like navigating your way along a highway by looking back over your shoulder at the center line as you drive.

JIM: *Zits* is in over one thousand newspapers and twenty countries after five years, which, they tell us, is something of a record. The highest compliment we hear from readers is "You must have a camera hidden in our house!" It's gratifying to think that this world we've created resonates for so many readers. But I can't help but wonder what they make of Jeremy's life in Estonia.

LYNN JOHNSTON AND
FOR BETTER OR FOR WORSE

Story from Issue No. 137, March 2003

We asked Lynn Johnston, the creator of *For Better or For Worse,* an interesting question: Cartoonists have known for a long time that newspaper syndicates haven't been anxious to receive "story strip" submissions. They have claimed that the public can see a complete story in an hour on TV and won't stick with a continuing story running for weeks on the comics pages. So how did Lynn manage to come up with a story strip that has been one of that genre's very most popular examples over the years? Here is what she told us.

by Lynn Johnston

Like everyone else in this business, I receive many folios and comic strip samples. Some are rudimentary, some are professionally done, but almost all these artists have submitted their work and are wondering why they continue to receive rejection notices. All seem to have the same problem—they are working for themselves, not an audience. Like a new-age musician carried away by his own lyrics and discordant strum, they wonder why they are given polite encouragement and nobody buys their stuff.

I have written the same advice letter so many times, it's number 36 in the computer.

You are working for an audience, people who know nothing about your characters or your story lines, and you have maybe ten seconds a day to convince them that it's worth their while to take another look.

An editor can see immediately if a strip has a chance, and success depends entirely on the willingness of the artist to take direction. Most artists are not.

Most submissions give you the outlines of the characters, a sketch of each, and then plunge you into the middle of an actual story without introducing the players, showing clearly how they relate to one another and

why they behave the way they do. Readers don't get a chance to see your folio, guys; they don't know and don't *want* to know what's going on if there's no hook. The hook has to come right at the beginning!

Each strip has to have a reasonable punch line. Each one must be easy to follow, written as if you were writing poetry with an economy of words, carefully and purposely chosen.

Gag-a-day is difficult to write. I envy and admire all those who produce successful gag-a-day strips. Story strips must also begin with a gag-a-day format. Even if the next day's panels have a consecutive theme, it must be funny or meaningful or alliteratively clever or you lose your readers.

Going back to the submission. Most artists are so engrossed in their stories and characters they are unable to climb out of their fantasy world and look at their strip objectively. It's difficult to hear "I don't get it" when the meaning is perfectly clear to *you*! But the friend who's honest enough to say "I don't get it" is telling you what you need to hear. This is your editor, this is your audience, this is the reaction you're getting from everyone outside your adoring family circle, and you have to listen.

I have given lengthy advice, gone over every strip, rewritten punch lines, redrawn expressions, and asked for the changes to be sent back. Generally, I hear no more from my "student," but the ones who do return their packages (after a very long hiatus) send me the same drawing with no changes and new strips with the same errors.

Without exception, my best students have been women—and men under the age of eighteen. They are willing to listen, to take direction, and to make changes. The others wonder why I'm not helping to promote them and seem agitated by criticism. In any business, criticism from someone whose *been there* is *help*!

I know there's an edge to the way I'm writing this. I am actually angry as I express my real frustration with people who have great potential but throw it away because they won't change. They are married to their dream world, it cannot be interrupted, and they're stuck in a rut, submitting the same stuff over and over, eventually turning to self-publication and the Internet.

Something I've noticed, too, is that many people don't think backgrounds are important. They are. If

Lynn Johnston

you can't tell where the characters are, what their workplace, home, or neighborhood is like, how can you identify with them? Static figures, talking heads, can only survive if the punch line is worth the effort of looking at four equally interesting panels!

It's work, but make your characters *act*, draw them in different positions, show the staircase in the background, show the dashboard of the car. Make them come alive in a *visible* environment! It's work, but it's going to bring believability to your characters and encourage your audience to *come in* to your fantasy world.

For Better or For Worse began as a gag-a-day strip. I was used to doing single-panel gags, so my effort when I first began was to produce something funny (if possible), every day about a family of four.

Because a strip would often beg the question "And *then* what happened?" I started to do consecutive strips

Cartoon Success Secrets

but never more than three or four at a time. Real story lines didn't happen until I'd been published for a couple of years, and by then I had a readership who knew the characters, had walked around their neighborhood, and even knew what kind of furniture was in each room.

I never started the strip with a soap opera in mind. The kids were going to stay small, and everything would be simply drawn. That didn't happen. As the years went by, I kept my interest—and the audience's, as well—by challenging myself to write about sensitive issues and revealing as much as possible in the backgrounds, so that each panel was a good piece of art in its own right (or as good as I could make it).

I use a lot of reference material. I have toy cars, chairs, animals, furniture, a wheelchair, and so on: things I can hold up and turn to the position they're seen in the strip. I use a Polaroid camera and pose people the way I want the characters posed, so they look more realistic and the acting is believable.

It frustrates me no end when I see a strip where a chain saw is being used, for example, and the machine looks absolutely nothing like a real chain saw. Sears still sends out catalogs and so do the big hardware stores. Know what the thing looks like and *then* turn it into a cartoon!

This whole agitated monologue was spurred on by Jud Hurd's asking me to answer the question, "Why are there so few modern successful story strips?" I think I've answered that question. The formula I'd give to someone wanting to do a story strip is eightfold.

1. Be funny. Be honest, and accept "I don't get it" as a clue.

2. Introduce your characters clearly and slowly. Let them sink in (you have ten seconds a day to do this).

3. Do a gag-a-day for at least three years. It takes this long to establish a faithful readership.

4. Do uncomplicated story lines, never longer than a week at first and still ending each panel with a good punch.

5. Challenge yourself to draw well. It's time-consuming, but it's so worthwhile.

6. Be professional. This means taking advice, changing something, even throwing out an entire page.

7. Listen to your audience and work for them. They are the ones who keep you in the paper. Respond to them, answer their questions, congratulate them on the birth of their children, acknowledge their correspondence, and a bond will exist between you that goes far beyond your daily four-panel insights.

8. Never let a poor strip go through. Even though it's a ten-second read, make each and every daily and Sunday the best you possibly can.

I think I've learned to follow these eight steps. I haven't always been open to criticism. I haven't always taken my own advice, but at the age of fifty-five with over twenty years of practice, I've learned to write and draw a successful newspaper comic strip. Perhaps this information will be useful and encouraging to someone else. Good luck!

HECTOR CANTÚ AND CARLOS CASTELLANOS AND *BALDO*

Story from Issue No. 134, June 2002

Breaking Barriers
by Sonya Cole

Sometimes, two heads are better than one. Especially when bringing a completely new flavor to an already established environment.

The newspaper comic strip *Baldo,* created by Hector Cantú and Carlos Castellanos, features a Latino family in the funny pages. Baldo Bermudez, dad Sergio, Tia Carmen, and little sister Gracie bring a different perspective to the comics pages.

"We're basically two guys who love comics and decided to create one," said Cantú. "You write about what you know. Carlos and I grew up as Latino kids in the United States. That's the story we tell. Some things we experienced are unique. Some things are very normal."

To get their strip out in the market, the team sent a month's worth of dailies to the major newspaper syndicates. The first batch was well received, and syndicate editors encouraged Hector and Carlos to produce a second round. By summer 1999, they had a contract. In April 2000, Universal Press Syndicate launched *Baldo* nationwide in about a hundred daily and Sunday papers. It's one of the syndicate's most successful new strips.

Cantú studied journalism at the University of Texas at Austin, and his writing has appeared in the *Los Angeles Times Magazine* and the *Hollywood Reporter.* He also wrote a syndicated business news column for the Knight Ridder news service.

Castellanos has been doodling since he was a kid. He credits his high school math teachers for being his best art instructors: "I did most of my drawing in math class." He began his freelance career as an illustrator in 1981, while still in college. He's done work for magazines, book publishers, ad agencies, and corporate clients.

SONYA: What first got you interested in comics and cartooning?

CARLOS: I'd like to start by telling you what a rush it is to be featured in *CARTOONIST PROfiles.* I remember picking up my very first issue on one of my weekly

by Hector Cantú and Carlos Castellanos

BALDO

The star of the show. A teen with a penchant for magical daydreaming who longs to date the prettiest girl in school. In the meantime, he'll settle for a good game of soccer and building his very own lowrider car one piece at a time.

DAD

The anchor of the Bermudez family. A business owner who wants only the best for his "perfect" children.

GRACIE

Little sister with a cause. No ribbons and fluffy dresses here. It's earth-saving campaigns and "Chica Power!" gritos for this strong-willed, yet cute, rebel.

CRUZ

Baldo's best friend and cohort. if Baldo has second thoughts about building his lowrider or talking to the prettiest girl in school, Cruz is always right there, ready to shove him forward.

TIA CARMEN

The live-in aunt who hovers over her sobrino and sobrina with a bag full of Old World ways, common-sense advice and magical remedies.

THE STARS OF BALDO

trips to the local comic-book store when I was sixteen: Issue No. 35, September 1977. I still have that magazine in my office. It was so exciting for me to read about all the behind-the-scenes stuff. I thought, *Wow! This is so cool!*

Sorry, back to your question. I guess I was always interested in comics. My dad used to draw cartoons for me when I was growing up, so I suppose he planted the seed. I was pretty shy growing up, so for me, drawing

funny pictures and gags was an easy way to break the ice with other kids. Initially, though, I was more interested in the superhero comic-book genre. When I was about ten years old, I used to draw and write these ten-to-fifteen-page full-color action comic books with superheroes that I had made up. My friends would all take turns reading them and passing them around. I would literally spend my whole day drawing all of the Marvel comic book heroes with huge muscles. I had a

So this is your house?

Where's the tortilla maker? Don't you decorate with pinatas? I don't see any Ricky Martin posters!

Britney, that would be called a preconceived *noción*.

Where? Is it some exotic Latin American ceiling decoration?

Look what I found!

It's a photo of me and a tour guide I met *years* ago!

It brings back such good memories.

"I remember my trip to old Mexico like it was yesterday."

Are you my tour guide?

Para servirle, señorita.

My name ees Lopez... but ev'ry one calls me *Gordo*.

You don't really talk like that, do you?

Only if you find it irresistibly romantic.

A tip of the sombrero to Gus Arriola.

problem drawing women, though. I couldn't make them look soft; they always looked like guys in drag.

HECTOR: I'd like to send a shout-out to all my homies in the 214 and 818.

SONYA: Were there particular comic strips or artists that inspired you?

HECTOR: I was always reading *Mad* magazine, Sergio Aragones, Dick DeBartolo, Al Jaffee. When I was maybe thirteen, I submitted a drawing and got a rejection letter. I was so mad I wadded it up and threw it in the trash. I remember the stationery had a watermark of Alfred E. Neuman's face. I'm sure his grin wasn't

BALDO MEETS GORDO:
HOW THE GUS ARRIOLA CROSSOVER TRIBUTE CAME TOGETHER
by Sonya Cole

For five days, beginning November 20, 2001, comic strip readers got a peek at Latino comic history. That's when Gordon the Mexican tour guide—who appeared in his own strip from 1941 to 1985—made a special guest appearance in *Baldo*.

Gus Arriola's Gordo appeared in a flashback, as Baldo's Great-aunt Carmen stumbled across a vacation photo and fondly recalled her romantic encounter with the tour guide.

"This was just a way to tip our hats to Gus," said Hector Cantú, co-creator with Carlos Castellanos of *Baldo*. November marked *Gordo's* first appearance in newspapers sixty years ago. "*Gordo* broke ground by bringing Latino characters to the comics page on a daily basis."

It didn't come without controversy. The dialect initially used by the characters in *Gordo* faced criticism from those who saw the phonetic spellings as stereotypes of Mexican people. Gordo Lopez was a chubby Mexican bean farmer. "Mees Ruiz!" he would say. "Don't you reckonize os?" Or, "The hot sun an' all this talk 'bout work is making me a leetle sick!"

But Cantú said Gordo evolved over the years, eventually losing his pronounced accent. The last *Gordo* comic strip appeared in 1985. At its peak, the comic ran in 275 newspapers.

"*Gordo* is interesting," Cantú said, "because you see how dominant culture influenced the strip at the beginning and how Gus slowly got away from that over the years." Along the way, Arriola introduced millions of readers to Mexican culture and customs.

The retired Arriola, who lives in Carmel, California, with his wife, was flattered by the memorial. "I thought that was very kind of them to remember us," Arriola said. "We've been retired for sixteen years. I thought it was very clever how they worked Gordo in."

Cantú had met Arriola over the phone a few years back, "so we just called Gus up and asked what he thought of the idea and he said, 'Let's do it.'"

A few story lines were tossed around, such as having Gordo visit Carmen in the *Baldo* universe ("We had him knocking on the door as a surprise visitor," Cantú said). In the end, a flashback worked best. "We didn't bring Gordo into the *Baldo* universe. We took a *Baldo* character to the *Gordo* universe," Cantú said. "We figured if anyone could go back twenty, twenty-five years and interact with Gordo, it was Tia Carmen. In comic strip years, they are about the same age."

To re-create Gordo, the *Baldo* creators asked Arriola to do the drawings. A space would be left in each panel for Gus to draw his Gordo. But Arriola said he would rather leave it in their hands. Castellanos considered scanning Gordo images from compilation books into his computer. But the quality of the scan alone did not hold up. So Castellanos redrew them.

In the end, Arriola said he was pleased with the results. "I think he [Castellanos] did well enough," Arriola said. "I think former readers recognized Gordo, and I was happy that someone else did the work."

The *Baldo* team passed the final strips by Arriola and he gave them a thumbs-up, offering just a few Gordo dialogue changes. Cantú could not resist poking gentle fun at Gordo's accent in the sequence's second day. "Gus was cool about it," Cantú said. "It's great that he has a sense of humor about the controversy over Gordo's early dialect."

The day the strips hit newspaper, e-mail starting hitting the *Baldo* Web site.

"We received e-mails from *Gordo* fans around the country thanking us for bringing back memories and for once again putting Gordo on the comic pages," Cantú said. "I think Gus would be happy to know there are lots of people with fond memories of *Gordo*."

If there was another benefit, say the *Baldo* creators, it was correcting the notion that *Baldo* is the first U.S. strip with Latino characters. "We always have to remind newspaper reporters of *Gordo*," Cantú said. "I guess you can say we're the first strip about a Latino family, but not the first Latino strip, period."

taunting me, but I think that rejection was very inspirational.

CARLOS: As far as comic book art is concerned, I liked Gil Kane, Jim Starlin, Neal Adams, and my all-time favorites John Buscema and Alfredo Alcala. The art was stunning when these two guys worked together on *The Savage Sword of Conan.* As far as strips go, I was heavily influenced by Berke Breathed's *Bloom County* and Bill Watterson's *Calvin and Hobbes.* Those are the two that really inspire me.

SONYA: What was it about their work that drew you in?

CARLOS: It was the characterization and the way they combined the writing and the art. I think the writing in those strips is incredible—so poignant and creative—and the art was so animated it made the strip come alive. I still look at their work and just laugh. Great stuff!

SONYA: How did you guys meet?

HECTOR: I was a magazine editor in California, and I made assignments to freelancers. One day I needed an illustration for a story, so I picked up one of those huge artist directories that get sent to magazines and found Carlos's work. I liked it, so I called him up and gave him an assignment. That was—oh, about five years before we launched *Baldo.*

SONYA: How did you guys end up working together on the strip?

HECTOR: I was looking for a career change and thought, "Hey, I can do a comic strip!" It was kind of naïve, but I had been writing all my professional life and had been a comic fan for even longer than that, so I called Carlos and asked if he wanted to do a strip. I'm sure the first thing he thought was, "Oh, brother, not another writer who can't draw!"

CARLOS: Yes, I get offers from individuals all the time asking if I would illustrate a book they have or a comic strip idea they've been stirring around in their noodle. After viewing said material, I would usually gag and then politely turn the opportunity down due to lack of time or a scheduled appointment to have bamboo shoots hammered underneath my fingernails. So,

CHARACTER DEVELOPMENT:
HOW THE CAST WAS CAST
by Sonya Cole

The *Baldo* characters went through several stages before they reached their final design for launch in April 2000.

Artist Carlos Castellanos started sketching characters when the concept—a teen boy and his family—began taking shape. As writer Hector Cantú further developed the stories and characters, Castellanos deviated from his early sketches.

CARLOS: I was just feeling around for something different from anything that was on the comic strip pages—a different-shaped head with different proportions. We wanted him really approachable and friendly. I thought the round head would inspire that.

BALDO

1/98

4/98

1/99

Castellanos described his task as similar to that of a casting director. "You can't quite put your finger on it, but you know it's not working, so you continue to look."

Here's a glimpse at what went into developing each character's appearance.

JANUARY 1998

HECTOR: We were looking for a good-looking teenager, maybe fifteen. We're talking "leading man" material, except it's not a slick movie but a goofy, fun comic strip.

APRIL 1998

CARLOS: I looked at the opposite end of the spectrum and went more angular to make him look more Latino.

JANUARY 1999

CARLOS: I settled somewhere in between. There's some roundness to soften it up. I found the middle ground and was really happy where he ended up.

HECTOR: For me, this was Baldo. When I saw it, I was like, "That's the guy—that's the character!"

TIA CARMEN

1/98

1/99

4/98

JANUARY 1998

HECTOR: The idea was an older relative who lived with the family who was a widow. That's all Carlos had to work with in the beginning.

CARLOS: As the character developed, she looked too normal, too material. That's what I was originally shooting for, but her character became zanier.

APRIL 1998

CARLOS: I started to play with her expressions and body proportions more. She looks like she's hyped up on caffeine to reflect her personality. She looks more vibrant, with more energy. I was on the right track, I just wasn't there yet.

JANUARY 1999

CARLOS: Here she's just an evolution of April '98 with exaggerated glasses and hairdo. I gave her a triangular head to make her different and her jowls more pronounced. When I drew this, I knew she was Tia Carmen.

HECTOR: By this time, Tia Carmen was a much kookier character. She was still a widow, but she was not wearing black all the time. She was dealing with her loss in a different way and the image conveyed this.

needless to say, when Hector called, I was like, *Oh, here we go!* But as fate would have it, I was also looking for a change of direction, as far as creating work that was more personal and meaningful (having your first child will do that). I was looking into producing a line of CD-ROM games and characters geared to the Hispanic-American market. The concept Hector proposed seemed like the perfect fit. The only question remaining for me was, Could he write it and be funny?

After some verbal exchange about the characters and the different scenarios, he went back and wrote about four weeks' worth of daily gags. As it turned out, they were pretty good. It does take a while to develop the timing and pace for writing strips. It's a tough medium. So as we got closer to developing the characters, I started to develop the sketches.

SONYA: So do you guys ever fight?

HECTOR: Only with big fluffy gloves. Actually, we let our wives fight each other, and we just sit back in our lawn chairs with a beer and watch. No, seriously, we get along swell. I live in Texas, and Carlos lives in Florida, so everything we do is by phone and e-mail. We may have little disagreements over dialogue or art, but I think we both know our only goal is to make the strip the best it can be.

WOW! THIS **GORDO** GUY REALLY LEFT AN IMPRESSION ON YOU, DIDN'T HE?

AS A TOUR GUIDE, HE WAS A RASCAL! BUT HE WAS SWEET AND KIND, TOO...

HE SHOWED ME THAT IN MANY WAYS, ALL PEOPLE, NO MATTER WHERE THEY LIVE, ARE ALIKE IN MANY WAYS.

IT'S NICE TO REMEMBER HIM THAT WAY.

HAPPY 60TH ANNIVERSARY, **GORDO!**

I CAN'T GO IN THERE!

DO YOU KNOW WHAT PEOPLE SAY ABOUT THAT PLACE? IT'S SCARY! IT'S CROWDED! WE'RE SO VULNERABLE!

TIA CARMEN, IT'S OUR PATRIOTIC DUTY. IT'S FOR THE GOOD OF THE COUNTRY.

PLAZA MALL

AT LEAST LET ME SPLASH ON SOME HOLY WATER!

$10? I'LL GIVE YOU $5!

$24.99? WOULD YOU TAKE $15?

$50? MY FINAL OFFER IS $24!

TIA CARMEN!

WE'RE AT PLAZA MALL... NOT FLACO'S FLEA MARKET!

AWESOME BUY, DUDE.

THE RIGHT CLOTHES GIVE YOU MATURITY AND SET YOU APART FROM THE CROWD...

WHOA, CHECK OUT MINI-YOU.

"ALL SALES FINAL."

GRACIE

1/98

1/99

4/98

JANUARY 1998

CARLOS: Originally, she was Baldo's older sister. She was curvaceous and sexy—a school hottie. I was pretty happy with the sketch the first time out.

HECTOR: But then we stepped back and looked at the big picture. Was she too close to Baldo's age? Would a younger sister give us more comic possibilities?

APRIL 1998

CARLOS: I knew I wanted her wide-eyed and spunky. We didn't want her girly and frilly. I added just a couple of ponytails because we didn't want her too cute. [Overall], the glasses made her bookwormish— she didn't look very active."

HECTOR: I think Carlos really liked this image and still uses it. When we do flashbacks of Tia Carmen as a little girl, she looks like this!

JANUARY 1999

CARLOS: She looks confident and spunky. I wanted her to have a compact little body so she could have the "cute factor" and get away with things.

HECTOR: She could be running around with Charlie Brown and Lucy. On paper, she was very smart for her age and a little mischievous. Carlos captured that.

Hector Cantú and Carlos Castellanos and *Baldo*

DAD

1/98

1/99

4/98

JANUARY 1998

HECTOR: Dad was the anchor-of-the-family character. We saw him as an immigrant, coming to the United States as a young boy.

CARLOS: Here, he was more rounded, but he looked too stuffy and unapproachable.

APRIL 1998

CARLOS: I made him a little younger with a little more energy so he wasn't quite so stuffy. But there was something wrong with it. His face wasn't quite right.

JANUARY 1999

CARLOS : There's a gradual progression from the previous dad—his hairstyle and face shape. He has a softer look, friendlier and approachable.

HECTOR : This dad is more fun to look at. With his receding hairline and mustache, he's a character you can smile at.

BALDO
BY CANTÚ AND CASTELLANOS

CARLOS: Look, let's be honest. There's no doubt partnerships can be difficult. But all in all, we see eye to eye 90 percent of the time. There's no room for egos here. The only thing that matters is producing the best-quality strip we can do. Period! When we do have a difference of opinion, we handle it like professional adults. We call each other names.

SONYA: Why a team? Why didn't you each do a strip on your own?

HECTOR: I did a lot of drawing as a kid. In elementary school, a friend and I wrote and drew our own satire magazine, like *Mad* magazine. It was like twenty pages, and our big movie spoof was "Planet of the Grapes." I even drew a one-shot comic strip for my high school newspaper. But I had no confidence at all that my art abilities were anywhere near good enough to be nationally syndicated.

CARLOS: Writing and drawing a daily strip doesn't leave time for much else. I knew early in my twenties I wouldn't want to do both. I like variety, and I really enjoy the collaboration process. Coming from an advertising background, I've come to appreciate the value of brainstorming sessions. Having the chance to bounce ideas off someone else works magic.

SONYA: You went with Universal Press Syndicate. What happened after you signed on the dotted line?

HECTOR: We immediately went on a monthly production schedule, producing *Baldo* for UPS eyes only. I think their main goal is to see if you have more than thirty days' worth of gags in you and if you can meet deadlines. We did this for three months, and then the syndicate decided to launch us.

SONYA: Did you hire an attorney before signing?

HECTOR: Yep. A lawyer friend of mine in Los Angeles hooked us up with Peter Eichler, who had done work for the *Tank McNamara* guys, for Cathy and Robb Armstrong. And yes, most attorneys let you pay in monthly installments. Believe it or not, they have the sweetest collections people.

CARLOS: They are, they've very nice. They call us every month, and send us reminders so we know they're thinking about us.

SONYA: What about trademarking your character? How was that experience?

HECTOR: I guess it's possible to handle it yourself, but it's one of those things you don't want to mess up.

Hector D. Cantú created his first newspaper cartoon when he was twelve. "It was a small-town community newspaper that just happened to be owned by my brother, but I think I can add that to my résumé," Hector says. He went on to study journalism at the University of Texas at Austin and today is an assistant features editor at the *Dallas Morning News*. He also writes a nationally distributed business column for Knight Ridder Tribune News Service. He spent nearly six years at award-winning *Hispanic Business* magazine in Santa Barbara, California. His writing has appeared in the *Los Angeles Times Magazine* and the *Hollywood Reporter*. He lives in Dallas with his wife, Linda, and three kids: Maya, Sofia, and Max.

We did the initial paperwork on our own but then had to go back and correct some stuff. A good attorney will get it right the first time.

SONYA: So what's the process for producing your strip? How does it come together?

As a child, Carlos Castellanos was always interested in creating art. At age seven, he saw his first episode of *Bewitched.* Watching Darin Stevens sitting behind a large drawing table and working from home inspired Carlos to do the same. He began his freelance career as an illustrator in 1981 while still in college. "And I've never looked back," Carlos says. He keeps busy doing work for magazines, book publishers, ad agencies, and corporate clients—in Florida and nationally. Carlos lives in West Palm Beach, Florida, with his wife Maria; sons Chase and Alec; dogs Indy and Sai Hung, and a cat named Lagger.

HECTOR: For me, the hardest part is coming up with the situations. What's going to happen? What if Tia Carmen goes to the hospital? What if Baldo enters a car magazine contest? I'm always walking around with a pocket note pad, jotting down stuff at the mall or at my kids' school. Carlos and I will be on the phone talking about our families, old aunts and abuelitas—grandmothers—and when we were teens, and that

sparks ideas. Then I shut myself in a room and try to finalize the dialogue. Some ideas pan out. Others don't go anywhere. I shoot for twelve to fifteen written strips that Carlos and I can go through each week.

CARLOS: As I read through each script, I visualize the action in my mind, trying to figure out the best way to lay out and pace what I'm reading, first deciding on the minimum number of panels that are absolutely necessary to make the gag work, while allowing room for text.

Keeping the strip from appearing too cluttered is always a priority for me, while still working in enough detail to keep it visually interesting. Deciding between using close-ups or a wide shot, showing a single character vs. multiple characters in a panel, is all dependent on what will help tell the story or gag the best. Often, by the time I start to sketch, I have a crystal-clear picture in my mind of what I'm going to do. I just project that image onto the computer screen and start to draw.

SONYA: How do you draw *Baldo*? What supplies do you use?

CARLOS: I draw *Baldo* completely on my Apple computer using a Wacom tablet and Adobe Photoshop software. I had switched over to using the computer as my tool of choice for illustration work about three years before I started working on *Baldo,* so I was already very comfortable using the technology to acquire the look I wanted. I start with a grayscale template for the daily strip to the height and width required for publication. Once I have my template open, I move the panels around and change their placement to accommodate the dialogue and the action I see taking place. First I add the dialogue to each panel. Next, I add a new "layer" in my Photoshop file that I'll use for my sketch. I then lower the opacity on this new layer so that my sketch is lighter, resembling a light pencil sketch. Once the sketch is complete, I create another layer above the sketch layer and trace over my sketch with the finished black line. After the final line art is done, I delete the sketch, flatten the file, and save in tiff format. The line art for the Sunday strip is handled the same way.

SONYA: How do you do the Sunday strips? Do you color your own Sundays?

CARLOS: Yes, I color my own strip using Photoshop. It gives me total control on how I see the color being applied. I start by opening the line art file on the Sunday strip and convert the grayscale file to a CMYK file, open a new layer above the line art for my color and set the mode to MULTIPLY. This allows me to paint over the line art in the above color layer while allowing the line art underneath to show through. When I'm done with my week's worth of strips, the tiff files are stuffed and sent to an online bulletin board the syndicate maintains for attached e-mail submissions. The upload takes only about forty-five seconds. I love working on my computer and would never go back to working traditionally. The computer allows for so much more freedom and experimentation in my work. It's a wonderful tool.

SONYA: Do you feel you've ever stereotyped Latinos in *Baldo*?

HECTOR: We try to stay away from that. People are looking at us and trying to catch us being stereotypical. When you're writing comedy, you can go for easy surface stereotypes or something a little deeper. Baldo chasing the cute girl, a guy who likes sports and cars, dealing with older relatives, dealing with personalities—those are the stereotypes we play with, not language and food and accents.

SONYA: There's a fine line between portraying Latinos and not being Latino enough for your readers. Have you had any complaints either way? What about other minority characters in the strip?

HECTOR: Most of the debate happened before we launched. We had discussions with syndicate editors. Some said the characters were too Latino. Some said they weren't Latino enough. We just did what was comfortable for us. And we really haven't received any complaints.

CARLOS: We introduced a Middle Eastern substitute teacher named Mr. Ali shortly after the attack on the World Trade Center.

HECTOR: We used that story as a way to open a discussion about preconceptions. You see a Middle Easterner and expect certain things, but we flipped it. He's catching flak for giving Fs to students, not for September 11. We got e-mails from people saying "Keep him" and others saying, "How dare you? You crossed the line."

CARLOS: A few people felt we were stereotyping, but we weren't. It was the complete opposite. These folks made some huge assumptions and read a lot into the strips. It's funny, because it just brings their own prejudices to the surface.

SONYA: Some cartoonists tackle political or social issues in their strips. Does *Baldo* have an agenda?

HECTOR: We've received mostly positive response. *Baldo* is just bringing a different point of view to the comics, a peek into a particular household. That's mostly our agenda: showing a different perspective and seeing how this family deals with things. The number-one agenda is to have fun and be funny.

CARLOS: I think the strip is more character driven. We're not out trying to knock people over the head to teach them something. We want to keep it fun and entertaining. When a message is appropriate, we do it.

SONYA: Is Baldo going to grow up?

CARLOS: None of the characters are going to age for now. We plan on keeping cars and girls just out of Baldo's reach for as long as we can. We'd like to torment him a little longer. The poor guy is going to be in need of some serious therapy.

SONYA: How far in advance do you guys work?

HECTOR: Not far enough! We're about a month in advance of publication for dailies. Some creators are two months, some two weeks. For Sundays, we're almost two months in advance.

SONYA: Do you have any new projects in the works with Baldo?

CARLOS: Well, we just had our first *Baldo* book released—*The Lower You Ride, the Cooler You Are*—with a second one scheduled for sometime next year. Also, we're in early talks with a network concerning a possible *Baldo* TV series, nothing concrete yet.

SONYA: What advice do you have for aspiring cartoonists?

HECTOR: Never say never. We're the last guys to say, "It's a long shot, you'll never make it." We put out our proposals and got nibbles and then got syndicated. We had a lot of experience going into this thing, working for newspapers and publishers, but it was still a long shot for us. It's a long shot, but you gotta try.

CARLOS: My advice is don't drink and draw. I've seen what can happen. It's not pretty. No, really, find what makes you different and pursue it. Look at what you bring to the table, what your talents are, and put them together. Enjoy the journey, and be passionate about what you do.

AFTERWORD

TRIBUTES

CLAUDIA

For a number of years now my wife, Claudia, seen in this 1990 photo of the two of us, has ably assumed the office details connected with publishing *CARTOONIST PROfiles*. Not only has she handled those welcome subscriber renewals, logged the names of new readers, dealt with the many changes of address required, and prepared the updated mailing label lists each March, June, September, and December, she has written those countless friendly and informative letters that many of you have received—letters which, unfortunately, I never seemed to have time to write in the early days of the magazine. I apologize at this late date—there just weren't enough forty-eight-hour days available to get everything done.

In addition to all her other abilities, Claudia writes poems in both French and English. On the opposite page is one for cartoonists.

Claudia and me at the marriage of our son, Philip, to Janet Kelley, July 14, 1990

TRIBUTE

When cogs of justice falter out of sync,
Or tangled prose obscures the truest path,
Who champions the right in dauntless ink
With forceful reasoned strokes, a tempered wrath?
The cartoonist.

When wearied we become by stress, and sore,
When duties with their urgencies deceive,
Who draws us through imagination's door
And costumes us, too brief, in make-believe?
The cartoonist.

When published indiscretion strips us bare,
Self-conscious in defection do we blush;
Endearing human frailties we all share
Are tickled into laughter by his brush.
The cartoonist.

The history of man, pretensions chaffed,
Examined, changed, recorded by his pen,
In silent solitude he plies his craft
On broadest board, the loneliest of men.
The cartoonist.

claudia hurd
april 24, 1982

PHILIP HURD AND ED REED

During the summer of 1983, after our son Philip had graduated in electrical engineering from Rensselaer Polytechnic Institute, he and I flew to Europe, rented a car, and found ourselves one day near the town of Broadway in the beautiful Cotswold section of England.

Keith Mackenzie, art editor of the *London Daily Mail* who had become a regular *CARTOONIST PROfiles* correspondent, had visited the colorful town some years previously and done a story about a very funny syndicated cartoonist and local resident, Ed Reed. I had been laughing at his cartoons for the Register and Tribune Syndicate for many years, so we were delighted when a phone call to Ed in Broadway brought a quick invitation to Philip and me to drop by.

Just as we parked in the front courtyard of his home, he came walking with his two King Charles Cavalier spaniels, Benedict and Bede, and gave us a tour of the grounds—whose sculptured hedges looked like a slightly smaller version of Versailles. When Philip and I enthused about the lavishness of his property, Ed quipped, "My wife's been a very thrifty woman!" It developed in conversation later that day that he hadn't acquired this layout entirely with pen and ink. In his early days, when he had worked in Dallas, he had occasionally bought up oil rights with some of his cartoon income.

How did he happen to wind up in this beautiful spot? Years ago he had begun to spend five or six months at a time in various world capitals and then he would return to the United States and visit newspapers in twenty or more cities. He finally decided, after seeing and living in a number of these far-flung spots, to settle permanently in Broadway, England.

OFF THE RECORD   **By Ed Reed**

"Bob, it's a sort of minor victory over the budget. I'm using PINK INK."

OFF THE RECORD   **By Ed Reed**

"If you prefer a firmer mattress, you can always add ice cubes!"

MIGHTY MOUSE

©Terrytoons

Paul Terry and Jud Hurd

TO WHOM IT MAY CONCERN:

I believe that the best days of these United States are ahead of us and not behind us. A better United States can only be achieved by creative thinking. *Jud Hurd* has created this new magazine, *CARTOONIST PROfiles,* to stimulate creative thinking. *Jud Hurd* operates with confidence born of skill, knowledge and experience. *Jud Hurd* is worthy of our support. God helps those who help themselves. Help yourself by supporting *Jud Hurd* and his new magazine, *CARTOONIST PROfiles.*

Paul Terry

Creator of *TERRYTOONS*

The first Terry advertisement

That JUD HURD is a menace!

You are sitting in your studio feeling sorry for yourself and CARTOONIST PROfiles arrives in the mail ... You drop everything and read the warmly perceptive stories about other Inkies —and learn that their problems often surpass your own (even the fancied ones)!

Trouble is, everyone else grabs at JUD'S magazine first— when I am fighting a mailing deadline. Then the entire staff knows the inside poop on this dirty-finger-nail-trade before I do!

I'd show JUD how independent I am by cancelling my subscription— except that I can't wait to see the next issue of PRO-files!

Palm Springs
November 1975

THE WHITE HOUSE

WASHINGTON

May 14, 1975

Dear Jud:

Nothing is more lasting than humor or the
pleasure of laughter. Despite the passing of time since I met with the members
of the Association of American Editorial
Cartoonists, my family and I continue to
find new enjoyment in the outstanding
collection of caricatures each time we
look at them.

I was especially pleased to have one of
your cartoons in this collection, and I
appreciate the toast! I trust it has
contributed to my good health these past
months!

This collection of cartoons will be
treasured by all of the Fords for years
to come, and I hope there will be an
opportunity for me to thank you personally some day. Until then, may your
hand be steady, your mind creative and
your perspective sharp.

With my continued appreciation and very
best wishes,

Jerry Ford

Mr. Jud Hurd
United Feature Syndicate
220 East 42nd Street
New York, New York 10017

RONALD SEARLE

Dear Mr. Hurd,   12th March 1981

     I think it is remarkable that you have managed to not only keep "Cartoonist Profiles" going, but have also managed to maintain its original substance and quality.

     Even though it remains basically an 'American' magazine we Europeans don't feel completely shut out. There is always something of a more general interest to keep us absorbed.

     "Cartoonist Profiles" is obviously going to become an essential source of documentation and a vital part of the recorded history of American Graphic Humour. Meanwhile that doesn't prevent it from being thoroughly entertaining now!

     Congratulations on your single-mindedness.

With kind regards.

Sincerely,

CARTOONIST'S PROFILE
COMPLETES MT. RUSHMORE

NOVEMBER 12, 2002

• • •

HAPPY 90TH BIRTHDAY, JUD!
YOU ARE UP THERE WITH THE
GREAT ONES.

KEN. JUDY ALVINE

HAPPY BIRTHDAY, JUD !!!

Bill
JANOOMA

Neal
Walker

ALF
THORSIO

GREG
WALKER

MORT
WALKER

BRIAN
WALKER

WILL YOU BECOME
A CARTOONIST?

If you're pulled and prodded by a pesky plethora of persistent promoters of perennially popular professions, but still proclaim that you prefer pens and Pelikan ink in perpetuity to portray the perfidies of the planet's peculiar people, yes—*you will be a cartoonist!*

ACKNOWLEDGMENTS

The author and publisher gratefully acknowledge the following syndicates, publications, artists, and contributors for permission to reprint the cartoons, sketches, photographs illustrations, and letters contained herewith (in order of appearance):

The Landon Course of Cartooning © 1914–1926 by C. N. Landon.

E. C. Segar letters and *Popeye* art created especially for *Red Cat* magazine, 1931.

Professor Butts by Rube Goldberg © King Features Syndicate

The Thrill That Comes Once in a Lifetime and personal letter © Estate of H. T. Webster

Down on the Farm by F. B. Opper © 1922, by King Features Syndicate

Opper illustrations from Bill Nye's *History of the United States,* published by Stanton and Van Valet Co., Chicago

Krazy Kat comic and personalized drawing by George Herriman © 1922 by King Features Syndicate

Krazy Kat and *Scrappy* illustrations and letter or recommendation © Charles Mintz Studio

Just Hurd in Hollywood by Jud Hurd © King Features Syndicate

NEA logo and Dance of the Pensioneers © 1939 Newspaper Enterprise Association

Bulk Station News magazine cover art © 1948 Standard Oil Company, Ohio

Columbia Capers © Columbia Transportation Co.

Playmate magazine cover art and *Inspector Hector* © Children's Playmate Magazine

Ticker Toons © King Features Syndicate

Health Capsules ® by M. Petti, M. D., and Jud Hurd, © 1993, 1995 United Features Syndicate

Harold Gray photograph courtesy of the National Cyclopedia of American Biography

Little Orphan Annie character sketches and strips by Harold Gray courtesy of the Boston University Special Collections Department © Tribune Media Services

Gumba news clipping © Tribune Media Services

Harry Hershfield caricature by Emidio Angelo

Abie the Agent by Harry Hershfield © King Features Syndicate

Heart of Juliet Jones logo, photos and strips by Stan Drake © King Features Syndicate

Buz Sawyer by Roy Crane © King Features Syndicate

Roy Crane portrait by Bob Zschiesche

The Born Loser by Art and Chip Sansom © Newspaper Enterprise Association

Art Sansom photos by Rebman Photo Service, Inc.

Wizard of Id by Brant Parker and Johnny Hart © King Features Syndicate

Peanuts by Charles Schulz © United Features Syndicate

B.C. by Johnny Hart © Creators Syndicate, Inc.

Johnny Hart photo by Perri Hart.

Frank and Ernest by Bob Thaves © Newspaper Enterprise Association

Mort Walker and Dik Browne art by Stan Drake

Hagar the Horrible by Dik Browne © King Features Syndicate

Bringing Up Father and *Rosie's Beau* by George McManus © King Features Syndicate

Doonesbury illustration and letter by Garry Trudeau © Universal Press Syndicate

Blondie by Chic and Dean Young, Stan Drake and Denis Lebrun © King Features Syndicate

Dennis the Mennace by Hank Ketcham, Ron Ferdinand and Marcus Hamiltion, © King Features Syndicate and Hank Ketcham Enterprises

Ron Ferdinand and Hank Ketcham photos courtesy of *Monterey Peninsula Herald*.

Calvin and Hobbes by Bill Watterson © Universal Press Syndicate

Garfield by Jim Davis © Universal Press Syndicate

Mother Goose and Grimm by Mike Peters © Grimmy Inc. and Tribune Media Services

Mike Peters Editorial cartoons © United Features Syndicate

Dilbert by Scott Adams © United Features Syndicate

FoxTrot by Bill Amend © Universal Press Syndicate

Moose & Molly by Bob Weber © King Features Syndicate

Curtis by Ray Billingsley © King Features Syndicate

Luann by Greg Evans © King Features Syndicate

Hi and Lois by Brian and Greg Walker and Chance Browne © King Features Syndicate

Shoe, Pluggers and editorial cartoons by Jeff MacNelly © Tribune Media Services

Boondocks by Aaron McGruder © Universal Press Syndicate

Aaron McGruder photo courtesy of Khui Bui, *The Washington Post*

Family Circus by Bil Keane © Bil Keane, Inc. and King Features Syndicate

Cathy by Cathy Guisewite © Universal Press Syndicate

Zits by Jerry Scott and Jim Borgman © ZITS Partnership and King Features Syndicate

For Better or For Worse by Lynn Johnston © Lynn Johnston Productions, Inc. and United Features Syndicate

Baldo by Hector Cantu and Carlos Castellanos © Baldo Partnership and Universal Press Syndicate

Off the Record by Ed Reed © 1977 The Register and Tribune Syndicate

Mighty Mouse by Paul Terry © Terrytoons

Andrews McMeel Publishing has made every effort to contact copyright holders.